The Art of Pasta

Lucio Galletto
& David Dale

Artwork by Luke Sciberras
Photography by Anson Smart

GRUB STREET • LONDON

For my children,
Matteo
and Michela

Contents

Introduction

My earliest memory is of my mother sprinkling flour on a big wooden board in anticipation of making a batch of ravioli, while the fragrance of slowly simmering meat sauce drifted through the house. So pasta is as much a part of my personal history as it is a part of the history of Italy.

Now, maybe I have to admit that the origins of fresh pasta lie with the Greeks, who passed it on to the Etruscans and the Romans some 3000 years ago. And maybe I have to admit that the origins of dried pasta lie with the Arabs, who started manufacturing it in Sicily about 1100 years ago. But I am absolutely confident that it was the Italians who perfected it, developing flavour, texture and shape to the point where, in the second decade of the twenty-first century, I can offer you 165 wonderful pasta recipes – a collection of classics and personal favourites that still barely scratches the surface of the regional repertoire.

The word 'pasta' actually comes from an ancient Greek term for barley porridge, but it wasn't used in its contemporary context until the nineteenth century. The Romans used the word *lagana*, or 'layers', for the sheets of dough they mingled with cheese and meat sauce and baked, while the Arabs in Sicily used the term *itriyya* for the ribbons of dried dough they sold around the Mediterranean. In the year 1154, a geographer named Mohammed al-Idrisi wrote a report for the King of Sicily in which he praised the hardworking citizens of 'a delightful settlement called Trabia' (a town to the west of Palermo). He wrote: 'Its ever-flowing streams propel a number of mills. Here there are huge buildings in the countryside where they make vast quantities of *itriyya* which is exported everywhere: to Calabria, to Muslim and Christian countries. Very many shiploads are sent.'

In the thirteenth century, names more familiar to us started to appear – vermicelli, maccheroni and ravioli. In the epic tales of *The Decameron*, which dates from around 1350, Giovanni Boccaccio described a place somewhere in Italy that sounds like paradise:

'There was a mountain made entirely of grated parmesan cheese, and on this mountain lived people who did nothing but make maccheroni and ravioli and cook them in chicken broth, after which they threw them down the mountainside and whoever got most of them had most of them to eat.' Well, all I can say is that mountain must have been very close to my birthplace in Liguria, because the obsession with fresh pasta (and parmesan) continues to this day – and it is what inspired me to undertake this book.

And what a wonderful trip it has been, learning about the origins of the dishes I already knew and discovering new favourites. It was like travelling in a time machine through the regions of Italy to discover the events that influenced the birth of a new taste sensation. I began to appreciate the creativity – often necessitated by poverty – that has given us such simple masterpieces as ravioli filled with potato and dressed with olive oil and pecorino cheese, or 'spaghetti with no sauce' (dressed with cheese and pepper) that was cooked and sold in the streets of nineteenth-century Naples and eaten with bare hands.

I came to understand the importance of social pressures in shaping what we eat. My mother often told me about two contrasting periods in recent Italian history. Before the war, when people couldn't afford to buy dried pasta, they had to make their own. Then, after the war, at the height of the country's economic boom, they felt compelled to buy dried pasta to avoid looking poor to their neighbours, even if they preferred the taste of fresh. Nowadays, of course, attitudes have come full circle, and eating fresh pasta is once again fashionable – a sign of wealth, even though well-made dried pasta goes better with certain sauces.

Of course, geography is as important as history. In the south, where the sun is warm and shines most of the time, they grow the best wheat and have developed the best ways of drying and storing pasta. That is why they eat mostly *pasta secca* (dried pasta), such as spaghetti and linguine. The same sun ripens the tomatoes and the sea air helps to give them their unique flavour. The south enjoys more immediate and spontaneous cooking methods, and the sauces and the dressings for the pasta mainly involve vegetables, seafood, herbs, garlic, fresh cheeses and, of course, olive oil. Southern Italians also love to add a kick with chilli.

In the north, where the sky is grey most of the time and the air is full of humidity, the pasta is made fresh – to be eaten quickly, before it turns mouldy! Butter and cheese enrich the slow-cooked meat ragùs and the mushroom sauces that dress ravioli, lasagne and tagliatelle. Root vegetables and beans are turned into beautiful soups thickened with fragments of pasta, and cheaper cuts of meats are used to make great clear broths to have with cappelletti, tortellini, passatelli and other tiny pasta types.

But it's not just the regional and social story that I want you to enjoy in this book. It's the pleasure of discovering pasta for yourself. I want you to become confident about making and cooking pasta. Timing is important. I don't want you to be afraid to put a large pot of water on the heat or to salt it at the right time. I don't want you to be afraid of immersing the pasta in the boiling water, or getting in there with a fork to separate its strands. Or of testing the pasta a few times towards the end of the cooking time, so it doesn't end up being overcooked. I don't want you to be afraid to pick up the pot for draining. I want you to be ready with the colander in the sink, the sauce in the pan and your family and friends around the table.

MAKING THIS BOOK

Since childhood, I have been fascinated by art and artists – as much as I've been fascinated by food. My family's restaurant in Liguria was filled with the works of visiting painters and sculptors, and now the walls of my restaurant in Sydney are crammed with the work of Australian artists who seem to enjoy what comes out of my kitchen. One of the most colourful of them is Luke Sciberras.

I wanted this book to reflect my two passions, so I asked Luke if he would read the recipes and apply his imagination to conveying the essence of the ingredients on the page. The result was beyond my wildest hopes.

Luke carried his brushes and colours to the studio of photographer Anson Smart, and watched chef Logan Campbell prepare and compose the dishes we wanted to illustrate. Then he literally painted around the plates, while Anson snapped them. I've seen illustrations in cookbooks before, and I've seen photos, but I've never seen a collaboration quite like this.

Back in Liguria, my family used to take great care to make the dishes look beautiful before they left the kitchen. They used to say *'L'occhio vuole la sua parte'* (The eye needs its share). Now we have applied that same principle to the art of making a cookbook. I am proud to present it to you.

Buon appetito e buon divertimento – Enjoy the food and enjoy the view.

A FEW WORDS FROM LOGAN CAMPBELL,
EXECUTIVE CHEF AT LUCIO'S

As a boy, I had no idea I was going to become a chef, even though my father was one. I actually wanted to be a pilot, but that's another story.

What I did know was that I loved the feijoas that grew in our backyard. Dad had planted six trees and every year the fruit (closely related to the guava) would grow fat and fall off the tree, releasing a heady, almost quince-like aroma. I would take them to school and trade them, always keeping some aside for myself, of course. The feijoa was one of the first flavours I can remember.

As I grew older, my father's influence began to assert itself: I became amazed at the transformation of raw ingredients to cooked, even if I didn't quite understand why things changed the way they did. 'Cooking is a life skill,' my father would say, but I still didn't appreciate the levels of dedication and painstaking effort involved in making genuinely good food.

Entering the world of commercial cooking as an apprentice, I became very disillusioned with what I saw: it was a world of cranky megalomaniacs and over-caffeinated pastry chefs where you had to fight to be shown anything. But I was also lucky enough to encounter a handful of chefs who would impart their knowledge freely – and their guidance has made all the difference. The most important thing I've learnt is that cooking is a tactile thing; you feel it through your hands, through smells and tastes, and a close observation of ingredients.

Following a recipe is not always the easiest thing in the world, and many people struggle to match the words in a book to the immediate events happening in the pan in front of them. Before you start any of my recipes, I suggest you give it a read through first, so that you understand what the final outcome will be, and can plan what you will need before you need it. I have tried to give as much explanation and guidance as I can in the methods without them resembling a novel.

Let me finish by saying it was also my intention to push the boundaries a little with some of my recipes here, so that you might increase your confidence and be inspired to try new things. This is a creative hands-on process, and I encourage you to keep an open mind and trust your instincts.

Making and cooking Pasta

Pasta is the most convivial of foods – the international symbol of Italian family cooking and the spirit of the Italian people. *Ci facciamo un piatto di pasta* ('Let's make a plate of pasta') is probably the most spoken phrase in Italy. Every Italian knows how to make at least one very good plate of pasta, and every Italian thinks he or she has got the best recipes, left by a mother or grandmother, rarely a father or grandfather.

One image from my childhood that will never leave my mind is of lunch on schooldays. Being of different ages and going to different schools, my brother and I came home at 2 p.m. and 2.30 p.m. respectively, but my mother used to cook pasta fresh for each one of us. She would never even have considered cooking a double quantity at 2 o'clock and keeping it warm for half an hour. She always had the salted water ready and boiling – then, when one of us walked in, she would throw in the pasta. By the time we had said hello, put down our bags and washed our hands, the pasta would be on the table, steaming, covered with sauce, al dente and wonderful. This recollection tells you all you need to know about the importance of freshly cooked pasta in Italian daily life.

On weekdays my mother was too busy looking after the chickens, the rabbits and the three men in her life to make fresh pasta, so she would send my brother Aulo down to the local shop to replenish our supply of dried pasta. There he would reach into a deep wooden drawer and pull out a handful of spaghetti, penne, orecchiette or fusilli, depending on the sauce my mother was planning to make. The pasta was paid for by weight, then Aulo would bring the bag of pasta home, where it was stored in a big jar near the stove.

But the weekend was different. Early in the morning, out came the large wooden board that had been in the family for generations: *bang* it went, as it was slapped down on top of the kitchen table. Out came the big apron, the flour, the eggs and the rolling pin, smooth and shiny – just like we want our dough to be!

For the next few hours, the kitchen became a temple to honour fresh pasta in all its forms. The flour was heaped into a mound and the eggs broken into it, then mixed, then kneaded with precise and elegant movements. While the dough was resting in a warm place away from draughts, the sauce would go onto the stove. Mostly it was just garlic, oil and tomato, perhaps with some vegetables from our garden or a handful of mushrooms we'd picked in the forest, but on special occasions there might be a little meat or seafood. The sauce slowly simmered, its distinctive bubbling sound and enticing aroma a foretaste of the joy that lay ahead.

Before she cut the pasta, my mother would give my brother and me little balls of dough, which we would make into animal shapes. That was a big event! Then, with just a knife, a rolling pin and nimble fingers (no machines in those days), she would produce tagliatelle, farfalle, tagliolini and ravioli.

We can make the same pasta in our kitchen today. Here's the story on making, cutting, shaping and cooking fresh pasta – and it's easier than you might think. The steps in the procedure are as follows:

Mix together flour, eggs and salt
Knead by hand for 8 minutes
Cover the ball of dough with cling wrap and let it rest for at least 20 minutes
Roll out the dough by hand or with the pasta machine
Stretch the dough by hand or with the pasta machine
Cut into the desired shapes.

BASIC PASTA DOUGH

The best work surface for making pasta is a large wooden board, but any clean surface will do. Try to avoid marble as its lower temperature makes the kneading more difficult. Ideally, the room where you make the pasta should be warm and free of draughts.

It's difficult to give the exact quantities of flour and eggs because it depends on the size of the eggs, the humidity in the air, and how much egg the flour will absorb. Having said that, a good rule of thumb is to use 1 egg for every 100 g flour, and allow 100 g flour per person. Adding more eggs, or even just egg yolks, and adjusting the amount of flour accordingly results in a richer pasta – you'll soon learn what kind of pasta you prefer. If possible, try to use Italian 'oo' wheat flour. It's very fine and high in gluten, which makes the dough more workable and gives it a good texture. Always use the best and freshest eggs at room temperature.

400 g plain flour, plus extra
    for dusting
4 eggs
pinch of salt

SERVES 4

Shake the flour through a sieve to form a mound on the board or benchtop. Make a well in the centre, but not too deep – the work surface shouldn't be exposed.

Break the eggs into the well and, using a fork, beat the eggs together until combined. Then, still with the fork, start incorporating some flour into the eggs, a little at a time, until the eggs aren't runny any more. Put the fork aside and get ready to use your hands.

Push some of the flour to one side – the aim is to add just enough to stop the dough being too moist and sticky. Using your fingers, draw the mound in towards you and work the mixture with the palms of your hands, pushing outwards. Continue in this way, drawing in with your fingers and pushing out with your palms, until the dough is well mixed. When you feel that the dough is reaching the right consistency – that is, not too dry, nor too crumbly or sticky – put it aside and scrape the work surface and your hands clean. (If the dough seems too dry, you may add a little warm water.)

Wash your hands and dry them well. Now it is time to start kneading. Sprinkle some extra flour on the work surface, then place the ball of dough on it. Using the heel of one hand, press down and away from you, giving the dough an oval shape. Fold the oval in half with the other hand, and give it half a turn. Press the dough down and away from you again with the palm of your hand and repeat the folding and pressing process, always turning the dough in the same direction. When you have strongly kneaded the dough in this manner for about 8 minutes – and you are feeling a pleasant glow in your shoulders – the dough should be smooth and elastic. To check if it is ready, press it with the tip of your finger. If it springs back, it has reached the desired texture.

Wrap the pasta dough in cling wrap and let it rest for a minimum of 20 minutes at room temperature away from draughts – or for up to 24 hours in the fridge.

Now the dough is ready to be rolled in the pasta machine or with a rolling pin and cut into the shape you need.

COLOURED PASTAS

It is simple and fun to make different pastas. Just keep in mind that although we will give recommended quantities, it may take a little trial and error to obtain the desired strength of colour and flavour.

Some flavoured pastas have such a pronounced personality that they require their own special sauce – for example, chocolate pasta benefits from a rich, gamey sauce. Similarly a particular sauce may require a certain pasta, such as a ragù of oxtail, which goes perfectly with capsicum pappardelle.

For most coloured pastas, it is a simple matter of replacing one of the eggs with a puree of the colouring ingredient. Other times you just add the ingredient directly to the eggs. Sometimes other adjustments are required. When adding vegetables with a high water content, such as spinach or capsicum, you need to reduce the number of eggs. The moisture content of the vegetables will vary from batch to batch, so be ready to add more flour if necessary. The important thing is that the pureed ingredient must be completely cooled before it is added to the eggs and then placed in the flour well.

The pasta dough is kneaded and rolled in the usual way (see pages 17–18), though some additives will reduce the elasticity of the pasta, so you may not be able to make the sheets as thin as you can with plain pasta.

Saffron

Herb

Chocolate

Capsicum

Squid Ink

Porcini

HERB PASTA DOUGH

This is a delightful and surprising pasta, as it can be made with so many different herbs.

The exact quantity of each herb used is entirely up to you, taking into account the strength of flavour of each one – for example, I would be more generous with parsley than with strongly scented rosemary. Or just use sage. The important thing is that you pick all the leaves from the stems and chop the leaves very finely.

small handful of finely chopped herbs – flat-leaf parsley, sage,
   rosemary, thyme or whatever else you like
4 eggs
400 g plain flour
pinch of sea salt

Simply stir the finely chopped herbs into the eggs, then work this mixture into the flour and salt as described for basic pasta dough (see page 11).

BLACK PASTA DOUGH

Despite its dramatic black colour, this pasta has a delicate flavour with just a hint of the sea. Fresh squid ink is available in sachets from good fishmongers.

1 tablespoon squid ink
4 eggs
400 g plain flour
pinch of sea salt

Mix the squid ink with the eggs, then work this mixture into the flour and salt as described for basic pasta dough (see page 11).

ALL THE RECIPES ON THIS PAGE SERVE 4.

PORCINI PASTA DOUGH

60 g dried porcini mushrooms
3 eggs
400 g plain flour
pinch of sea salt

Soak the porcini in hot water for about 10 minutes, drain well and puree in a blender. Allow the porcini puree to cool completely, then mix with the eggs. Work this mixture into the flour and salt as described for basic pasta dough (see page 11).

GREEN PASTA DOUGH

This is generally made with spinach or silverbeet, but you could also try using wild greens or nettles. When you clean and cook the silverbeet, it will lose more than half of its weight, so you need about 300 g raw silverbeet to yield 100 g of cooked squeezed greens.

300 g silverbeet (Swiss chard)
3 eggs
400 g plain flour
pinch of salt

Separate the white stems from the leaves and discard. Wash the leaves, then roll them up and slice them finely. Put the shredded silverbeet leaves into a saucepan of boiling water and blanch for about 4–5 minutes, then drain and plunge into iced water to stop it cooking further and to preserve its wonderful green colour.

As soon as the silverbeet is cool enough to handle, squeeze out as much of the water as you can. Puree the silverbeet in a blender, then mix with the eggs. Work this mixture into the flour and salt as described for basic pasta dough (see page 11).

CHOCOLATE PASTA DOUGH

This is not at all sweet – the chocolate simply adds depth and complexity of flavour. This pasta goes especially well with boar ragù (see page 191) and other sauces made with rich gamey meats such as venison or hare.

Simpler alternatives include a tomato and chilli sauce (see page 99), sage butter (see page 219) or walnut sauce (see page 221).

75 g unsweetened cocoa powder
4 eggs
400 g plain flour
pinch of sea salt

Mix the powdered cocoa into the eggs, then work this mixture into the flour and salt as described for basic pasta dough (see page 11).

PUMPKIN PASTA DOUGH

400 g pumpkin, skin on, seeds removed and cut into wedges
50 ml olive oil
sea salt and freshly ground black pepper
2 eggs
400 g plain flour

Preheat the oven to 250°C.

Place the pumpkin wedges in a bowl and mix with just enough olive oil to coat them. Season with salt and pepper.

Line a baking tray with baking paper. Place the pumpkin wedges in a single layer on the tray. Roast, turning once, for 20 minutes or until golden and tender.

When the pumpkin is cool, scrape the flesh from the skins, then puree in a blender and add to the eggs, along with a pinch of salt. Work this mixture into the flour as described for basic pasta dough (see page 11).

SAFFRON PASTA DOUGH

This golden-hued pasta is best matched by a delicate sauce that won't swamp the saffron's subtle flavour – try it with zucchini flowers, tomatoes and basil (see page 153).

large pinch of saffron threads
400 g plain flour
4 eggs
pinch of sea salt

Soak the saffron in 1 tablespoon warm water and leave to infuse. When cool, add to the eggs. Work this mixture into the flour and salt as described for basic pasta dough (see page 11).

CAPSICUM PASTA DOUGH

This flavourful pasta goes well with rich sauces such as the oxtail ragù on page 185.

1 large red capsicum (pepper)
pinch of paprika (optional)
3 eggs
400 g plain flour
pinch of sea salt

To roast the capsicum, cook it skin-side up under a hot grill or, using tongs, hold it over a naked gas flame, until its skin becomes blistered and charred all over. Put the capsicum in a plastic bag until it is cool enough to handle and the skin can be easily removed. Discard the stem and seeds then puree the capsicum flesh in a blender. If you want a deeper and more intense colour and flavour, add a little paprika.

When the capsicum puree is completely cool, mix it with the eggs then work this mixture into the flour and salt as described for basic pasta dough (see page 11).

ALL THE RECIPES ON THIS PAGE SERVE 4.

ROLLING AND STRETCHING
PASTA DOUGH BY HAND

This method does not use downward pressure on the dough, rather you are lightly stretching it along the pin. The whole procedure should not take more than 10 minutes.

Your rolling pin needs to accommodate the whole width of the sheet of pasta. Keep in mind that a two-egg dough should result in two sheets of pasta about 60 cm in diameter. Before you start rolling, divide the dough into two or more pieces, depending on the size of your rolling pin.

Knead the dough quickly a couple of times to remove any excess moisture. Flour and knead again a couple of times, if necessary. Place the dough comfortably in the centre of your floured work surface and press down with the palm of your hand to flatten it slightly.

Place the rolling pin on the dough about a third of the way in, making sure it is parallel with the edge of the work surface closest to you. 'Open out' the ball of dough by placing your hands on top of the rolling pin and pushing energetically away from you, then letting the pin roll back towards you; do not push the pin onto or over the far edge of the dough. Repeat this action four or five times.

Turn the dough a full quarter turn and repeat the same action four or five times. Continue in this manner until the pasta dough is flattened into an even disc about 20 cm in diameter.

You are now ready to stretch the dough. Place the rolling pin at the far edge of the pasta sheet and curl the dough over the pin. Start rolling the pin back towards you, taking up enough of the dough to fit around the pin. With one hand, hold the nearest edge of the pasta sheet to keep it from moving, then use the heel of your other hand to push the pin away from you, thus stretching the sheet of dough between your two hands. You must work quickly and there must be no downward pressure, only an outward stretching action.

Roll the pin back towards you and repeat the procedure (holding, pushing, rolling), wrapping more of the dough around the pin each time, until all of the dough is wrapped around the rolling pin.

Next you have to turn the dough through a half turn: do this by placing the dough-wrapped pin on the table with the end pointing towards you and unrolling the dough, opening it out flat again. Continue stretching, rolling and turning the dough until the sheet measures about 30 cm in diameter.

Now comes the final tricky part, where you stretch the dough to a 60 cm sheet. Lightly dust your hands with flour.

1. Lay the sheet on the board in front of you. Place the rolling pin at the far edge of the dough and gently roll towards you, wrapping about 10 cm of the sheet around the pin.

2. You are going to roll out and roll back this 10 cm section of the dough, and simultaneously you are going to lightly slide your palms from the centre of the pin to the edges of the pin and back again very quickly. It is important that as the pin rolls out, your palms brush the surface of the dough, literally pulling it, as they move away from the middle. If you press downwards, the dough will stick. You need to press sideways for the dough to stretch, and only in one direction – outwards – then let the pin roll back towards you again as your hands come back to the centre. Working quickly and lightly, repeat this step three or four times.

3. Now you can wrap more of the dough around the pin and repeat step 2 again, and again, until you have all the dough on the pin.

Rotate the fully laden pin through a half turn then lay the sheet out in front of you and repeat steps 1, 2 and 3.

When you have rotated the sheet a complete turn, your dough should measure about 60 cm in diameter. If the edges are a little thicker than the rest of the sheet, simply run the pin over them until they are uniform. Likewise, if there are any tears or holes, they are easily repaired by gently pulling the edges together and sealing with a little water, then running the pin over the top.

These rolled pasta sheets will dry out very quickly, so you need to start cutting them straight away.

ROLLING AND STRETCHING PASTA DOUGH USING A PASTA MACHINE

For home use, I recommend the Italian-made Imperia pasta machine. The standard model will roll and stretch a 15 cm strip of pasta to six different thicknesses, and it comes with two cutters for long pasta – 2 mm and 6.5 mm. Additional cutting accessories are readily available, but you can always roll up the pasta sheet and use a sharp knife if you want other widths.

The pasta machine takes a lot of the hard work out of the rolling and stretching process. Just remember that you still need to take the time to work the dough through all the settings until you reach the final (or second-last) setting, to obtain the elasticity and silkiness that characterises the best pasta.

Divide the dough into four equal portions. Take one portion and, with the palm of your hand, flatten the dough so it will fit through the widest setting on the machine. Keep the remaining portions of dough covered in cling wrap so they do not dry out.

Set the machine on the widest setting. Feed the dough through and then fold it into thirds onto itself – as you might fold a business letter – pressing lightly to eliminate any bubbles of air. Feed the dough through the machine again another four or five times until it is the same width as the machine, folding it into thirds each time. Feed through one last time and, without folding it, lay the sheet on a nearby tea towel then repeat with the remaining portions of dough. Do not let the sheets touch, or they will stick together.

Now you are ready to stretch the dough. It is handy at this point to have a helper to manage the pasta sheets, as they get longer and more unwieldy as they pass through each setting of the rollers. If they become too long to manage, you can cut them with a knife to the desired length.

Move the setting on the machine down one notch and feed each sheet through again. Keep reducing the setting a notch and feeding each sheet through, thinning the pasta until all the sheets have been stretched to the desired thickness.

These rolled pasta sheets will dry out very quickly, so you need to start cutting them straight away.

CUTTING PASTA

Have plenty of clean dry tea towels ready to accommodate the pasta, plus some flour or semolina for dusting.

Start by cutting the pasta sheets into manageable lengths, covering any part of the pasta that is waiting to be cut with a clean damp tea towel to protect it from the air.

Everyone seems to have an opinion as to exactly what width each type of ribbon pasta should be. My recommendations for the recipes in this book are as follows, but you will come across many variations. The length of ribbon pasta also varies, but as a rule of thumb, thinner pasta can be longer than thicker pasta. For tagliatelle and fettuccine, I would suggest that somewhere between 25 and 30 cm is manageable. Remember too that all fresh pasta will expand slightly during cooking.

PASTA WIDTHS

Capelli d'angelo 1.5 mm
Tagliolini 2.5 mm
Tagliatelle 5 mm
Fettuccine 8 mm–1 cm
Pappardelle 2.5 cm
Lasagnette 3 cm

All of these pastas can be cut by hand, and the standard widths can be cut using the appropriate fitting on a pasta machine.

By hand, cut the pasta dough into sheets about 25 cm long. Flour lightly and roll each sheet into a loose cylinder then, using a very sharp knife, cut through the dough at the required intervals – for example, every 5 mm for tagliatelle.

With floured hands, gently unravel the noodles and place them on a lightly floured tea towel. Sprinkle with a little more flour and continue with the next sheet of dough until they are all made. Cover them with a damp tea towel if you think they are drying out too much, or alternatively sprinkle with a little more flour if they seem to be sticky.

CANNELLONI

Using a sharp knife, cut the pasta sheet into 10 cm squares (or whatever size best suits your baking dish). Lay the cannelloni sheets on a floured tea towel while you flatten and cut the remaining dough. You can stack each cannelloni sheet on top of the previous one with a floured tea towel in between each layer until you are ready to roll them round your filling.

LASAGNE

Using a sharp knife, cut the rolled pasta sheet into 15 cm × 10 cm rectangles (or whatever size best suits your baking dish). Lay the cut sheets on a floured tea towel while you flatten and cut the remaining dough. You can stack each lasagne sheet on top of the previous one with a floured tea towel in between each layer.

FARFALLE

With a sharp knife, first cut the pasta into 4 cm strips and then, using a fluted ravioli cutter or pastry wheel, cut these strips every 6 cm so that you have rectangles measuring 6 cm × 4 cm. If you don't have a ravioli cutter or pastry wheel, just use a sharp knife – the edges won't be so pretty, but the flavour will be the same.

Using your thumbs and index fingers, squeeze these rectangles in the centre to form a butterfly shape. Squish the edges together so that they stick – you may need to brush the centre with a little water to make the edges stick to it. Lay the farfalle on a floured tea towel and continue until they are all made.

GARGANELLI

Using a sharp knife, cut the pasta sheet into 2.5 cm squares. Pick up one square and dab a little water on one corner. Place a clean pencil on the opposite corner of the pasta square and roll the pasta around the pencil until you reach the opposite water-dampened corner, then push down to secure and slide the pencil out. You have made one garganello. Place it on a lightly floured tea towel and repeat the process until you have made them all.

MALTAGLIATI

Maltagliati means 'badly cut' and that is exactly what this pasta is. Leftovers and scraps can be roughly cut into strips, diamonds, triangles and rectangles about 3–4 cm a side – the more irregular, the better.

QUADRETTI

Using a sharp knife, and with the help of a ruler, cut the pasta sheet lengthways at 2 cm intervals and then crosswise at 2 cm intervals to produce 2 cm squares. Sprinkle the quadretti with flour before lifting them from the work surface to a clean, lightly floured tea towel. Cover with a damp tea towel until ready to use.

Ravioli/pasta ripiena

Silky fresh pasta sheets can also be made into little parcels stuffed with various fillings – the 'Filled pasta' chapter, starting on page 211, has full instructions, as well as ideas for basic fillings and recipes.

HOW TO COOK PASTA

To ensure that it cooks properly, pasta should be boiled in a lot of water – about 1 litre for each 100 g of pasta – and ideally in a low and wide pan (but still with sides higher than its diameter) for more uniform heat distribution. The water should not reach the top of the pan, or it will overflow during cooking, and it must be salted only after it has started boiling – if you add salt before, the water will take longer to boil. You will need about 1 teaspoon of rock salt or sea salt for each litre of water. Oil should never be added to the water when cooking dried pasta, but I do suggest adding a few drops when cooking filled pasta such as ravioli, to help stop the parcels from sticking together.

The pasta must be put in only when the water has reached a rolling boil – all at once for long pasta like spaghetti, and a bit at a time for short pasta such as penne.

To bring the water quickly back to the boil, cover two-thirds of the pan with a lid. When the water has reached boiling point again, take off the lid and turn the heat down a little. Stir with a fork so the pasta does not stick, and keep stirring occasionally during the cooking to separate the pasta.

Dried pasta should be cooked until it is al dente – that is, soft on the outside but still firm to the bite on the inside. Not only does it taste better this way, but it is also easier to digest because it hasn't absorbed too much water. Note, though, that al dente does *not* mean raw – undercooked pasta is as bad as overcooked. Al dente is generally achieved by cooking dried pasta for 1 or 2 minutes less than the suggested time on the packet. While the pasta is cooking, pick out a piece occasionally with a fork and chew on it, to see if it has reached the desired texture. I personally like pasta very al dente ('standing up', as the Italians put it), so I cook my spaghetti for only 5 minutes or so – this way, the strands still have a white spot in the middle.

Fresh pasta is a bit more particular, because it depends on whether you cook it as soon as it is made or if you have let it dry a little. For example, if you're cooking tagliatelle within an hour of making it, you should not need to boil it for more than 2 minutes. But if you're cooking it the next day, after it has dried, it could take 5 minutes.

As soon as the pasta is cooked to your satisfaction, remove it from the heat and drain it, retaining a little of the cooking water, which can then be used to moisten the finished dish if it seems too dry. Never run cold water through the pasta when draining, as it will wash off the layer of starch necessary to enable it to amalgamate better with the sauce. I usually like to add the drained pasta to the pan containing the sauce, so the pasta absorbs the sauce in the final minutes of cooking.

Eat pasta as soon as it's cooked, when it is at its best: pasta doesn't wait for you, but rather you have to wait for the pasta. And remember that there should be enough sauce to coat the pasta, not drown it.

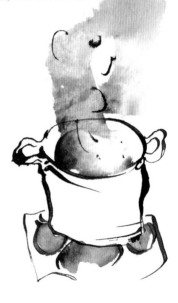

Soups
and
broths

For centuries, homes in the Italian countryside have been scented by the pot of soup that hangs permanently over the coals in the fireplace, welcoming the farmer home from the fields and the hunter home from the forest. Soups are among the most ancient staples of Italian cuisine. Very much of peasant origin, they are the ultimate comfort food: economical to prepare, yet tasty and nourishing. Mainly made of vegetables and legumes, they are often flavoured with a soffritto of olive oil, onion and pancetta, and bulked up with a handful of pastina (tiny pasta shapes) or fragments shaken from the bottom of the container where the dried pasta has been stored. Eaten with bread, and topped with some olive oil or pesto, the soup becomes a meal in itself.

Then there are the lighter soups, made with a clear broth (*brodo*) to which pasta has been added, and designed to be eaten as an appetiser. In Italy, broths are very popular in the months from autumn to spring. Many houses have pots of broth simmering on the stove, in preparation for *tortellini in brodo*, *passatelli in brodo*, or simply to be sipped as a consommé before the hot entrée at an elegant dinner party, served in those beautifully delicate cups with two handles.

In this chapter we discuss both types of *pasta in brodo*, and tell you how to make some great basic stocks. Stock will keep in the fridge for three days, or in the freezer for up to six months. You can freeze it in ice-cube trays, then pop the cubes out of the trays and store them in a ziplock freezer bag.

Chicken broth

BRODO DI POLLO

1 large chicken (about 1.5 kg), skin removed
1 onion, peeled but left whole
1 carrot, cut in half
1 celery stalk, cut in half
handful of flat-leaf parsley (optional)
large pinch of sea salt
a few black peppercorns

MAKES ABOUT 1.5 LITRES

For a complete meal, prepare this lovely chicken broth and have pasta cooked in the broth as an entrée, then serve the poached chicken (from the stock) as a main course with salsa verde and salad or vegetables. A memorable lunch – and very balanced for the colder seasons.

Place all the ingredients in a stockpot or large saucepan. Pour in 2 litres of cold water, adding more to cover, if necessary. Bring to the boil and cook for 15 minutes, then reduce the heat and allow to barely simmer for at least another 2 hours. During this time, skim any foam from the surface as it forms.

Remove the chicken (keeping it to serve later with salsa verde and salad or vegetables), then strain the stock through muslin or a fine sieve into a bowl, and refrigerate for at least 2 hours.

Remove and discard the layer of solidified fat that will have formed on the surface of the stock. You are now left with a deliciously full-flavoured, gelatinous stock that can be used as is, or diluted with water if necessary.

Fish stock

FUMETTO DI PESCE

500 g fish heads and bones
    (mainly heads, if possible)
1 onion, cut into segments
1 celery stalk, roughly chopped
1 carrot, roughly chopped
1 large slice of lemon
2 sprigs each of sage and thyme
1 bay leaf
150 ml dry white wine
large pinch of sea salt
a few black peppercorns

MAKES ABOUT 1.5 LITRES

With fish, most of the flavour lies in the head and the bones, so don't throw them away. When you buy fish and ask the fishmonger to fillet it for you, be sure to keep the bones and the heads, taking them home in a separate bag.
    You can serve this broth as a delicate consommé, or freeze it in ice-cube trays for later use. It retains its flavour well, and the cubes are perfect for adding to a seafood sauce for pasta if it seems too dry.

Place all the ingredients in a stockpot or large saucepan. Pour in 2 litres of cold water, adding more to cover, if necessary. Bring to the boil, then reduce the heat and simmer for 40 minutes, skimming any foam from the surface as it forms.

Strain the stock through muslin or a fine sieve into a bowl and store in the refrigerator or freezer; it will keep for 3 days chilled or 4–6 months frozen.

Beef broth

BRODO DI MANZO

During winter, particularly in the countryside of northern Italy, you're likely to find a pot of meat broth bubbling away in most kitchens, enriching the whole house with its scent. This nourishing broth wouldn't always be served with pasta; sometimes it might be sipped as a lovely clear consommé, just to warm everyone up before the serious eating begins.

In this recipe, we explain how to remove the fat, but you might prefer to live like the citizens of Bologna, who love to see glistening sparkles of fat on top of their broth, calling them *stelline* ('little stars').

500 g meaty beef bones (such as shank, short ribs, shin bones)
500 g cracked beef bones (ideally knuckle – ask your butcher)
2 carrots, cut in half
2 celery stalks with leaves, cut into 5 cm lengths
2 onions, peeled and cut in half
2 large ripe tomatoes, cut in half
handful of flat-leaf parsley
1 bay leaf
1½ teaspoons sea salt
a few black peppercorns

MAKES ABOUT 2 LITRES

Preheat the oven to 220°C. Place all the bones in a large heavy-based roasting tin and roast for 30 minutes. Stir well, then add the carrots, celery and onions and roast for a further 45–60 minutes, stirring occasionally, until the bones are a very deep brown.

Transfer the roasted ingredients to a large stockpot. Spoon off the fat from the liquid in the roasting tin, then add 500 ml of water. Place over medium heat, bring to the boil and scrape to loosen any browned drippings from the tin – this is all the good stuff. Add to the stockpot, along with 2 litres of water. Bring to the boil, then reduce the heat and simmer, partially covered, for 30 minutes. During this time, skim any foam from the surface as it forms. Add the tomatoes, parsley, bay leaf, salt and peppercorns and simmer over low heat, partially covered, for 3 hours.

Remove the bones, then strain the broth through muslin or a fine sieve into a bowl. Check the seasoning, adding more salt if needed. Leave to cool, uncovered, in the refrigerator. If desired, remove the layer of solidified fat from the surface before using.

This stock will keep in the refrigerator for 3 days, or in the freezer for up to 6 months. You can freeze it in ice-cube trays, then pop the cubes out of the trays and store them in a ziplock freezer bag.

Vegetable broth

BRODO DI VERDURE

1 onion, peeled and cut in half
1 carrot, cut in half
2 young celery stalks with leaves, cut in half
1 clove garlic, peeled
6 button mushrooms, left whole
3 sprigs each of marjoram, thyme and
    flat-leaf parsley
3 bay leaves
1 teaspoon sea salt
1 teaspoon black peppercorns

MAKES ABOUT 1.5 LITRES

When I was growing up, we didn't make a big distinction between chicken broth and vegetable broth. When there was a chicken to be eaten, we'd make a broth with it. When there wasn't, we'd make a broth with vegetables from the garden, being sure to include some leafy young celery stalks and plenty of fresh herbs to boost the flavour.

    This broth is delicious with vegetable-filled ravioli (see page 215), tortellini, or with passatelli (see page 37), whether or not you're vegetarian.

Place all the ingredients in a stockpot or large saucepan, cover with 2 litres of water, and bring to the boil. Reduce the heat to low and simmer for about 1 hour.

Strain the stock through muslin or a fine sieve into a bowl, and you have a beautiful vegetable stock.

Spring minestrone with ditalini

MINESTRONE LEGGERO CON DITALINI

3 carrots, diced
2 celery stalks, diced
1 large white onion, diced
300 g zucchini (courgettes), diced
300 g potatoes, diced
150 g shelled peas
150 g green beans, trimmed and
    cut into 1 cm lengths
200 g spinach, chopped
200 g ripe tomatoes, peeled and seeded
    (see page 51), then diced
sea salt and freshly ground black pepper
300 g ditalini
60 ml extra virgin olive oil
handful of chopped basil *or* 2 tablespoons
    pesto, if you have it to hand
freshly grated parmesan, to serve (optional)

SERVES 4–6

Colourful and wholesome, this spring minestrone soup is not only tasty, but also a feast for the eyes. Aesthetically, it's important to cut all the vegetables to a similar size, slightly bigger than the pasta pieces. I've suggested a tube-shaped pasta called ditalini, but equally good is the slightly longer sedanini.

Place all the vegetables in a stockpot or large saucepan and add enough cold water to cover by 2 cm. Place over a high heat and bring to the boil. Mix thoroughly with a wooden spoon and season with salt and pepper. Turn down to a gentle simmer, cover and cook for 15 minutes. Add the pasta, stir well and simmer for a further 8–10 minutes or as indicated on the pasta packet.

Remove from the heat and stir in the olive oil and the chopped basil or pesto. If using pesto, you could sprinkle on a little parmesan, if you like.

Ditalini and potatoes in vegetable broth

PASTA E PATATE IN BRODO

This is what Italians call a *minestra*, which is a kind of thick hearty soup that is very popular in Tuscany. Potatoes were only deemed an acceptable part of Italian cuisine in the nineteenth century, although they had arrived in Europe from South America much earlier than that. Some 200 years ago in the area of Liguria where my family comes from, the local bishop put out a pamphlet reassuring his parishioners that potatoes were not poisonous and urging them to plant them, as they were such good nourishment for poor people.

100 g flat pancetta
2 sprigs rosemary, leaves picked
80 ml extra virgin olive oil
3 spring onions, finely chopped
1 large ripe tomato, peeled and seeded (see page 51), then sliced
300 g waxy potatoes, peeled and diced
sea salt and freshly ground black pepper
1 litre vegetable broth (see page 32)
200 g ditalini or other small pasta
freshly grated parmesan, to serve (optional)

SERVES 4–6

Place the pancetta and rosemary leaves on a chopping board and chop them together finely – a mezzaluna is ideal for this, but otherwise a big, sharp knife will do.

Pour the olive oil into a large saucepan over medium heat, add the spring onions and the pancetta and rosemary mixture and cook for 4 minutes, stirring with a wooden spoon. Add the tomato and potato, sprinkle on a little salt and pepper, and stir for a minute.

Add the broth, bring to the boil, and cook for 10 minutes. Add the pasta and continue cooking for the time recommended on the packet.

Serve the *minestra* very hot – with a sprinkle of parmesan, if you like.

Bean and Pasta soup

PASTA E FAGIOLI ALLA MONTANARA

Pasta e fagioli is one of the few dishes that unify Italy: from *pasta e fasoi*, the northern version, to the Calabrian *pastafazool* made immortal by Dean Martin. This version *alla montanara* ('from the mountains') calls for large white beans, called *fagioli di Spagna* in Italian, and the presence of chilli makes it instantly recognisable as Calabrian.

You'll need to start this soup ahead of time, as the beans need to be soaked overnight and the cooked soup is rested for a couple of hours before serving.

1 kg large white beans (*fagioli di Spagna*)
1 carrot, cut in half
1 celery stalk, cut in half
75 ml olive oil
3 cloves garlic, peeled and lightly squashed
2 red chillies, finely chopped
1 kg white onions, peeled and
    roughly chopped
200 g prosciutto, diced
200 g ripe tomatoes, peeled and seeded
    (see page 51), then diced
sea salt
300 g potatoes, peeled and diced
400 g maccheroncini, ditalini or
    broken spaghetti
freshly grated nutmeg, to serve

SERVES 4–6

Cover the beans with cold water and leave to soak overnight.

Next day, drain the beans and place in a large saucepan or stockpot. Add enough cold water to cover the beans by 5–10 cm, then add the carrot and celery. Bring to the boil, then turn down to a simmer and cook gently over low heat for 45 minutes.

In the meantime, make the soffritto. Heat the olive oil in a heavy-bottomed frying pan and sauté the garlic and chilli until the garlic is just golden, then remove and discard the garlic cloves. Add the onion to the pan and sauté, stirring with a wooden spoon, until it is soft and translucent, then add the prosciutto and cook for another 3 minutes. Add the tomato, stir well and cook for a further 2 minutes.

Now, back to the beans. After they have cooked for about 45 minutes, discard the carrot and celery and add the soffritto you have just made. Stir well, season with salt, then continue cooking over low heat for another 45 minutes. Remove the pan from the heat and add the potatoes and pasta. Mix well, cover the pan with a lid and let the soup rest off the heat for about 2 hours. After this time, you will find that the potatoes and pasta are both cooked to perfection!

Gently reheat the soup, sprinkle with a few gratings of nutmeg and serve.

Chickpea soup with quadretti

ZUPPA DI CECI CON QUADRETTI

Chickpeas are a wholesome element of the Mediterranean diet, adding a pleasant nutty flavour. They appear in ancient Roman recipes, and the world's first great lawyer, Cicero, supposedly got his name from *cicer*, the Latin word for chickpea (*ceci* in Italian) because his grandfather had a wart on his nose that looked like one. I find that dried chickpeas soaked overnight then cooked have a better flavour and texture than tinned chickpeas.

400 g chickpeas
200 g basic pasta dough (see page 11)
10 g dried porcini mushrooms
15 sage leaves, roughly chopped
1 clove garlic, finely chopped
2 celery stalks, finely chopped
2 large ripe tomatoes, peeled and seeded
 (see page 51), then sliced
sea salt
60 ml extra virgin olive oil
60 g freshly grated parmesan

SERVES 4

Soak the chickpeas in cold water for 24 hours, then drain and place in a stockpot or large saucepan. Cover them with double their volume of cold water and simmer gently for 2 hours, stirring regularly with a wooden spoon. Skim off and discard any scum that rises to the surface, adding more boiling water if necessary.

While the chickpeas are cooking, prepare the pasta dough and set it aside to rest. Meanwhile, soak the dried porcini in warm water for about 15 minutes, then drain, pat dry and chop roughly. Mix the porcini with the sage, garlic and celery, and set aside.

Roll the pasta dough into a thin sheet (see pages 17–18). Using a sharp knife, and with the help of a ruler, cut the pasta sheet lengthways at 2 cm intervals and then crosswise at 2 cm intervals to produce 2 cm squares. Sprinkle the quadretti with flour before lifting them from the work surface to a clean, lightly floured tea towel. Cover with a damp tea towel until ready to use.

After the chickpeas have been cooking for 1½ hours, add the tomato, a large pinch of salt and the porcini mixture to the pan and stir thoroughly. Continue cooking for another half-hour or until the chickpeas are tender.

Cook the quadretti for 1 minute in plenty of boiling salted water, then drain, reserving a little of the cooking water. Add the pasta to the soup, stir thoroughly, and cook for another 2 minutes.

If the soup seems too dry, add a little of the reserved pasta-cooking water. Divide among four bowls and serve with a generous drizzle of olive oil (about 1 tablespoon per bowl) and the freshly grated parmesan.

Passatelli in broth

PASSATELLI IN BRODO

One evening when we were having a staff dinner at Lucio's restaurant, my then business partner (and still dear friend) Marino Maioli declared, 'I miss my mother's passatelli so much!' Marino, who comes from the hills near Rimini on Italy's north-east coast, went on to explain, 'It's a kind of pasta, but not really . . . a dough of parmesan and breadcrumbs is pushed through a special utensil with holes, so that little worms come out on the other side. These are cooked in boiling broth and when they come to the surface, they are ready. Passatelli is winter, it's Sunday, it's family and friends around a table feeling nurtured and warmed. Next time you are in Italy, you go and see my mother and she will make passatelli for you.' So I did! I drove right across Italy, from the Tyrrhenian Sea to the Adriatic Sea, and I visited Marino's mother. She made passatelli, and they were just as Marino had described.

Passatelli is a speciality from the Emilia Romagna region. They are usually eaten in broth and, as is often the case in Italy, are almost unknown outside their area of origin. In Emilia, people are crazy about nutmeg, so the passatelli is often scented with it, and they often sprinkle some more on the broth with the parmesan at the table. Down in Romagna, particularly by the sea, lemon zest may be added to the dough and, rather than being cooked in broth, the passatelli are cooked like pasta, drained and dressed with a vongole or mussel sauce.

There is one small problem: the special utensil used to make them is hard to find, even in Italy. I suggest you use a potato ricer – your passatelli will be thinner, but just as delicious.

3 eggs
a few gratings of nutmeg
sea salt
150 g freshly grated parmesan,
    plus extra to serve
150 g stale bread, grated finely
    (or packaged breadcrumbs are fine)
20 g butter or bone marrow
1 tablespoon plain flour
1.5 litres chicken broth (see page 30)

SERVES 4

Break the eggs into a large bowl, preferably ceramic, then add the nutmeg and season with salt. Start mixing with a fork, adding the parmesan, breadcrumbs and butter or bone marrow and mixing well. Using your hands, knead the mixture well until a soft dough forms, sprinkling with flour if necessary to stop it from sticking. If the dough seems too stiff, add a little water to soften it. Form the dough into a ball, cover with cling wrap and leave the dough to rest for 2 hours at room temperature.

Divide the rested dough into smaller balls that will fit into the potato ricer. (The bigger the ball, the longer the passatelli will be – and you don't want them too long!)

To make the passatelli, press the dough through the potato ricer onto a lightly floured tea towel. When all the passatelli are made, bring the broth to the boil, then take it off the heat and immediately add the passatelli. Mix delicately. When the passatelli rise to the surface, they are ready. Serve immediately sprinkled with parmesan – and more nutmeg, if you want.

Pasta soup with peas

PASTA E PISELLI

This hearty soup is so quick and simple to make that it easily becomes addictive. We use ditalini or tubetti for this, but broken spaghetti or a mixture of pastas will do just fine.

In the old days, when dried pasta was sold from huge sideboards with glass-fronted drawers in Italian grocery stores, there was always lots of broken pasta left in the bottom of the drawers. Sold cheaply to make way for the next batch, this pasta often found its way into soups.

90 ml extra virgin olive oil

25 g butter

1 small white onion, finely chopped

70 g pancetta, cut into small strips

400 g fresh or frozen peas

sea salt and freshly ground black pepper

200 g tubetti, ditalini or broken spaghetti

1 tablespoon finely chopped flat-leaf parsley

80 g freshly grated parmesan

SERVES 4

Heat the olive oil and butter in a large saucepan or stockpot over a low–medium heat. Add the onion and pancetta and sauté for about 6–8 minutes, stirring with a wooden spoon, until the onion is soft. Add the peas, then season with a little salt and pepper and stir for a couple of minutes to allow the peas to absorb the flavours.

Add 1 litre of water or broth, bring to the boil and cook the peas for 10 minutes (5 minutes if using frozen peas). Add the pasta and cook for the time indicated on the packet, stirring often with a wooden spoon.

When the pasta is ready, stir in the parsley and serve immediately with the parmesan.

Veal and pork tortellini in chicken broth

TORTELLINI IN BRODO

Tortellini are a speciality of Emilia Romagna, particularly Bologna and Modena. They are very good eaten with various sauces (try the Ragù alla Bolognese on page 56 or any of the tomato sauces on pages 51–52), but served in broth they make any day a festive day, and any festive day an unforgettable one.

If you buy your minced meat from the butchers, ask them to run it through the mincer twice for you – this will give the filling a finer and lighter texture.

400 g basic pasta dough (see page 11)
1.5 litres chicken broth (see page 30)
freshly grated parmesan, to serve

FILLING

20 g butter
100 g minced veal
100 g lean minced pork – ideally pork loin
6 sage leaves, finely chopped
sea salt and freshly ground black pepper
30 g ricotta
50 g prosciutto, finely chopped
2 eggs
a few gratings of nutmeg
100 g freshly grated parmesan

SERVES 4

First make the pasta dough according to the instructions on page 11.

While the dough is resting, heat the butter in a frying pan over high heat. Add the minced veal and pork and the sage, season with salt and pepper, and brown for a few minutes just until the meat changes colour. Place in a bowl and allow to cool, then add the ricotta, prosciutto, eggs, nutmeg and the parmesan. Mix well.

Roll out the pasta and shape into tortellini (see page 217), filling them with the veal and pork mixture.

Bring the broth to a simmer, add the tortellini and cook for 4–5 minutes (they will rise to the surface when they're ready). Transfer the tortellini and broth to a beautiful tureen and serve immediately. Make sure there is plenty of freshly grated parmesan on the table.

Pasta in broth with meatballs

PASTA IN BRODO CON POLPETTINE

Tiny meatballs added to soups or stews are apparently part of an Arab cooking tradition that arrived in Sicily more than 1000 years ago. Here they are like little explosions of flavour that contrast with the smoothness of the zucchini and the lightness of the pasta. As with all *in brodo* dishes, the quality of the broth is critical here – it's best to be able to stand back at the end of the meal and proudly tell your guests you made it yourself.

2 × 1.5 cm thick slices Italian-style bread,
    crusts removed
250 ml milk
200 g minced veal or beef
1 egg
handful of chopped flat-leaf parsley
80 g freshly grated parmesan
sea salt and freshly ground black pepper
500 g large zucchini (courgettes), diced
2 litres beef broth (see page 31)
400 g pastina or other short pasta for soups
freshly grated parmesan, to serve

SERVES 4

Break the bread into small pieces and soak in the milk, then squeeze and place in a bowl with the minced meat, egg, parsley and the 80 g of parmesan. Season with salt and pepper and, using your hands, mix well. With the help of a spoon, shape the mixture into little meatballs – about the size of an almond is perfect for eating easily from a spoon with some broth, I think, but you can make them larger if you prefer.

Bring the broth to the boil in a large saucepan. Add the meatballs, then lower the heat and simmer gently for 3–4 minutes or until cooked through – the time needed will depend on the size of the meatballs. Add the pastina and the zucchini and simmer gently until the pasta is al dente.

Transfer to your favourite soup tureen and serve immediately, sprinkled with parmesan.

Stuffed quadretti in beef broth

QUADRETTI SPALMATI IN BRODO

This stuffed pasta differs from ravioli in that the filling is spread uniformly over one sheet of pasta before the second layer is gently pressed on top to hold the filling in place before it is cut into squares.

First prepare a half quantity of basic pasta dough and set it aside to rest.

While the dough is resting, prepare the filling. Break the eggs into a large bowl, sprinkle in a little salt and pepper, and beat with a fork. Add the ricotta, mascarpone and grated parmesan and mix thoroughly with a spoon.

Flatten the pasta dough into a long rectangular sheet (see pages 17–18). Spread the filling evenly over one half of the pasta sheet, then fold the other half over it. Press down gently all over and around the edges with your fingertips, making sure the filling is in contact with both the top and bottom sheets of pasta. Cut the stuffed pasta into 2 cm squares and let them dry for 10 minutes.

Bring the broth to a simmer in a large saucepan, carefully slip in the stuffed quadretti and cook for 3–4 minutes.

Serve very hot, with a sprinkling of parmesan.

200 g basic pasta dough (see page 11)
1.5 litres beef broth (see page 31)
freshly grated parmesan, to serve

FILLING

2 eggs
sea salt and freshly ground black pepper
100 g ricotta
100 g mascarpone
100 g freshly grated parmesan

SERVES 4

Some
basic
sauces

It's a debate like the chicken and the egg. What's more important: the pasta or the sauce? Is the pasta just the logical base for a great stew, or is the sauce just an afterthought that might enhance a beautifully worked sculpture in dough?

In this chapter we come down on the side of the sauce (having taken the other side elsewhere in this book). We discuss some classic accompaniments, dressings and condiments that can be made separately, kept and used whenever a dish needs elevation.

You'll encounter words such as sugo, salsa and ragù here, used to indicate variations in the way Italians describe sauces: a ragù (or *tocco* in Ligurian dialect) is usually a meat sauce; a sugo is a thin sauce, often tomato; and a salsa is a thicker vegetable sauce, containing pieces of vegetable, not pureed.

We begin, naturally, with the king of sauces – pesto, which is the pride of Liguria, where I come from.

PESTO

Three things define the cooking of Liguria: simplicity, poverty and originality. We keep it simple because we like the flavour of every ingredient to speak for itself; a history of economic hardship has taught us never to waste anything; and the influence of other seafaring cultures – like the Normans, the Vikings and the Arabs – has made our cooking unique in Italy.

The sauce called pesto (which literally means 'pounded') is a perfect example. Simple to make, with inexpensive ingredients, its origin seems to lie with the Arabs hundreds of years ago. Authentic *pesto alla Genovese* has seven and only seven ingredients: basil, garlic, salt, pine nuts, olive oil, parmesan and pecorino. The crucial thing is to achieve a perfect balance, with no one ingredient overpowering the other. Having said that, there is still much debate in Liguria about the desirable strength of the pesto, the amount of garlic used and the sharpness of the pecorino: the closer you travel to Genoa, the more garlicky and sharper with pecorino the pesto becomes.

While the Ligurians settled on basil as the focus of flavour and colour in pesto during the nineteenth century, other parts of Italy have adapted pesto to local tastes. To give you a taste of the many regional variations, we've included some pesto recipes from other regions, especially those in the south of Italy:

- Linguine with Tuscan pesto (page 78)
- Fusilli with Sicilian pesto (page 79)
- Spaghetti with pistachio pesto (page 81)
- Rigatoni with Calabrian pesto (page 82)
- Fusilli with almond and mint pesto (page 78)
- Linguine with orange pesto and eggplant (page 85)
- Trofie with basil and walnut pesto (page 159)

Classic Pesto

PESTO ALLA GENOVESE

Because pesto is so simple, it is important that all the ingredients are the best you can get. The basil leaves should be small and tender with no stalk – if the leaves are large, I suggest you remove the central stalk and tear the leaves into smaller pieces. The garlic should be the freshest you can find and the pine nuts should be used raw, not toasted. The cheeses should be of the best quality and freshly grated, and the sea salt should be the finest available. Most important of all is the olive oil, which should ideally be Ligurian, for its delicate fruity flavour. The colour of the pesto should be pea green: this is achieved by using young basil leaves and the right amounts of pine nuts and cheese.

While using a blender is acceptable and gives a good result, it is only by pounding the ingredients with a mortar and pestle that you can obtain the perfect emulsion. The order the ingredients are added to the mortar is another source of contention. I am of the school that believes it better to start with the garlic and salt, followed by the basil (which will retain its beautiful green colour), then the pine nuts, the cheeses, and finally the oil.

50 small basil leaves

1 clove garlic, peeled

pinch of sea salt

1 tablespoon raw pine nuts

2 tablespoons freshly grated parmesan

1 tablespoon freshly grated mild pecorino, preferably Sardinian

about 3 tablespoons extra virgin olive oil

SERVES 4

Carefully wash the basil leaves and dry them gently between two paper towels without applying pressure.

If using a mortar and pestle, begin with the garlic and a pinch of salt (this will help to keep the basil green). Crush the garlic, then add the basil leaves and continue pounding against the sides of the mortar with a rotary movement, not just beating the pestle against the base. Add the pine nuts, the two cheeses and a tablespoon of olive oil and continue mixing with the pestle. When the mixture is reduced to a creamy consistency, transfer it to a bowl. Add enough olive oil to amalgamate everything nicely, mixing well. Pour on more oil to cover the pesto. If you are keeping the pesto for a while (it will keep for a month in the fridge), make sure it is always covered with olive oil to maintain its freshness and stop it from going black.

If you prefer to use a blender, put all the ingredients in at once and use the lowest speed. Stop often to let it cool down, because hot oil will affect the aroma of the basil. Pulse until the pesto reaches the desired consistency.

Pesto is a sauce *a freddo*; it should never be cooked or heated. Add it to pasta – traditionally trenette (see page 76) – off the heat and serve immediately.

TOMATO SAUCES

In people's minds, tomato sauce is so inextricably linked with Italy that many are surprised to learn that until 1700, no tomatoes were used in Italian food. For that was when the new 'golden apple' from America was finally accepted by Europeans. The southern Italians and the Spanish were the first to embrace it, while the English continued to believe it was poisonous for another 100 years.

Of course, there are many kinds of tomatoes, and at least as many ways of making a tomato sauce. The soffritto or base for the sauce is very important, as it determines the ultimate flavour, and it will often be matched to the type of pasta, occasion or mood. Some cooks use only onion in the soffritto, while some add finely chopped garlic; others slice the garlic for a stronger taste, or infuse the oil with a whole garlic clove for a more subtle flavour. Some add celery and carrot, then pass the sauce through a mouli for a smooth, velvety and quite elegant sauce; others prefer to melt an anchovy into the oil and include chilli and capers for extra pungency, or add chopped pancetta or lardo to give the sauce a rich savoury note. And then there are herbs to consider: parsley, basil or thyme, added at the beginning or the end of the cooking time. Some finish the sauce with a drop of olive oil, others with a knob of butter. Some use parmesan; others don't. Then there are the cooking times: short, for a fresher, more acidic taste; or longer, for a more traditional, reduced sauce.

Here I give you three of my favourite tomato sauces, but I want you to feel free to improvise – just as they would in Italy – to make them your favourites.

Pasta al pomodoro – pasta (usually spaghetti) with tomato sauce – is probably the most-eaten dish in the whole of Italy, from the small islands south of Sicily to the mountain villages perched high in the Alps. Wonderfully simple and very tasty, it couldn't be easier. Make the sauce while the pasta is cooking. When the pasta is al dente, drain it and, while it is still steaming, toss it with the tomato sauce, and there you have it. You will soon understand why Italians are addicted to *pasta al pomodoro* . . .

50

Tomato Sauce I

SALSA DI POMODORO I

This is a fantastic, fresh and quick sauce that relies on good, ripe tomatoes for its flavour. I recommend using vine-ripened tomatoes for their lovely balance of acidity and sweetness, or roma tomatoes. (If the tomatoes seem too watery when you cut into them, place the diced tomato in a colander over the sink and leave to drain for about half an hour so it loses some of its moisture.) I want the tomato and basil to be the stars of this sauce, with nothing to get in the way of such a fine balance of flavours.

1 tablespoon extra virgin olive oil
2 cloves garlic, peeled and lightly squashed
1 red chilli, cut in half lengthways (optional)
600 g very ripe tomatoes, peeled and seeded
    (see below), then diced
sea salt
2 tablespoons chopped basil leaves

MAKES ENOUGH FOR 4

Heat the olive oil in a large heavy-based saucepan over low heat, add the garlic and chilli (if using) and stir with a wooden spoon until the garlic just starts to colour. Discard the garlic and chilli.

Increase the heat to medium–high. Add the tomato and salt to the oil and simmer gently until the tomato has broken down and the liquid starts to boil away. Stir often and take care not to let it burn. When the sauce starts to emulsify and thicken (after about 4–5 minutes), remove the pan from the heat. At this point you can stir in the basil.

The sauce is now ready to receive your chosen pasta – spaghetti would be my first choice.

How to peel and seed tomatoes

Cut a cross at the base of the tomatoes and plunge into boiling water for about a minute. Remove with a slotted spoon and place the tomatoes in iced water until the skin starts to wrinkle. When cool, drain and peel the tomatoes – the skin should slip off easily – then cut them in half and use a teaspoon to scoop out the seeds.

Tomato Sauce II

SALSA DI POMODORO II

1 × 400 g tin peeled tomatoes
60 ml extra virgin olive oil
1 clove garlic, minced
½ red onion, finely diced
3 sprigs basil
pinch of sea salt
1 teaspoon butter

MAKES ENOUGH FOR 4

Every home in Italy has tins of peeled tomatoes in the cupboard, so don't worry, there is nothing wrong with it – especially in winter, when fresh tomatoes are not at their best. But I do suggest you buy the best quality, either 'San Marzano' style imported from Italy, or locally produced. And whatever you do, make sure that what is in the tin is only tomatoes and their juices, and nothing else!

This sauce goes best with tube-style pasta, such as rigatoni.

Pass the tomatoes through a mouli or squish them with your hands. Set aside.

Heat the olive oil in a large heavy-based saucepan over medium heat. Add the garlic and stir until it just starts to colour. Add the onion and sauté until it becomes soft and translucent. Add the crushed tomato, the basil and salt to taste. Simmer gently for 20 minutes until the sauce is nice and thick. Discard the basil, add the butter and stir.

Tomato Sauce III

SALSA DI POMODORO III

3 tablespoons extra virgin olive oil
2 cloves garlic, peeled and lightly squashed
1 red onion, chopped
1 small carrot, chopped
2 celery stalks, chopped
1 kg ripe roma tomatoes, cored and
    roughly chopped
pinch of sea salt

MAKES 500 ML – ENOUGH FOR 4

When tomatoes are cheap and in abundance, you can make a large batch of this sauce to use over the winter months. Just increase the quantities here and transfer the sauce to sterilised jars or bottles. A nice touch if doing this is to add a single fresh basil leaf to each jar or bottle before sealing.

I think of this as the 'grande dame' of these three tomato sauces – it reminds me of a great soprano: strong and confident, but at the same time delicate and elegant. Rather like an instant passata, this sauce captures the essence of tomato, with added depth of flavour from the celery, carrots and onions and the final touch of the basil. The results inspire optimism – somehow, all is well with the world when you have a sauce like this on hand!

Heat the olive oil in a large heavy-based saucepan over medium heat. Add the garlic cloves and stir with a wooden spoon until they just start to colour, then discard. Add the onion, carrot and celery and sauté until the onion becomes translucent. Add the tomato and salt, then reduce the heat to a simmer. Cover the pan and continue cooking, stirring from time to time, until the tomatoes begin to fall apart – about 45 minutes.

Now pass the sauce through a mouli or coarse sieve and return it to the pan. Check the seasoning and continue cooking (without a lid) until the sauce has thickened. The time will depend on how watery the sauce was to begin with, but it should be around 20 minutes. To check if the sauce is ready, place a drop on a plate: if a large watery halo does not form around it, then the consistency is right.

This sauce will keep in the fridge for up to a week, or can be preserved for later use (see left).

RAGÙS

Present in all regions of Italy, ragùs are interpreted in different ways from the north to the south. The word comes from the French *ragout*, which is a meat stew cooked slowly over low heat; it might contain veal, beef, lamb, goat, rabbit, hare or other meats.

In Italy, there are also differences in the herbs and spices used, the type of wine and the base (soffritto) of the sauce in which the meat cooks. Some ragùs are served as a two-course meal. The sauce is used to dress pasta, which is eaten first, then the meat, sometimes with vegetables, becomes a *secondo*. Sometimes the meat is minced and used to dress pasta, but it still makes for a substantial meal.

For Italians, all ragùs have two important things in common: Sundays and family memories. They are usually made on a Sunday, because that is when there is more time to spend on cooking. Every Italian recalls a mother or grandmother stirring a big pot of ragù as it bubbles away in the kitchen – and the distinctive scents it gives off, from the strong and sharp smell of the onions in the soffritto to the more reassuring aroma that indicates the meat is almost ready. Ragù is the sense memory of conviviality!

I hope you can build up memories for your family and friends with one of the following ragùs. Just remember that the most important ingredient for making any ragù is time.

In addition to the recipes for classic Bolognese and Ligurian ragùs given here, I've also included recipes for some of my other favourite ragù-style pasta sauces on the following pages:

- Neapolitan ragù (page 58)
- Neapolitan meat sauce – La Genovese (page 60)
- Sicilian meat sauce (page 61)
- Lasagnette with a tomato ragù (page 172)
- Lasagnette with rabbit sauce (page 186)
- Capsicum pappardelle with oxtail (page 185)
- Chocolate tagliatelle with wild boar (page 191)

Ligurian meat sauce

TOCCO DI CARNE

This meat ragù comes from Genoa, the capital of Liguria, where a substantial sauce is called a *tocco* (or *tuccu* in the local dialect). It can be eaten in several different ways. The first is to pass the ragù through a mouli and then use it to dress pasta (as my mother used to do); another way is to serve the sauce with pasta, followed by the meat as a main course with vegetables (as my Aunty Anna preferred). Or you can even use the meat to fill ravioli and serve these with the sauce – with lots of parmesan, of course.

The traditional recipe includes some bone marrow for richness, and I suggest you use it too, if your butcher will oblige.

25 g dried porcini mushrooms
100 ml extra virgin olive oil
   (a light Ligurian oil, if possible)
40 g butter
50 g bone marrow (optional)
1 celery stalk, finely chopped
1 small carrot, finely chopped
1 small white onion, finely chopped
1 garlic clove, peeled and lightly squashed
2 bay leaves
500 g veal or beef – shoulder or belly, rolled
   and tied in one even piece like a roast
2 sprigs rosemary
120 ml dry white wine
4 large ripe tomatoes, peeled and seeded
   (see page 51), then diced
1 tablespoon tomato paste
sea salt
freshly ground black pepper
250–500 ml veal or beef stock

SERVES 4

Soak the dried porcini mushrooms in warm water for 15 minutes, then drain, pat dry with paper towels and chop finely. Discard the soaking water.

Pour the olive oil into a heavy-based saucepan with high sides that is just large enough to hold the meat. Place over medium–high heat and add the butter and bone marrow, if using. When melted, add the celery, carrot, onion, garlic, bay leaves and porcini. Sauté for 6–8 minutes or until the vegetables have softened, stirring constantly with a wooden spoon and discarding the garlic clove as soon as it starts to colour.

Add the meat and the rosemary to the pan and brown the meat on all sides for about 15 minutes, stirring delicately. Add the wine and, when it has evaporated (about 5 minutes), stir in the tomato and the tomato paste. Season with salt and pepper and mix well, shaking the pan to make sure nothing is sticking to the bottom.

Turn the heat down to low and cook gently for 10–15 minutes, then add enough stock to cover the meat. Cover the saucepan, turn the heat down to very low and cook for 1½ hours. Check on the sauce often, turning the meat and shaking the pan to avoid sticking; if it starts to look too dry, add a little more stock or water. When it is ready, the meat should be very tender and the sauce reduced and velvety.

If you want to eat the ragù with pasta as a main course, break up the meat with a fork and then pass everything through a mouli (or pulse at low speed in a blender).

However, if you want to serve the meat as a second course, take it out of the pan and keep it warm. Discard the bay leaves and rosemary sprigs and pass the sauce through a mouli. Serve with pasta as a first course, followed by the meat as a main course, accompanied with vegetables.

Classic Bolognese sauce

RAGÙ ALLA BOLOGNESE

'When you see something that comes from Emilia Romagna, you must bow, because it deserves it!' So says Pellegrino Artusi, the patriarch of Italian cooking, in his wonderful cookbook, *La scienza in cucina e l'arte di mangiare bene* ('*Science in the Kitchen and the Art of Eating Well*'). And I certainly bow in front of this delicious ragù, so rich, delicate and elegant – and the basis, in bastardised form, of Australia's adopted national dish, the spag bol. Traditionally, Bolognese sauce is mainly eaten with tagliatelle, sometimes with rigatoni or conchiglie, but never with spaghetti. It is also a vital element of a Bolognese-style lasagne (see page 251).

Of course, there are many versions, even in Bologna itself, so in 1982 a delegation of the Accademia Italiana delle Cucina confined the ingredients to beef, pancetta, onion, carrot, celery, tomato paste, broth, white wine and milk or cream. However, I find that quite boring – and, being a bit of a rebel, here I give you the Bolognese that my mother used to make, which includes three kinds of meat, mushrooms and chicken livers. There are a few things that everybody agrees with, though: onion, carrot and celery in equal quantities; no garlic and no fresh or tinned tomatoes – only tomato paste.

In Bologna, they say that you make ragù *col naso* ('with your nose'), meaning that you do not use cooking times. From the smell alone, you should know when the soffritto is ready, when the meat has browned enough, when the wine has evaporated, when to add the tomato paste and, finally, when it is ready. But that experience comes with time.

60 g dried porcini mushrooms
50 g butter
100 ml extra virgin olive oil
100 g pancetta
100 g onions, finely chopped
100 g carrots, finely chopped
100 g celery, finely chopped
4 chicken livers (about 75 g), cleaned
    of membrane and finely chopped
300 g minced veal
300 g minced beef
2 mild pork sausages, skin removed
2 sprigs each of rosemary, sage, thyme
    and oregano
125 ml dry white wine
3 bay leaves
3 tablespoons triple-concentrated
    tomato paste
sea salt and freshly ground black pepper
150 ml full-cream milk

SERVES 8–10

Soak the dried porcini mushrooms in warm water for 15 minutes, then drain, pat dry with paper towels and chop finely. Discard the soaking water.

Place the butter and olive oil in a large heavy-based saucepan and place it over medium heat. When the oil is hot and the butter has melted, add the pancetta, onion, carrot and celery. Mix thoroughly and sauté for about 15 minutes, stirring most of the time, until the vegetables have become soft and the flavours have become one. Remember that particular smell!

Now add the porcini, chicken livers, minced meats and sausage meat and stir everything together. Sauté for about 15 minutes, stirring regularly, to give the meats time to brown nicely, and to let the water they release evaporate. While the meats are browning, prepare your *mazzetto odoroso* by wrapping the herb sprigs in a piece of muslin and tying it securely; if you don't have muslin, simply tie the herb sprigs together in a bundle with string.

When the meats have all browned nicely, stir in the wine, then add the *mazzetto odoroso* and bay leaves. Let the wine evaporate for about 5 minutes. As the wine evaporates, the fumes will permeate the herbs and transmit the aroma into the meats. Try to memorise the smell when the wine has completely evaporated!

Now add the tomato paste and 250 ml water, season with salt and pepper, and mix everything thoroughly. Turn the heat down to low and cover the pan with a lid, leaving it slightly ajar to allow the steam to escape. Let the sauce simmer very gently for 1 hour, stirring from time to time and adding more water as necessary.

At this point, add the milk and cook for another 30 minutes. Taste for seasoning; discard the bay leaves and the *mazzetto odoroso*. Your *ragù alla Bolognese* is ready.

RAGÙ ALLA NAPOLETANA

The Neapolitans are crazy about their ragù. They consider it an offering to God for making Neapolitans so special! Eduardo de Filippo, the great Neopolitan *commediografo* and actor, wrote a wonderful poem about this ragù called *O'rrau* (as the sauce is known in the local dialect). It basically says that his mother used to make the best ragù, but since he got married he is just eating meat cooked in tomato! This, of course, is exactly what we do not want.

There are two ways of preparing and cooking the meat in a Neopolitan ragù: one is to use a couple of types of stewing meat cut into big chunks that are slowly cooked to melting tenderness; the other is to form the meat into thick rolls called involtini (*braciole* in the local dialect) with spare ribs added for extra flavour, as in the version given here. Over the years the sauce has become lighter, using much leaner meats, olive oil in place of pig fat, and lean pancetta instead of lardo. The soffritto, the base of the sauce, is only onions, and a lot of them; no celery, no carrots. Even the cooking times have been shortened, but it still takes more than two hours on a very low heat.

This ragù cannot be taken lightly: it is (for the Neapolitans) the king of sauces. Traditionally made in a terracotta pot, it should be stirred only with a wooden spoon, and it demands dedication and concentration. In return, it will fill your house – and those of your neighbours – with a wonderful aroma.

500 g beef topside or rump, cut into four or six slices, each about 5 mm thick
sea salt and freshly ground black pepper
3 cloves garlic, very finely chopped
100 g sultanas
30 g pine nuts
2 tablespoons finely chopped flat-leaf parsley leaves
150 ml extra virgin olive oil
500 g pork short ribs, cut into smaller pieces to fit the pot
50 g pancetta, trimmed of most of the fat and diced
2 red onions, finely diced
150 ml dry white wine
2 kg ripe tomatoes, peeled and seeded (see page 51), then diced
15 small basil leaves
500 g rigatoni or bucatini
180 g freshly grated parmesan

SERVES 4–6

First prepare the *braciole*. Lay the beef slices on the benchtop and season with salt and pepper, then sprinkle each slice with the chopped garlic, sultanas, pine nuts and parsley. Roll up the slices and secure them with toothpicks or tie with kitchen string.

Heat the olive oil in a large heavy-based saucepan or flameproof casserole over medium heat. Brown the beef rolls and pork ribs all over for about 10–12 minutes, then remove from the pan. Add the pancetta and onion to the pan and sauté gently, stirring regularly with a wooden spoon (only) until the onion has softened and the flavours of the soffritto have amalgamated – about 10 minutes. Return the meats to the pan, pour in the white wine and simmer until it evaporates. Add the tomato and basil and season with salt and pepper, mixing thoroughly but delicately with the wooden spoon. Reduce the heat to very low and cook for 2 hours, every so often shaking the pan, turning the meat around and stirring the sauce – if it seems too dry, add a little water.

When the ragù is ready, remove the meat and set aside for the second course.

Cook the pasta in plenty of boiling salted water until al dente. Drain the pasta, dress with the sauce and serve as a first course, generously sprinkled with parmesan.

Neapolitan meat sauce

LA GENOVESE

Just because it's called *La Genovese*, don't assume it comes from Genoa. This particular ragù is familiar only to the Neapolitans and is completely unknown in Liguria or, for that matter, in the rest of Italy. The origins of the sauce are still a mystery and the Neapolitans, a bit embarrassed by the foreign name for their own sauce, insist that although it was not invented in Naples or by a Neapolitan, they are the first and only people in Italy to appreciate it! Apparently it was created some time in the 1600s by some cooks from Genoa, which doesn't surprise me as it is very similar to Ligurian *Tocco di Carne* (see page 55).

La Genovese is a sauce in the ragù style and is eaten in the same way, with the sauce used to dress the pasta, and the meat served as the main course. Like ragù, it needs time, and the point at which you add the ingredients is most important. One peculiarity of this ragù is that a large amount of onions are used, and various *salumi*, prosciutto and fresh herbs enhance the flavour of the sauce. Remember: while it is cooking, stir it only with a wooden spoon.

50 g pancetta, finely diced
50 g prosciutto, finely diced
50 g salami, finely diced
1 carrot, finely diced
1 celery stalk, finely diced
1 kg white onions, finely diced
5 large ripe tomatoes, peeled and seeded
   (see page 51), then diced
1 teaspoon thyme leaves
1 tablespoon rosemary leaves
1 tablespoon flat-leaf parsley leaves
1 teaspoon marjoram leaves
50 g butter
120 ml extra virgin olive oil
1 kg beef (such as shoulder or belly),
   rolled and tied in one piece like a roast
sea salt and freshly ground black pepper
150 ml dry white wine
celeriac or mashed potatoes, to serve

SERVES 8

Place the pancetta, prosciutto, salami, carrot, celery, onion, tomato and all the herbs in a bowl and mix well.

Put the butter and olive oil in a heavy-based saucepan large enough to hold all the ingredients. Add the pancetta mixture and the beef and season with salt and pepper. Cover the pan and cook over very low heat for 1½ hours, shaking the pan regularly and turning the meat every 15–20 minutes with a wooden spoon.

Remove the lid, push the sauce to one side and increase the heat to medium–high to brown the meat all over. Add the wine in three batches, waiting each time for it to evaporate before adding the next batch. Turn the heat down to low, then cover and cook for 1 hour, checking frequently to make sure that nothing is sticking to the bottom of the pan – add some water (2–3 tablespoons at a time) if it becomes too dry.

And there you have the wonderful Genovese, where the meat is very tender but not dry: enjoy it as a main course, with a side of celeriac or mashed potatoes. The sauce – the star of the ragù – is beautifully dark and shiny, ready to be enjoyed with large rigatoni or ziti or penne or bucatini or maltagliati or . . .

Sicilian meat sauce

RAGÙ ALLA SICILIANA

The Sicilian ragù is similar to the Neapolitan one, still with plenty of onions and the meat done in one big *braciole* (called *falsimagro* or *farsumagru* – 'false thin' – because the meat looks lean, but all the fat is on the inside). The *braciole* is stuffed and rolled, pork spare ribs and/or whole sausages are added with fresh herbs, and again, it is a two-course dish.

500 g lean shoulder of veal, in one
    rectangular slice
75 g minced veal
4 pork and fennel sausages
10 basil leaves, finely chopped
1 clove garlic, finely chopped
sea salt
100 g mortadella, in thin slices
2 hard-boiled eggs, peeled and thinly sliced
150 ml extra virgin olive oil
2 onions, thinly sliced
100 ml red wine
2 kg ripe tomatoes, peeled and seeded
    (see page 51), then crushed in a blender
1 teaspoon oregano leaves, chopped
2 bay leaves
freshly ground black pepper
freshly grated parmesan, to serve
green salad, to serve

SERVES 8

Let's prepare the *falsimagro* first.

Place the veal shoulder on the benchtop and pound it a little to make it a uniform thickness all over. Combine the minced veal and the meat of one sausage in a bowl and then add the basil, garlic and a pinch of salt. Mix thoroughly, then spread over the flattened veal. This will also fill any holes on the surface of the meat, to make it smooth and leakproof for the rest of the fillings.

Now arrange the mortadella slices over the minced meat and on top of that, in the middle, arrange the slices of egg. Now roll up the veal, being careful not to squeeze out the filling, and tie securely.

In a small non-stick frying pan over medium heat, cook the remaining sausages for about 10 minutes to brown them on all sides and get rid of the fat. Set aside to cool slightly, then pat well with paper towels to remove any excess fat and cut them into 4 pieces each. Now we are ready to start the ragù.

Heat the olive oil in a large heavy-based saucepan over medium heat and sauté the onion with a pinch of salt for a few minutes until soft and golden, mixing constantly with a wooden spoon. Do not let the onion burn. Add the rolled veal and brown it all over, then pour in the wine and simmer until it has evaporated. At this point, add the crushed tomato, oregano and bay leaves and season with salt and pepper. Add the sausage pieces and mix thoroughly. Reduce the heat to low and cook for about 2 hours. Shake the pan regularly during this time, turning the meat every 15–20 minutes and stirring with a wooden spoon. Add some water, or hot stock if you have it, as necessary.

Serve the sauce with pasta (keeping a little aside for the main course) and plenty of parmesan. To follow, remove the string from the *falsimagro*, slice it carefully and serve with the reserved sauce and a lovely tender green salad dressed with extra virgin olive oil and red wine vinegar.

Bechamel sauce

BESCIAMELLA

Credit for this classic sauce of butter and flour must be given to the French, for it was named after Louis de Bechamel, chief steward of Louis XIV's household, who created a recipe that appeared in a cookbook published in 1651. Legendary Italian gourmet Pellegrino Artusi elegantly Italianised the name to *belsamella* in his 1892 recipe collection *La scienza in cucina e l'arte di mangiare bene* ('*Science in the Kitchen and the Art of Eating Well*'), but nowadays it's called *besciamella* – and is an important ingredient to enrich and hold together baked pasta dishes.

450 ml milk
50 g butter
50 g plain flour
sea salt

MAKES ABOUT 420 ML

Heat the milk in a small saucepan just until a few bubbles start to appear on the surface, then remove from the heat.

Melt the butter in a heavy-based saucepan over low heat. Add the flour and cook for 2 minutes, stirring constantly with a wooden spoon and making sure that the flour does not colour. Remove from the heat and slowly add the hot milk a little at a time, stirring constantly to stop lumps from forming. When all the milk has been amalgamated, place the sauce back over low heat, season with salt and cook, stirring continuously, until the mixture has the consistency of thick cream.

Dried pasta

Dried pasta (*pasta secca*) is the most-eaten pasta in Italy and all over the world. Light and comfortable to digest, it is easier to handle than fresh pasta and can be stored for longer, so you can keep a wide selection of shapes in the pantry to suit different moods and sauces.

Don't scrimp when it comes to buying dried pasta. Go for quality rather than price, and be sure the pasta is made with proper durum wheat (which allows the pasta to be cooked al dente). With cheaper pasta, the quality will likely be compromised by the use of inferior wheat and too rapid a drying process. Your safest option is to buy Italian: the south of Italy is where the best durum wheat is grown and where, over the centuries, the art of slow-drying has been perfected.

There is nothing more horrible than overcooked pasta – mushy pasta can spoil the best sauces. I beg you to cook dried pasta only until it is al dente, which means 'to the tooth', or giving a slight resistance to the bite. I suggest boiling the pasta for one or two minutes less than the time recommended on the packet, but you should learn your own preferred al dente point by pulling out strands of pasta during the last three or four minutes of cooking and biting on them to test their readiness. Always reserve a little of the cooking water before you drain the pasta. You can use it to loosen the sauce if it has become too thick, and its starch content will also help the sauce to cling to the pasta.

Of course, when it comes to combining dried pasta with sauces, the possibilities are almost infinite, but to get you started here are some of the most popular shapes of dried pasta and their 'perfect match' sauces:

- ribbon pasta, such as spaghetti, vermicelli, linguine and bavette, goes with light tomato sauces, seafood, butter- and oil-based sauces, pesto and light cream sauces

- shaped pasta, such as cavatelli, conchiglie, farfalle, fusilli, gemmelli, lumache and orecchiette, goes well with tomato sauces, meat sauces, pesto, chunky sauces and cheese sauces

- tubular pasta, such as rigatoni, tortiglioni, ziti, paccheri, penne, manicotti, maccheroni and garganelli, goes with thick tomato salsas, rich ragùs and thick cream sauces.

As a footnote, I would suggest that you never serve dried cappelli d'angelo (angel hair) with a sauce; the strands are much too thin to hold a sauce and are better eaten in a broth.

UNCOOKED SAUCES

Pasta with *salsa a crudo* (uncooked sauce) is hot pasta tossed quickly with a cold, uncooked sauce and served immediately, while still warm.

Most dressings of this kind cannot be prepared and used right away, but rather need to rest for fifteen minutes to an hour, to allow all the ingredients to macerate and infuse their flavours. Those that are used straight away will benefit from a squeeze of lemon juice.

These preparations must not be confused with cold pasta salads. When you make a pasta salad, the pasta is cooked al dente, then drained and refreshed under cold water to stop the cooking process. The pasta is dressed when it is cold. Personally, I am not a fan of pasta salads – I see no point in ruining a beautiful salad with cold pasta.

But when you make pasta with *salsa a crudo*, it is only the sauce that is cold; the pasta must be hot and cooked al dente. For these sauces, I suggest you use a Ligurian olive oil for its beautifully delicate, fruity flavour.

A crudo sauces are excellent for hot summer days and nights – for full enjoyment, I urge you to act quickly and eat the pasta immediately, while it is still warm.

Spaghettini with tomato and basil dressing

SPAGHETTINI SALSA A CRUDO SEMPLICE

1 clove garlic, peeled and cut in half
600 g ripe tomatoes, peeled and seeded
   (see page 51), then sliced into strips
100 ml extra virgin olive oil
large handful of basil leaves,
   roughly chopped
handful of oregano leaves, roughly chopped
sea salt and freshly ground black pepper
400 g spaghettini or vermicelli

SERVES 4

This is a very delicate sauce. No strong flavours here – just tomato, basil, oregano and olive oil, and the strength of the sun that nurtured these beautiful ingredients.

Rub the inside of the serving bowl with the cut surfaces of the garlic. Place the tomato in the bowl and dress with the olive oil, basil and oregano. Season with salt and pepper and mix thoroughly. Cover and leave to rest at room temperature for 1 hour.

Cook the spaghettini or vermicelli in plenty of boiling salted water until al dente. Drain well, then tip into the serving bowl and toss quickly through the sauce. Serve immediately.

Linguine with everything

LINGUINE CON TUTTO

600 g ripe tomatoes, peeled and seeded
   (see page 51), then diced – you could use
   multi-coloured cherry tomatoes here
80 g black olives, pitted
8 anchovy fillets in oil, drained
50 g capers in salt (ideally small Sicilian
   ones), rinsed and dried
1 clove garlic, peeled and cut in half
½ red onion, finely chopped
2 celery stalk hearts (the young yellow
   ones), finely chopped
handful of flat-leaf parsley leaves, chopped
handful of basil leaves, chopped
1 teaspoon oregano leaves, chopped
4 tablespoons extra virgin olive oil
sea salt and freshly ground black pepper
400 g linguine

SERVES 4

This is what the Italians call a *fuori dall'uscio* dish, which literally means 'outside the door', the notion being that the householder just pops out into the garden and grabs a few handfuls of whatever is fresh. Here I've suggested what I like to eat with my pasta in the summer, but you should feel free to improvise around your own favourite ingredients that may be ready and waiting outside your door – or inside the door of your local greengrocer.

Place the diced tomato in a colander over the sink and leave to drain for about half an hour so it loses some of its moisture.

In the meantime, cut the olives in half lengthways and then in half again. Chop the anchovies into small pieces and mix together with the olives and capers in a small bowl. Set aside.

Rub the inside of the serving bowl with the cut surfaces of the garlic – this adds a very subtle flavour. Place the drained tomato in the bowl and add the onion, celery and herbs. Splash in the olive oil, season with salt and pepper, and mix well. Cover and leave to rest for at least 30 minutes.

Cook the linguine in plenty of boiling salted water until al dente.

Add the olive mix to the sauce and stir to combine. Drain the pasta, then add to the sauce and toss until well mixed. Serve immediately.

Spaghetti with tomato and mozzarella dressing

SPAGHETTI ALLA CAPRESE

This is a lovely dish for summer, when tomatoes are at their most luscious. It involves hot spaghetti and a simple sauce of raw ingredients at room temperature. The cheese in this case is not parmesan but mozzarella. Try to avoid those rubbery yellow balls sold as mozzarella in some supermarkets. What you need is the fresh, moist white cow's milk mozzarella that is known as *fior di latte* by the Neapolitans. If you can find the version made with buffalo milk, all the better.

500 g ripe tomatoes, peeled and seeded
  (see page 51), then finely diced
1 clove garlic, peeled and cut in half
1 teaspoon chopped oregano leaves
15 basil leaves, roughly torn
150 ml extra virgin olive oil
150 g fresh mozzarella, cut into the
  same-size dice as the tomatoes
sea salt
400 g spaghetti
handful of small basil leaves, to serve

SERVES 4

Place the diced tomato in a colander over the sink and leave to drain for about half an hour so it loses some of its moisture.

Rub the inside of the serving bowl with the cut surfaces of the garlic – this adds a very subtle flavour. Add the drained tomato, oregano, basil, olive oil and mozzarella, and season with salt. Stir everything together, then set aside to rest for about half an hour.

Cook the spaghetti in plenty of boiling salted water until al dente. Drain well, then tip into the serving bowl, add the small basil leaves and toss quickly through the dressing. Serve immediately.

Small maccheroni with ricotta and rosemary

MACCHERONCINI RICOTTA E ROSMARINO

200 g fresh ricotta
2 tablespoons rosemary leaves,
    finely chopped
2 tablespoons freshly grated parmesan
2 tablespoons freshly grated pecorino
sea salt and freshly ground black pepper
3 tablespoons extra virgin olive oil,
    plus extra to serve (optional)
400 g maccheroncini
10 g blanched almonds, roughly chopped

SERVES 4

This light and fresh dressing is served at room temperature with warm pasta. The sharpness of the rosemary is invigorating and stands up well to the salty pecorino, which is softened with ricotta to help coat the pasta.

Place the ricotta in a ceramic or glass bowl, add the rosemary, parmesan and pecorino and season with salt and pepper. Mix thoroughly, then gradually add the olive oil, stirring constantly until smooth.

Cook the maccheroncini in plenty of boiling salted water until al dente. Drain the pasta, reserving a little of the cooking water.

Working quickly, tip the pasta into a large serving bowl. Moisten the cheese mixture with 1–2 tablespoons of the reserved cooking water, mix well and then pour over the pasta.

Toss delicately, then sprinkle with the almonds. Pour a little extra olive oil over the pasta before serving, if you like.

Penne with fresh tomato and mint

PENNE AL SUGO CRUDO QUASI COTTO

120 ml extra virgin olive oil
1 clove garlic, very finely chopped
1 tablespoon flat-leaf parsley leaves,
    very finely chopped
500 g ripe tomatoes, peeled and seeded
    (see page 51), then finely diced
1 tablespoon mint leaves,
    very finely chopped
sea salt and freshly ground black pepper
400 g penne
2 tablespoons freshly grated pecorino

SERVES 4

This sauce is *quasi cotto*, or 'partly cooked'. Made from *crudo* (raw) ingredients, it is then added to the pan containing the just-cooked pasta to heat through. This warmth maximises the flavours without spoiling the freshness of the effect in the mouth.

Put the olive oil in a large bowl, add the garlic and parsley and mix well. Now add the tomato and mint, season with salt and pepper and mix thoroughly. Set aside.

Cook the penne in plenty of boiling salted water until al dente.

Drain the pasta and place in a flameproof casserole (preferably terracotta) over low heat. Add the sauce and pecorino and toss quickly. Keep over the heat for 2 minutes, stirring constantly, then serve immediately.

Rigatoni with tomato and chilli dressing

RIGATONI PICCHI PACCHIU

500 g ripe tomatoes, peeled and seeded
  (see page 51), then diced
150 ml extra virgin olive oil
2 cloves garlic, finely chopped
2 red chillies, seeded and finely chopped
10 small basil leaves
sea salt
400 g rigatoni
3 tablespoons freshly grated pecorino

SERVES 4

Picchi pacchiu is a Sicilian dialect term for the local little snails, but it's also a metaphor for carrying your life on your back. Here, it is a way of saying that this is a pasta dish made by poor people from simple but tasty ingredients. In the recipe below, the sauce is served as a cold dressing, but in some parts of Sicily the tomato is lightly cooked with the oil and garlic.

Literally meaning 'striped', rigatoni is a dried pasta that is mostly used in the south – just like the small red chillies in this sauce. I'm suggesting pecorino here instead of parmesan, because it fits better with the other pungent flavours.

Place the tomato, olive oil, garlic, chilli and basil in a large bowl. Season with salt and let it rest for about 1 hour.

Cook the rigatoni in plenty of boiling salted water until al dente. Drain and toss it well in the sauce. Sprinkle the pecorino over the top and serve immediately.

Spaghetti with cheese and pepper

SPAGHETTI CACIO E PEPE

400 g spaghetti
150 g freshly grated pecorino
freshly ground pepper

SERVES 4

I call this 'spaghetti with nothing'. *Cacio* is the Tuscan name for pecorino cheese and *pepe* is pepper – two things you would normally put on top of a pasta sauce. Here they *are* the sauce. This is a traditional dish from Lazio, the region that surrounds Rome, where they produce a wonderful pecorino that they don't want ruined by an elaborate dressing. Surprise your guests. They'll think you forgot the sauce – unless they are cheese connoisseurs.

I fondly imagine that this harks back to the way spaghetti was eaten in the streets of Naples in the nineteenth century: just pulled out of the boiling water, sprinkled with cheese and delivered to your mouth with your bare hands.

Cook the spaghetti in plenty of boiling salted water until al dente. Drain, but reserve about 125 ml of the cooking water.

Tip the spaghetti into a large serving bowl, add a little of the reserved pasta cooking water to loosen, then sprinkle the pecorino over the top and toss carefully. Sprinkle with plenty of pepper, then toss one more time and serve.

Spaghetti with garlic, oil and chilli

SPAGHETTI ALL'AGLIO E OLIO

This is one of the most basic sauces in the Italian repertoire, but when done properly, it is a little masterpiece. In Italy, this dish is usually eaten late at night or in the early hours for, whatever the reason you are still awake at that time, this pasta restores you. The Romans say it was invented in their city; the Neapolitans – scandalised, irritated and offended – say of course that it was invented in Naples. I would like to believe that Naples is the city of origin, simply because it seems a very Neapolitan way to deal with pasta.

The sauce is quick to prepare and can be improvised in the time it takes to cook the pasta. Chilli is not essential, so if you don't have any, use black pepper instead. You can also add olives, capers and anchovies. If you are not a big fan of garlic, infuse the oil with a subtle garlic flavour by leaving the garlic cloves whole and warming them in the oil just until they start to colour, then discarding them. You can also replace the parsley with basil, or use some of each.

400 g spaghetti
200 ml extra virgin olive oil
3 cloves garlic, finely chopped
1 red chilli, finely chopped
large handful of flat-leaf parsley leaves,
　　finely chopped
sea salt

SERVES 4

Cook the spaghetti in plenty of boiling salted water until al dente.

Meanwhile, heat the olive oil in a heavy-based frying pan over low heat and fry the garlic for a minute or so, stirring with a wooden spoon to spread the flavour through the oil. Add 2 tablespoons of the pasta-cooking water to the pan and stir in the chilli and parsley. Season with salt and cook for 3 minutes, mixing every now and then.

When the spaghetti is ready, drain it quickly so it is still rather wet and add it to the sauce. Gently toss to coat, then leave for about 1 minute over low heat before serving on hot plates.

Trenette with pesto, potato and green beans

TRENETTE AL PESTO CON FAGIOLINI E PATATE

This way of serving pesto with pasta, green beans and potato originated in the Ligurian fishing village of Portovenere, but it is now accepted and enjoyed all over the region. Trenette pasta is a local version of linguine, but where linguine noodles are flat, trenette noodles are rectangular. Use linguine if you can't fine trenette, but remember it's important to slice the green beans finely, so they are almost the same thickness as the noodles. This makes the dish look better and ensures it feels better in the mouth. Try to find a bean stringer if you can – they're inexpensive and make light work of stringing the beans and slicing them evenly. If you don't have one, finely slice the beans lengthways with a sharp knife.

50 small basil leaves

1 clove garlic, peeled

pinch of sea salt

1 tablespoon raw pine nuts

2 tablespoons freshly grated parmesan, plus extra to serve

1 tablespoon freshly grated mild pecorino, preferably Sardinian

about 3 tablespoons extra virgin olive oil

1 large potato (desiree or a similar waxy variety), peeled and cut into 1 cm cubes

300 g green beans, put through a stringer and slicer

400 g trenette or linguine

knob of butter

SERVES 4

Start by making the pesto. Carefully wash the basil leaves and dry them gently between two paper towels without applying pressure.

If using a mortar and pestle, begin with the garlic and a pinch of salt (this will help to keep the basil green). Crush the garlic, then add the basil leaves and continue pounding against the sides of the mortar with a rotary movement, not just beating the pestle against the base. Add the pine nuts, the two cheeses and a tablespoon of olive oil and continue mixing with the pestle. When the mixture is reduced to a creamy consistency, transfer it to a bowl. Add enough olive oil to amalgamate everything nicely, mixing well. Pour on more oil to cover the pesto. If you are keeping the pesto for a while (it will keep for a month in the fridge), make sure it is always covered with olive oil to maintain its freshness and stop it from going black.

If you prefer to use a blender, put all the ingredients in at once and use the lowest speed. Stop often to let it cool down, because hot oil will affect the aroma of the basil. Pulse until the pesto reaches the desired consistency.

Bring a large pan of salted water to the boil, then drop in the potato. After 5 minutes, add the beans and pasta and cook until the pasta is al dente. Drain the pasta, beans and potato, reserving a little of the cooking water.

Place 2 tablespoons of the pesto in a large serving bowl, along with 2 tablespoons of the reserved cooking water. Add the pasta, beans, potato and butter, then put the rest of the pesto on top, add a sprinkling of parmesan and toss well so that everything is evenly coated with pesto. Serve immediately.

Linguine with Tuscan pesto

LINGUINE AL PESTO DI NOCI

150 g mild pecorino (Sardinian, if possible)
200 g raw walnuts
2 large handfuls of small basil leaves
sea salt
100 ml extra virgin olive oil
400 g linguine

SERVES 4

This is a sauce from the north of Tuscany, clearly influenced by the *pesto alla Genovese* of neighbouring Liguria. No garlic is used in this pesto and the pecorino is not grated, but cut into pieces and then blended with the rest of the ingredients, giving an interesting texture. The basil and walnuts must not be too fine; they are left a bit rough. The walnuts should be as fresh as possible.

Cut the pecorino cheese into small cubes and place them in a blender with the walnuts, basil, a sprinkle of salt and 4 tablespoons of the olive oil. Pulse together for about 2 minutes until well mixed, leaving the walnuts a little chunky. Transfer to a bowl and stir in the remaining olive oil.

Cook the linguine in plenty of boiling salted water until al dente.

While the pasta is cooking, add a tablespoon of the pasta cooking water to the pesto and mix well. Drain the linguine and toss it gently with the pesto. Serve immediately – no extra cheese is required.

Fusilli with almond and mint pesto

FUSILLI AL PESTO DI MANDORLE E MENTA

4 tablespoons extra virgin olive oil
1 clove garlic, peeled and lightly squashed
250 g cherry tomatoes, quartered
10 basil leaves, chopped
sea salt
100 g blanched almonds, toasted
1 tablespoon chopped mint leaves,
    plus a few extra leaves to garnish
1 tablespoon oregano leaves
1 teaspoon capers in salt, rinsed and dried
400 g fusilli

SERVES 4

This quick and fragrant dish is the perfect meal to enjoy on a warm summer evening. It takes inspiration from the pesto Calabrese that features some cooked ingredients, but in this case we toss the pasta with hot cherry tomatoes then mix in the pesto.

Pour 1½ tablespoons of the olive oil in a heavy-based frying pan over high heat. Add the garlic and stir with a wooden spoon until just golden, then discard. Reduce the heat to medium. Add the cherry tomatoes and basil to the oil, season with salt and mix well. Cook for about 6 minutes, stirring from time to time. Transfer to a serving bowl big enough to hold the pasta.

In the meantime, place the almonds, chopped mint, oregano and capers in a mortar. Add the remaining olive oil, sprinkle with some salt and pound with the pestle until it is all amalgamated.

Cook the fusilli in plenty of boiling salted water until al dente. Drain and add to the tomato mixture, tossing gently to combine. Add the pesto and mix thoroughly, then serve immediately, garnished with a few mint leaves.

Fusilli with Sicilian pesto

FUSILLI AL PESTO SICILIANO

Sicilian food, like Ligurian, was influenced by centuries of Arab visits, so they too use the mortar to pound nuts and herbs with garlic. The presence of chilli and tomato is what distinguishes this sauce, which is also known as Trapani pesto, after the Norman town of the same name on Sicily's east coast.

4 ripe tomatoes, peeled and seeded
  (see page 51), then diced
sea salt
200 g blanched almonds
1 clove garlic, peeled
12 basil leaves
1 small red chilli, cut in half and
  seeds removed
100 g freshly grated parmesan,
  plus extra to serve
100 ml extra virgin olive oil,
  plus extra to serve
400 g fusilli

SERVES 4

Place the diced tomato in a colander over the sink, sprinkle with 1 teaspoon of sea salt and leave to drain for about half an hour so it loses some of its moisture.

Preheat the oven to 200°C. Spread out the almonds on a baking tray and put them in the oven for about 10 minutes until light golden, checking and stirring them often to make sure they toast evenly. Do not allow them to burn or the sauce will become very bitter. Set aside to cool.

Roughly chop the cooled almonds with the garlic and basil. Transfer to a blender and add the drained tomato, chilli, parmesan, 2 tablespoons of olive oil and ½ teaspoon of sea salt. Process until the mixture is creamy. Scrape down the sides of the bowl and process a little more if needed. Mix in the remaining olive oil.

Cook the fusilli in plenty of boiling salted water until al dente.

While the pasta is cooking, place the pesto in a serving bowl big enough to hold the pasta, add a tablespoon of the pasta cooking water and mix well. Drain the fusilli, and toss it gently with the pesto. Drizzle with some more olive oil, sprinkle with a little extra parmesan and serve immediately.

Buonissimo!

Spaghetti with pistachio pesto

SPAGHETTI AL PESTO DI PISTACCHI

This is another 'nut in the mortar' sauce from Sicily. And what a fantastic flavour! Sicily produces large amounts of pistachios, particularly in the Bronte area – and this is a beautiful way to use them, resulting in the most simple and delicate pesto with a vibrant green colour. This pesto is also excellent with gnocchi or penne.

150 g raw pistachios

1 small clove garlic, peeled

10 basil leaves

1 teaspoon raw pine nuts

40 g parmesan, cut into small pieces

pinch of sea salt

about 100 ml extra virgin olive oil

400 g spaghetti

handful of roughly chopped raw
    pistachios, to serve

SERVES 4

Blanch the pistachios by plunging them briefly into boiling water. Drain and, when cool enough to handle, peel off the skins.

Using a mortar and pestle, pound the pistachios well until fine, then transfer to a mixing bowl and set aside. Place the garlic, basil, pine nuts, parmesan and salt in the mortar and pound together until the mixture has a creamy consistency. Stir in 100 ml of olive oil, then transfer to the bowl with the pistachios. Mix thoroughly, adding enough olive oil to amalgamate everything nicely.

If using a blender, place the pistachios, garlic, basil, pine nuts, parmesan, salt and 100 ml of olive oil in the blender and pulse at the lowest speed until the mixture has a creamy consistency. Transfer to a bowl and stir in more olive oil, if necessary.

Cook the spaghetti in plenty of boiling salted water until al dente.

While the pasta is cooking, place the pesto in a serving bowl big enough to hold the pasta, add a tablespoon of the pasta cooking water and mix well. Drain the spaghetti, and toss it gently with the pesto. Scatter with chopped pistachios and serve immediately.

Rigatoni with Calabrian pesto

RIGATONI AL PESTO CALABRESE

In the southern Italian region of Calabria, they like it hot, and this fantastic version of pesto is fiery in both taste and colour, gaining its heat from red chillies and its intriguing orange colour from an unusual blend of capsicum and cheeses.

Traditionally, no garlic is used in this pesto, but if you like you can add a clove when the ingredients are in the blender.

180 ml extra virgin olive oil
½ white onion, finely chopped
sea salt
2 red capsicums (peppers), seeds and white
    membranes removed, cut into strips
10 basil leaves
150 g ricotta
1 large ripe tomato, peeled and seeded
    (see page 51), then diced
2 small red chillies, chopped
1 teaspoon oregano leaves
1 clove garlic, peeled (optional)
150 g freshly grated pecorino
100 g freshly grated parmesan
400 g rigatoni
handful of baby purple perilla leaves,
    to serve (optional)

SERVES 4

Heat 4 tablespoons of olive oil in a heavy-based frying pan over medium heat. When hot, add the onion and a pinch of salt and sauté until the onion is soft and translucent, stirring with a wooden spoon.

Add the capsicum and basil, season with salt and stir well. Sauté gently for a further 20 minutes or until everything has softened and melted together. Remove the pan from the heat and leave the capsicum mixture to cool for about 20 minutes.

Transfer the cooled capsicum mixture and its cooking oil to a blender. Add the ricotta, tomato, chilli, oregano and the garlic (if using), and the rest of the olive oil. Blend for about 20 seconds on medium speed. Stop the blender, add the pecorino and parmesan and blend again until the pesto is smooth and creamy. Transfer to a bowl big enough to hold the pasta.

Cook the rigatoni in plenty of boiling salted water until al dente. Drain and toss gently with the pesto. Garnish with the perilla leaves (if using), then serve immediately.

Linguine with orange pesto and eggplant

LINGUINE AL PESTO D'ARANCIA CON MELANZANE

This is a most unusual but fantastic pesto. The presence of oranges and almonds, which contribute subtlety of taste and colour, tells us that it probably originates from Sicily or the south of Italy. Here we have combined it with eggplant, ricotta and linguine, but this versatile pesto is also excellent stirred through any type of dried pasta, served with couscous or used as the basis of a salad dressing. For this recipe you will only need two or three tablespoons of the pesto, but the rest will last in the fridge for about 2 weeks, if kept covered with a thin layer of olive oil.

1 eggplant (aubergine)
sea salt
180 ml extra virgin olive oil
400 g linguine
1 clove garlic, peeled and cut in half
150 g ricotta
freshly grated parmesan, to serve

ORANGE PESTO

3 oranges, peeled, all pith and seeds
    removed, roughly chopped
80 g basil leaves
200 g blanched almonds
50 g capers in salt, rinsed and dried
pinch of sea salt
about 60 ml extra virgin olive oil

SERVES 4

For the pesto, place all the ingredients in a blender and blend on low speed until fine, adding more olive oil if necessary to make a smooth, creamy pesto. Transfer the pesto to a small lidded container and cover with a thin film of olive oil.

Cut the ends off the eggplant, then cut into 1 cm thick slices. Place the slices in a colander over the sink, sprinkle with sea salt and leave for 40 minutes to sweat out any bitter juices. Rinse the salt from the eggplant and pat dry with paper towels.

Heat the olive oil in a large frying pan until very hot, then fry the eggplant slices until golden on both sides, turning once. Drain on paper towels. When cool enough to handle, cut into strips about 5 cm × 0.5 cm. Set aside.

Cook the linguine in plenty of boiling salted water until al dente.

While the pasta is cooking, rub the inside of a large serving bowl with the cut surfaces of the garlic clove. Add the ricotta, eggplant strips, 2–3 tablespoons of the pesto and a tablespoon of the pasta cooking water. Mix well. Drain the linguine, add to the bowl and toss gently, adding more pesto to taste. Sprinkle with a little grated parmesan and serve immediately.

Spaghetti with eggplant and tomato

SPAGHETTI ALLA NORMA

This famous Sicilian dish is an homage to the musician Bellini: the inventor of the dish thought the flavours were so harmonious that it recalled the beautiful opera *Norma*. The spaghetti (or sometimes rigatoni or tortiglioni) is tossed in a tomato and basil sauce and then covered with a layer of fried eggplant. Traditionally, the cheese used for grating is salted ricotta, but I would suggest a good parmesan to achieve more harmony, because the ricotta can sometimes be too salty and you can't control that. At serving time I like to sprinkle the pasta with crumbled fresh ricotta, but this is optional.

350 g eggplants (aubergines)
sea salt
1 × 400 g tin peeled tomatoes
220 ml extra virgin olive oil
1 clove garlic, finely chopped
freshly ground black pepper
large handful of basil leaves, chopped
400 g spaghetti
200 g freshly grated parmesan
80 g fresh ricotta

SERVES 4

Cut the ends off the eggplants, then cut into thin slices. Place the slices in a colander over the sink, sprinkle with sea salt and leave for 40 minutes to sweat out any bitter juices.

Meanwhile, prepare the tomato sauce. Pass the tomatoes through a mouli or puree in a food processor. Heat about 100 ml of the olive oil in a heavy-based frying pan over low heat, add the garlic and cook for 1–2 minutes, mixing with a wooden spoon until the garlic starts to change colour. Increase the heat to medium. Add the tomato, season with salt and pepper and sauté for 15 minutes. Set aside a couple of pinches of basil and mix the rest through the sauce.

Rinse the salt from the eggplant and pat dry with paper towels. Heat the remaining olive oil in a non-stick frying pan over medium heat and fry the eggplant slices a few at a time until golden – about 2 minutes each side. Remove with a slotted spoon and drain on paper towels.

In the meantime, cook the spaghetti in plenty of boiling salted water until al dente. Drain, reserving a little of the cooking water.

Add the spaghetti to the sauce and toss gently, adding a little of the cooking water if necessary. Add the parmesan and the remaining basil, then transfer to a large hot serving dish. Season the eggplant slices with a little salt and place them on top of the spaghetti to almost cover it, then sprinkle with fresh ricotta and serve immediately.

Spaghetti with olives and capers

SPAGHETTI OMAGGIO ALL'EOLIE

100 g green Sicilian olives
100 g black olives
80 g capers in salt (ideally small
    Sicilian ones), rinsed and dried –
    and chopped if large
100 ml extra virgin olive oil
1 clove garlic, finely chopped
6 roma tomatoes, peeled and seeded
    (see page 51), then cut into thin strips
2 red chillies, finely chopped
sea salt
handful of tender small basil leaves,
    roughly chopped
1 teaspoon oregano leaves, chopped
400 g spaghetti

SERVES 4

This recipe is a fantastic homage to the Aeolian Islands, off the coast of Sicily, where they produce some of the best capers in the world: they are tiny and roundish, almost like peppercorns. A quick dish to make, this is strong in taste – powerful like the Aeolian sun. I recommend buying unpitted olives because they taste so much better. I also suggest a Sicilian olive oil, to achieve the true Sicilian flavour.

Cut the olives into fillets around the pit, then chop and place in a bowl. Add the capers to the bowl.

Heat the olive oil in a heavy-based frying pan over a medium heat and fry the garlic for a minute or so, then add the olives and the capers and cook for about 3 minutes, stirring regularly with a wooden spoon. Add the tomato and the chilli and cook for another 3 minutes. In the last minute of cooking, season with salt and stir in the basil and oregano.

Meanwhile, cook the spaghetti in plenty of boiling salted water until al dente. Drain, then add to the sauce, mixing gently but thoroughly. Serve immediately.

Bavette with broad beans

BAVETTE CON FAVE FRESCHE

1.5 kg fresh broad beans (the smaller
    the better)
120 ml extra virgin olive oil
1 white onion *or* 2 spring onions, chopped
sea salt and freshly ground black pepper
400 g bavette
60 g freshly grated parmesan

SERVES 4

This is a dish to look forward to in those few weeks of early summer when broad beans are young and fresh and need almost no cooking. It's the meaning and lifestyle of summer on a plate. Bavette is similar to linguine, which can also be used here.

Double-peel the broad beans by first removing them from the pod, then slipping the rough outer shell off the bean to reveal the tender, bright green bean inside.

Heat the olive oil in a large heavy-based frying pan over medium heat and sauté the onion for 5 minutes or until it is soft and translucent, stirring frequently with a wooden spoon. Add the broad beans and stir them around in the pan, then season with salt and pepper. Add 3 tablespoons of water to the pan, mix and let the broad beans cook gently until all the water has evaporated.

Meanwhile, cook the bavette in plenty of boiling salted water until al dente. Drain, then add to the broad bean mixture and season to taste. Toss in the pan for 1 minute, then sprinkle with the parmesan and serve immediately.

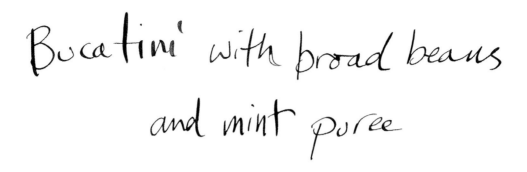

Bucatini with broad beans and mint puree

BUCATINI CON SALSA MARÒ

Broad beans are such a wonderful gift of spring. Growing up in Italy, every year we would wait anxiously for this season, so we could go to the vegetable garden and pick the beautiful green pods when they were small and tender. My mother used to give us a big basket that we would fill up and take inside for the whole family to shell together. Mostly we would just eat them raw for afternoon tea, dressed with a little sea salt and some fine Ligurian olive oil, and accompanied by a mild local pecorino cheese and crusty bread. What a joy!

In other parts of Liguria, broad beans are made into a pesto-like sauce called *marò*, which is usually spread on grilled bread to make bruschetta. But here I propose it as a pasta sauce.

1 kg fresh broad beans
  (the smaller the better)
1 clove garlic, peeled
5 small mint leaves
sea salt
100 g freshly grated pecorino
125 ml extra virgin olive oil
400 g bucatini

SERVES 4

Double-peel the broad beans by first removing them from the pod, then slipping the rough outer shell off the bean to reveal the tender, bright green bean inside. This is a little time consuming but well worth the effort.

You should have about 225 g double-peeled broad beans. Set aside a handful to garnish the finished dish, then place the rest of the beans in a mortar with the garlic, mint and a couple of pinches of salt. Pound with the pestle until you have a smooth paste, then transfer it to a serving bowl big enough to hold the pasta. Add the pecorino and stir well. Still stirring, slowly add the olive oil in a steady stream.

Cook the bucatini in plenty of boiling salted water until al dente.

While the pasta is cooking, dilute the broad bean sauce with 2 tablespoons of the pasta cooking water. Drain the bucatini, reserving a little of the cooking water. Tip the pasta into the serving bowl and toss well but gently, adding some of the reserved cooking water if it looks a little dry. Garnish with the reserved broad beans and serve immediately.

Fusilli with green beans and tomato

FUSILLI CON FAGIOLINI E POMODORO

For this dish, I have borrowed elements from two regional cuisines: Ligurian, where green beans are cooked with pasta when making *pesto alla Genovese*; and Sicilian, where almonds are used in many sauces. The dried tomatoes in oil give an intense flavour and a certain creaminess to the sauce, which then wraps itself around the corkscrew pasta. The herb of choice here has to be fresh oregano.

120 g dried tomatoes in oil, drained

80 g blanched almonds

4 tablespoons extra virgin olive oil

200 g green beans, trimmed and finely sliced lengthways (a bean stringer and slicer makes quick work of this)

400 g fusilli

2 cloves garlic, peeled and lightly squashed

200 g ripe tomatoes, peeled and seeded (see page 51), then diced

1 tablespoon roughly chopped oregano

sea salt and freshly ground black pepper

small handful of oregano leaves, to garnish (optional)

SERVES 4

Roughly chop the dried tomatoes and crush the almonds lightly with the flat of a large knife. Place in a blender with 1 tablespoon of the olive oil and blend on low speed, scraping down the sides every so often, until you have a smooth and homogenous paste. Transfer to a bowl and set aside.

Bring a large pan of salted water to the boil, then throw in the beans and the fusilli and cook until the pasta is al dente.

Meanwhile, heat the remaining olive oil in a heavy-based frying pan over low heat. Add the garlic and stir with a wooden spoon until just golden, then discard. Increase the heat to medium and add the tomato and almond paste, spreading it around the pan with the wooden spoon. After a minute, add the diced tomato and oregano. Season with salt and pepper and cook for 3 minutes, stirring regularly. Turn off the heat and set aside until the pasta is ready.

Drain the pasta and beans, reserving a little of the cooking water. Add the pasta and beans to the sauce, place over medium heat and stir everything together for about 1 minute, adding a little of the reserved cooking water if the sauce seems too dry. Garnish with oregano leaves, if desired, and serve immediately.

Rigatoni with eggplant and mushrooms

RIGATONI CON MELANZANE E FUNGHI

This eggplant sauce is *in bianco* – that is, without tomato – smoothed with a very good olive oil. I suggest using a Sicilian oil, but a strongly flavoured local extra virgin olive oil will do just fine. I put a bit of chilli in this recipe to represent the strength of the south, and I usually add some porcini mushrooms because they marry well with the eggplant. As for the herbs, I've gone with equal amounts of thyme and oregano for a touch of Ligurian northern flavour.

3 eggplants (aubergines)
sea salt
20 g dried porcini mushrooms
120 ml extra virgin olive oil
2 cloves garlic, finely chopped
2 red chillies, finely chopped
1 tablespoon thyme leaves, chopped
1 tablespoon oregano leaves, chopped
400 g rigatoni
50 g freshly grated parmesan

SERVES 4

Cut the ends off the eggplants and peel them, then cut into 1 cm cubes. Place in a colander over the sink, sprinkle with sea salt and leave for 40 minutes to sweat out any bitter juices. Rinse the salt from the eggplant and pat dry with paper towels.

Meanwhile, soak the porcini in warm water for 20 minutes. Drain and squeeze out the excess moisture, then pat dry with paper towels. Chop and set aside.

Heat the olive oil in a heavy-based frying pan over low heat, add the garlic and chilli and stir with a wooden spoon until the garlic just starts to change colour. Add the mushroom and eggplant, season with salt and mix thoroughly. Sauté over medium heat for 10 minutes, then stir in the thyme and oregano.

Meanwhile cook the rigatoni in plenty of boiling salted water until al dente. Drain, then add to the sauce and toss gently to coat. Sprinkle with parmesan and serve immediately.

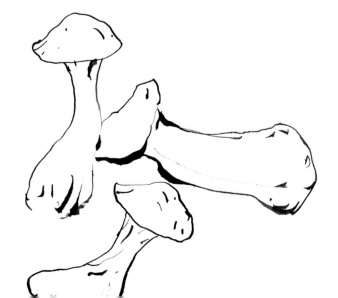

Maccheroni with silverbeet

MACCHERONI ALLE BIETE

A popular Ligurian side dish is spinach dressed with oil, sultanas and pine nuts, and I've often thought it would make a fine pasta dressing. Here I'm using silverbeet rather than spinach because it is more hearty and has a good sharp flavour. If you can, try to use a mild, fruity Ligurian olive oil as a contrast to the gutsy silverbeet.

20 g sultanas

2 bunches silverbeet (Swiss chard)

3 tablespoons extra virgin olive oil,
    plus extra to serve

1 clove garlic, peeled and lightly squashed

1 small red chilli, cut in half lengthways
    (keep the seeds in for a hotter result)

30 g pine nuts

40 g black olives, pitted and
    roughly chopped

sea salt and freshly ground black pepper

400 g maccheroni

45 g freshly grated pecorino

SERVES 4

Revive the sultanas by soaking them in warm water for 10 minutes. Drain them and pat dry with paper towels.

Trim, wash and spin-dry the silverbeet. Remove and discard the white stalks from the silverbeet and cut the leaves into thin strips.

Heat the olive oil in a heavy-based frying pan over low heat. Add the garlic and chilli and stir with a wooden spoon until just golden, then discard. Add the sultanas, silverbeet, pine nuts and olives to the olive oil. Sprinkle on a little salt and pepper and mix thoroughly with the wooden spoon. Cover the pan and let the mixture cook for about 5 minutes, stirring regularly. Add a little water if necessary.

Meanwhile, cook the maccheroni in plenty of boiling salted water until al dente. Drain, reserving some of the cooking water.

Add the maccheroni and half the pecorino to the sauce and toss to coat (add a tablespoon of the pasta cooking water if it seems too dry). Transfer the pasta and sauce to a serving bowl, drizzle with a little extra olive oil and sprinkle with the remaining pecorino. Serve pronto.

Maccheroni with vegetables

MACCHERONI ALLE VERDURE

I like to think of this pasta dish as *sogno di mezza estate*, which translates as 'a midsummer dream' – a reference to the time when these vegetables are at their seasonal peak. In order to retain their individual characteristics, the vegetables are cooked separately, before being combined with tomato, mozzarella and parmesan to create a symphony of colours and flavours that will please the eye as well as the palate.

1 large yellow capsicum (pepper)
2 long eggplants (aubergines)
3 zucchini (courgettes)
100 ml extra virgin olive oil
1 clove garlic, peeled and lightly squashed
300 g ripe tomatoes, peeled and seeded
   (see page 51), then diced
sea salt
400 g maccheroni
100 g fresh mozzarella, diced
60 g freshly grated parmesan
60 g basil leaves, finely chopped

SERVES 4

Remove the seeds and white membranes from the capsicum. Cut the ends off the eggplants and zucchini. Rinse all the vegetables and pat them dry, then cut into 1 cm dice.

Pan-fry each vegetable separately, using a tablespoon of olive oil for each: allow 5 minutes for the capsicum, 4 minutes for the eggplant and 3 minutes for the zucchini. As each is ready, remove from the pan and set aside.

Now you can start preparing the sauce. Heat the remaining olive oil in a large heavy-based frying pan over low heat, add the garlic and stir with a wooden spoon until just golden, then discard. Add the tomato and season with salt, then turn up the heat slightly and cook at a gentle bubble for about 10 minutes.

Meanwhile, cook the maccheroni in plenty of boiling salted water until al dente. Drain, then add to the sauce. Add the remaining ingredients one at a time – vegetables, mozzarella, parmesan and basil – delicately stirring to combine each ingredient with the pasta and sauce. Serve immediately.

Orecchiette with rocket and gorgonzola sauce

ORECCHIETTE CON RUCOLA E GORGONZOLA

The word orecchiette means 'little ears', a reference to the pasta's shape. To me, they look more like tiny bowls, each one ready to hold a few drops of sauce. They originated in Puglia, where they are usually handmade, and they get their concave shape and textured surface from the pressure of the cook's thumb as they are formed.

400 g orecchiette
50 g butter
4 tablespoons milk
50 g gorgonzola dolcelatte, cut into
    pieces and any crust removed
about 30 leaves of baby rocket,
    long stems removed, washed,
    dried and roughly chopped
sea salt and freshly ground black pepper
2 tablespoons freshly grated parmesan

SERVES 4

Cook the orecchiette in plenty of boiling salted water until al dente.

While the pasta is cooking, place the butter and milk in a heavy-based frying pan over low heat. Slowly add the gorgonzola, so that it melts into the butter and milk, mixing with a wooden spoon. Stir in the rocket and cook for 5 minutes. Season with a little salt and pepper to taste, remembering that gorgonzola can be salty.

Drain the orecchiette and add to the sauce. Sprinkle on the parmesan and stir well, then serve immediately.

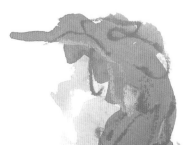

Sedani with four cheeses

SEDANI AI QUATTRO FORMAGGI

This is an Italian classic and a comfort-food favourite in our family. Here I pair it with sedani, a small macaroni-type pasta, but it is excellent with almost any kind of dried or fresh pasta (it's particularly good with gnocchi). Experiment to find your favourite. You can be equally adventurous with the cheeses – cheat and use only three if you like, although I think parmesan and gorgonzola are essential. I suggest using the dolcelatte variety of gorgonzola as it is creamier and more subtle, and therefore less likely to overpower the other ingredients. When you melt the butter at the beginning, you could add some fresh marjoram leaves. You could also add some crushed walnuts as you are tossing the pasta in the sauce.

400 g sedani
50 g gorgonzola dolcelatte
60 g emmental
60 g fontina
30 g butter
120 ml milk
nutmeg, to taste
freshly ground black pepper
60 g freshly grated parmesan

SERVES 4

Cook the sedani in plenty of boiling salted water until al dente.

Meanwhile, remove any crusts from the gorgonzola, emmental and fontina and cut the cheeses into small cubes.

Melt the butter in a heavy-based frying pan over very low heat. Add the cubes of cheese and the milk a bit at a time, and a few gratings of nutmeg. Stir with a wooden spoon until all the cheeses have melted and the sauce is smooth. Add a generous amount of black pepper and 1 tablespoon of the parmesan. Mix thoroughly.

Drain the pasta and add to the sauce. Toss gently to coat, adding a bit more nutmeg if liked and the rest of the parmesan. Serve immediately.

Penne with fiery tomato sauce

PENNE ALL'ARRABBIATA

Arrabbiata means angry – a reference to the hot chilli in the sauce. This robust sauce adheres to the ribbed pasta tubes of penne rigate, which act like little firebombs in the mouth. I first ordered this dish when I was a teenager, eating with my brother in a trattoria in Rome. Neither of us had tried chilli before. The waiter asked, 'Would you like it really angry?' and my brother, thinking that was a standard joke, replied, 'Yes, really, really angry – *arrabbiatissimo.*' When the pasta arrived, it was inedible!

It was only much later, living in Australia with its many cultures, that I came to appreciate the pleasures of chilli. The moral is: adjust the chilli to your taste. Try this recipe my way, and then reduce or increase the level of anger.

2 tablespoons extra virgin olive oil
1 clove garlic, peeled and lightly squashed
150 g guanciale or pancetta, cut into
    small cubes
2 red chillies, finely chopped
1 × 400 g tin peeled tomatoes
sea salt
400 g penne rigate
50 g freshly grated pecorino

SERVES 4

Heat the olive oil in a large heavy-based frying pan over low heat, add the garlic and stir with a wooden spoon until just golden, then discard. Add the guanciale or pancetta and chilli, and cook for about 5 minutes until the guanciale becomes crisp, stirring often with a wooden spoon.

Pass the tomatoes through a mouli or puree in a food processor. Add to the pan and season with salt. Increase the heat to medium and cook, covered, for 15 minutes, stirring regularly.

Cook the penne in plenty of boiling salted water until al dente. Drain, then add to the sauce and stir for about a minute. Serve immediately, sprinkled with pecorino.

Spaghetti and Meatballs

SPAGHETTI CON LE POLPETTINE

When I first heard about pasta with meatballs, I thought it was an American invention because I didn't know much about regional Italian food. The only cuisine I knew was my mother's cooking and the menu of our family restaurant by the sea. I had never seen a cookbook, as recipes were passed down verbally from one generation to the next. Everything changed when food became my passion in life: while studying regional cuisine I discovered that pasta with meatballs is a traditional dish from the south, particularly Sicily (although ironically, over the years, it has become more popular in the USA than in Italy). I must admit it is an amazing dish, full of love and flavour – a meal that unites family and friends. It is more a *piatto unico* ('one-dish meal') than an entrée.

30 g white bread, crusts removed

100 ml milk

200 g minced veal or beef

50 g pork and fennel sausages, skin removed

1 egg

1 tablespoon marjoram leaves, chopped

½ small white onion, finely chopped

2 cloves garlic, finely chopped

90 g freshly grated parmesan

sea salt and freshly ground black pepper

2 tablespoons olive oil

60 g butter

1 × 400 g tin peeled tomatoes

4 sprigs basil

400 g spaghetti

SERVES 4

Soak the bread in the milk until all the milk has been absorbed. Mash the bread with a fork.

Place the bread, minced meat, sausage, egg, marjoram, onion, a third of the garlic and 2 tablespoons of the parmesan in a large bowl. Season with salt and pepper and mix thoroughly. Form the mixture into meatballs the size of cherries.

Heat the olive oil and butter in a heavy-based frying pan over medium heat until the butter has melted. Add the rest of the garlic and cook for 1 minute, stirring with a wooden spoon. Add the meatballs and cook for about 8 minutes, turning them gently so they brown all over.

Pass the tomatoes through a mouli or puree in a food processor. Add to the pan and season with salt. Stir in the basil then simmer for 15 minutes, shaking the pan gently and stirring delicately.

Meanwhile, cook the spaghetti in plenty of boiling salted water until al dente.

Discard the basil sprigs from the sauce. Drain the pasta quickly and add to the sauce. Toss gently until well mixed, then transfer to a warm serving dish and take straight to the table.

Spaghetti carbonara

SPAGHETTI ALLA CARBONARA

Now we say *Buongiorno Roma* (instead of *Arrivederci Roma!*), because this dish is as Roman as the Colosseum, apparently taking its name from the coal sellers (*carbonari*) who used to make it as a snack. It first appeared at the end of World War II, becoming popular with American troops stationed in Italy because it reminded them of bacon and eggs. When they took the idea back home, some American chefs started adding cream and onions to the sauce, but I prefer to keep it simple.

It is important for the flavour that you use pecorino (sheep's cheese), rather than parmesan. I should really be just as strict about the guanciale (pig's cheek), but I know it can be hard to find, so if necessary you can substitute pancetta. You'll notice that there is no salt in this recipe, as both the guanciale and the pecorino are salty.

2 tablespoons extra virgin olive oil
150 g guanciale or pancetta, cut into
    1 cm cubes
freshly ground black pepper
3 eggs
400 g spaghetti
80 g freshly grated pecorino,
    plus extra to serve

SERVES 4

Heat the olive oil in a heavy-based frying pan over high heat. Toss in the guanciale or pancetta and a few pinches of pepper and cook for about 6–8 minutes or until crispy, stirring often with a wooden spoon. Remove from the heat.

Break the eggs into a bowl, add a pinch of black pepper and whisk with a fork. Set aside.

Cook the spaghetti in plenty of boiling salted water until al dente.

Meanwhile, put 2 tablespoons of grated pecorino in the bottom of each of four bowls. During the last minute of the spaghetti cooking time, return the pan with the guanciale to low heat and add 2 tablespoons of the pasta cooking water (the starch in the water will help the ingredients in the sauce to amalgamate).

Drain the spaghetti, reserving 125 ml of the cooking water, and toss it into the pan with the guanciale, stirring gently. Pour the whisked eggs over the spaghetti and stir for about 30 seconds, adding a little more of the pasta cooking water if the sauce seems too dry.

Divide the spaghetti among the four bowls and serve immediately, sprinkling on more pecorino if you wish.

Ham, mozzarella and spaghetti frittata

FRITTATA DI PASTA

Combined with a little sauce and eggs, some simply dressed spaghetti is transformed into a southern Italian favourite for a picnic or a long day at the beach. Just don't call it an omelette or a quiche – it's a frittata.

400 g spaghetti
1 quantity tomato sauce II (see page 52)
3 eggs
120 g freshly grated parmesan
1 tablespoon chopped flat-leaf parsley
sea salt and freshly ground black pepper
2 tablespoons extra virgin olive oil
20 g butter
150 g ham, cut into 1 cm cubes
150 g mozzarella, cut into 1 cm cubes
large handful of basil leaves, finely chopped

SERVES 4

Cook the spaghetti in plenty of boiling salted water for 2 minutes less than the suggested cooking time, then drain it and toss with the tomato sauce.

Beat the eggs in a large bowl with the parmesan and parsley. Season with salt and pepper, then add the spaghetti and mix well. Heat the olive oil and butter in a large (20 cm) non-stick frying pan over low heat. Lay half the spaghetti and egg mixture in the pan, pressing down a little to flatten the surface. Sprinkle the ham, mozzarella and basil over the surface and lay the rest of the spaghetti and egg mixture on top, pressing down firmly.

Cook over medium–high heat for about 6 minutes or until a crust forms on the bottom of the frittata. Flip the frittata by carefully sliding it onto a plate then up-ending it back into the pan. Continue cooking until the other side is browned.

Serve the frittata hot with a salad of tender leaves, or at room temperature for a picnic or a snack.

Rigatoni with potatoes and bacon

PASTA E PATATE

If you have ever wondered what the peasants of Italy ate when they didn't have much time and needed to fill themselves up cheaply, this is it. My father, who came from a large peasant family, used to tell me that when all else failed, there was always olive oil, potatoes and pasta in the kitchen, and some bacon hanging somewhere in the house. Here's a pasta based on that premise.

4 potatoes, peeled and cut into 1 cm cubes
400 g short pasta, such as rigatoni
   (or a mixture of pastas with the same
   cooking time)
3 tablespoons extra virgin olive oil
80 g bacon or pancetta, finely diced
sea salt and freshly ground black pepper
60 g freshly grated parmesan
handful of basil leaves, roughly chopped

SERVES 4

Bring a large saucepan of salted water to the boil and add the potato. After 3 minutes, add the pasta and cook until al dente.

In the meantime, heat the olive oil in a heavy-based frying pan over medium heat and cook the bacon or pancetta until crispy.

Using a slotted spoon, lift the pasta and potato from the water and add them to the bacon. The extra cooking water on the pasta adds to the creaminess of the dish. Mix well, then season with salt and pepper and sprinkle the parmesan and basil over the top. Serve very hot.

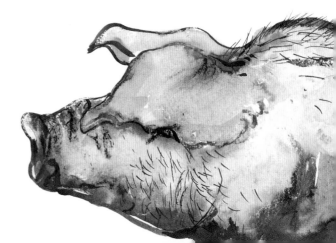

Orecchiette with veal involtini

ORECCHIETTE CON INVOLTINI

This lovely meal takes its inspiration from the Neapolitan or Sicilian ragù, but is much lighter and quicker to make. Orecchiette is a typical pasta from the southern region of Puglia, and it goes equally well with light or heavy sauces. Once handmade at home with flour and water, nowadays this versatile pasta is available commercially.

8 slices veal scaloppine

sea salt

40 g pine nuts, lightly crushed

large handful of mint leaves, very finely chopped

2 cloves garlic, 1 very finely chopped, 1 left whole but peeled and lightly squashed

200 g freshly grated pecorino

120 ml extra virgin olive oil

3 tablespoons dry white wine

1 × 400 g tin peeled tomatoes

freshly ground black pepper

400 g orecchiette

green salad, to serve

SERVES 4

Lay the veal slices on a board. Sprinkle with a little salt and then in equal quantities the pine nuts, mint and chopped garlic. Divide half the pecorino into eight portions and sprinkle over the top. Drizzle with a little olive oil, then roll up each piece of veal into a cylinder and secure with a toothpick to make the involtini.

Heat the remaining olive oil in a heavy-based frying pan over low heat. Add the whole clove of garlic and stir with a wooden spoon until just golden, then discard.

Increase the heat to medium, add the involtini to the pan and brown on all sides. Pour in the white wine and cook for about 5 minutes or until the alcohol has evaporated, shaking the pan a few times.

Pass the tomatoes through a mouli or puree in a food processor. Add to the pan, season with salt and pepper and mix thoroughly but delicately with the wooden spoon. Simmer very gently over low–medium heat for about 15 minutes, stirring from time to time.

Meanwhile, cook the orecchiette in plenty of boiling salted water until al dente. Drain and place in a serving dish. Pour the sauce and the involtini over the pasta and toss well to combine. Sprinkle with the remaining pecorino and serve immediately with a tender green salad.

Conchiglie with porcini mushrooms and pork sausages

CONCHIGLIE ALLA PAPALINA SBAGLIATA

I used to travel many kilometres from my home in Sydney to visit a restaurant that specialised in what I understood to be *pasta papalina*. Imagine my disappointment when I learned it was not the authentic recipe (for the traditional version, see page 176). I still loved the dish, though, and I could find it nowhere else. Although I never got their actual recipe, the cream sauce (ah, the eighties!) included sausages and a fresh, mild pecorino. I'm guessing they made it this way; *sbagliata* in the Italian recipe title means 'mistaken', but I think I've got it right . . .

10 g dried porcini mushrooms

3 teaspoons extra virgin olive oil

50 g butter

1 clove garlic, peeled and lightly squashed

200 g pork and fennel sausages

150 ml cream

sea salt and freshly ground black pepper

2 eggs

2 egg yolks

30 g freshly grated parmesan

30 g freshly grated mild pecorino

400 g conchiglie

SERVES 4

Place the dried porcini in a small bowl, cover with warm water and leave to soak for 15 minutes. Drain and pat dry with paper towels, then finely chop.

Heat the olive oil and butter in a heavy-based frying pan over medium heat until the butter has melted. Add the garlic and stir with a wooden spoon until just golden, then discard. Add the chopped mushroom to the pan and cook, stirring, for 3 minutes.

Remove the skin from the sausages and break them up a little. Add to the pan and cook for about 5 minutes until brown all over, stirring every so often. Reduce the heat to low. Add the cream, sprinkle with a little salt and plenty of pepper and cook for a further 5 minutes.

Meanwhile, beat the eggs and egg yolks in a bowl with the parmesan, pecorino and a pinch of salt. Set aside.

Cook the conchiglie in plenty of boiling salted water until al dente. Drain, reserving a little of the cooking water. Add the pasta to the sauce and toss gently, then take the pan off the heat and add the egg mixture and some of the reserved pasta cooking water if it seems too dry. Mix thoroughly and serve.

Spaghetti with seafood and tomato

SPAGHETTI IN GUAZZETTO

I have long been interested in adapting some of the classic main-course preparations so they can be served as pasta sauces, with the pasta being part of a *piatto unico* ('single dish') rather than something served on the side. I think *guazzetto* – a light braise, often with seafood – works very well in this context. This way of cooking fuses the flavours of the ingredients yet preserves their character, and the heat of the chilli adds a pleasing strength.

200 g baby octopus
200 g baby calamari
200 g baby cuttlefish
75 ml extra virgin olive oil
2 cloves garlic, peeled and lightly squashed
2 red chillies, thinly sliced
250 ml dry white wine
1 × 400 g tin peeled tomatoes
sea salt
400 g spaghetti
large handful of basil leaves, torn

SERVES 4

Hopefully you can buy the seafood already cleaned – it's worth the extra money! If not, roll up your sleeves, put on a big apron and head for the sink. Once you get started, you'll find it's not that bad.

To clean the baby octopus, cut the tentacles away from the head below the hard beak. Cut away and discard the beak, then turn the body inside out. Remove the ink sac and internal organs. Strip the skin away from the head and rinse it and the tentacles under running water. Rinse and drain well, then pat dry. Cut the body into bite-sized pieces and set aside with the tentacles.

To clean the calamari and cuttlefish, hold the tentacles in one hand and pull firmly with the other to separate the head from the body (try not to break the ink sac). Cut off the tentacles below the eyes and discard the head and guts, then push the beak (mouth) out and discard. Peel the skin off the body and rinse everything inside and out under running water. Leave the tentacles intact and cut the body open along the obvious seam, then cut into 1 cm strips. Set aside.

Heat the olive oil in a heavy-based frying pan over low–medium heat. Add the garlic and stir with a wooden spoon until just golden, then discard. Add the chilli and the octopus, stir with a wooden spoon and sauté for 5–8 minutes until the octopus becomes pink and shiny. Add the calamari, cuttlefish and white wine, stir well and simmer until the wine has evaporated.

Pass the tomatoes through a mouli or squish them with your hands. Add to the pan, season with salt and continue cooking over low heat for 30 minutes, stirring from time to time.

When the sauce is nearly ready, cook the spaghetti in plenty of boiling salted water until al dente. Drain and add to the sauce. Toss gently, sprinkle with the basil and serve.

Spaghetti reef-style

SPAGHETTI ALLO SCOGLIO

My uncle Ciccio was the cook in charge of the kitchen at my family restaurant in Italy, where his wife (my Aunty Anna) and my mother also worked, while my father was mainly in charge of the cold larder, the pantry and the cellar.

I fondly remember Ciccio as a very creative and very passionate chef. People would travel for hours to go to the restaurant and eat whatever he suggested. He had many specialities, but *spaghetti allo scoglio* – or 'reef-style', so called because all the seafood used comes from the waters surrounding the reef – was one of his most-requested, because it was like having the sea on a plate. Although not originally his invention, he made the dish his own to the extent that it became known as *spaghetti alla Ciccio*; even the way he described it would fill your mind with anticipation.

It was always a joy to watch him cook, with his long white apron flapping as he stood in front of the stove, adding all the ingredients to the sizzling soffritto at exactly the right time, one by one. When the sauce was ready, in would go the steaming-hot spaghetti, then he would be calling for the dish to be taken to the table immediately. It gives me great pleasure to share with you Ciccio's spaghetti with seafood.

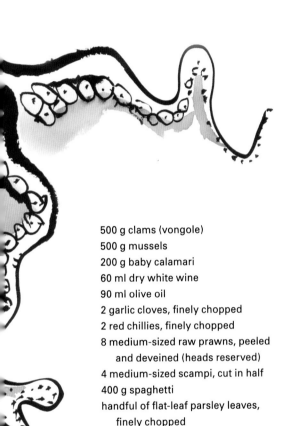

500 g clams (vongole)
500 g mussels
200 g baby calamari
60 ml dry white wine
90 ml olive oil
2 garlic cloves, finely chopped
2 red chillies, finely chopped
8 medium-sized raw prawns, peeled
    and deveined (heads reserved)
4 medium-sized scampi, cut in half
400 g spaghetti
handful of flat-leaf parsley leaves,
    finely chopped

SERVES 4

Soak the clams in salted water for about an hour (to purge them of any sand), then rinse several times in fresh water. Drain and set aside in a bowl. Scrub and debeard the mussels and add them to the bowl with the clams.

To clean the calamari, separate the tentacles from the body by holding the body in one hand and pulling away the tentacles with the other hand. Cut the tentacles straight across below the eyes and discard everything from the eyes up. Squeeze out and discard the bony beak and cut the tentacles in two. Remove and discard the quill and everything else from inside the body, then peel off the skin under running water and cut the body into thin rings. Wash the rings and the tentacles once more under running water, then pat dry with paper towels and set aside.

Place the clams and mussels in a heavy-based frying pan over high heat. Add the white wine and simmer until the shells open, removing the clams and mussels from the pan as soon as they open (one at a time if necessary – if they cook for too long, they become tough). Strain the cooking liquid left in the pan through a fine sieve into a large bowl. When the clams and mussels are cool enough to handle, take most of them from their shells, leaving a few in their shells for presentation, then return them all to the bowl with the cooking liquid so they don't dry out. Wash the pan thoroughly to remove any sediment.

Now heat the olive oil in the cleaned frying pan over low heat and sauté the garlic and chilli for 3 minutes. Add the calamari and cook for another 5 minutes. Add the prawns and scampi, together with the prawn heads. Using a wooden spoon, squash the prawn heads against the sides of the pan to release their flavour, discarding them when they have changed colour. Cook the prawns and scampi for another 3 minutes, then add all the mussels and clams, together with about 4 tablespoons of their cooking liquid. Cook for a further 3 minutes, mixing well to combine all the flavours, then remove the scampi and keep them warm.

Cook the spaghetti in plenty of boiling salted water until al dente, then drain and add to the sauce. Sprinkle on the parsley, gently toss everything together and serve immediately, topped with the scampi.

Spaghetti with Sardines

SPAGHETTI CON LE SARDE

This is from Sicily's capital, Palermo, but we can make it ours because Australia's markets offer beautiful fresh sardines, already cleaned and filleted. The fennel goes so well with the sardines, particularly when it is cooked to become soft and sweet, like the sultanas. I like to add a pinch of saffron for colour and finish the dish with toasted breadcrumbs for texture.

2 baby fennel bulbs

60 g sultanas

3 tablespoons extra virgin olive oil, plus extra to serve

6 anchovy fillets in oil

1 onion, finely chopped

30 g pine nuts

freshly ground black pepper

pinch of saffron threads

400 g fresh sardines, filleted and cut into 3 cm long pieces

400 g spaghetti

4 tablespoons breadcrumbs

SERVES 4

Cut off the top part of the fennel, leaving only the bulbs. Peel off and discard the tough outer layers. Boil the inner bulbs in lightly salted water for about 30 minutes or until tender. Drain, reserving some of the cooking water. Cut the bulbs into pieces and set aside.

In the meantime, soak the sultanas in warm water for 15 minutes. Squeeze them dry, then roughly chop them and set aside.

Heat the olive oil in a heavy-based frying pan over medium heat. Add the anchovies and, with the help of a fork, melt them into the oil. Add the onion, pine nuts and sultanas and stir gently for 5 minutes or until the onion has softened.

Add the fennel to the pan with 3 tablespoons of the fennel cooking water, and season with black pepper. Add a pinch of saffron, mix thoroughly and cook for 8 minutes. Stir in the sardines and cook for 15 minutes, stirring often.

In the meantime, cook the spaghetti in plenty of boiling salted water until al dente.

Toast the breadcrumbs in a small non-stick frying pan until just golden.

Drain the spaghetti and add to the sauce. Toss well, adding a little more of the fennel cooking water if needed, then sprinkle with the breadcrumbs and a little extra olive oil. Serve hot.

Spaghetti with clams

SPAGHETTI ALLE VONGOLE IN BIANCO

Here spaghetti, the king of pasta – long, thin and elegant – is paired with small clams and their juices to bring you the flavour of the sea, enhanced with garlic, chilli and the best olive oil. A celebration of life in summertime, this dish is available all around coastal Italy, particularly at those seasonal restaurants right on the beach where you can eat still wearing your swimming costume and dripping with sea water, with your feet in the sand and a glass of chilled white wine in your hand. *Classico* and *fantastico*!

I offer you two versions of *spaghetti alle vongole*: *in bianco* ('in white'), which is the way most Italians prefer to eat their clams, or with tomato. Try them both and choose your favourite. Just remember not to add salt to the clams at any point – let the sea speak for itself.

1 kg clams (vongole)
3 tablespoons white wine
100 ml extra virgin olive oil
400 g spaghetti
2 cloves garlic, peeled and lightly squashed
2 small red chillies, very finely sliced
2 tablespoons chopped flat-leaf parsley

SERVES 4

Rinse the clams thoroughly under cold running water to remove any sand or grit from the grooves of their shells. Place them in a large frying pan over high heat with the white wine and 1 tablespoon of olive oil and let them pop open – this should take less than 5 minutes. As they are popping, stir them with a wooden spoon. When all the clams have opened, lift them out with a slotted spoon and put them in a large bowl. Boil the liquid remaining in the pan until it has reduced by half, then strain it into another bowl through a fine sieve to remove any grit and sand. Set it aside. Wash the pan thoroughly to remove any sediment.

When the clams are cool enough to handle, take most of them out of their shells and put them in the bowl with the strained liquid; leave the rest of the clams in their shells, setting them aside separately.

Cook the spaghetti in plenty of boiling salted water until very al dente (2 minutes less than the cooking time on the packet).

Meanwhile, heat the remaining olive oil in the cleaned frying pan over medium heat. Add the garlic, chilli and 2 teaspoons of the parsley and stir with a wooden spoon until the garlic is just golden, then remove and discard the garlic cloves. Add the shelled clams and most of their cooking liquid and simmer for 2 minutes.

Drain the spaghetti and add it to the frying pan. Sprinkle on the remaining parsley, then add the reserved clams in their shells and a little more of the cooking liquid if it seems dry. Toss over low heat for about 1 minute to allow the flavours to mingle, then serve immediately.

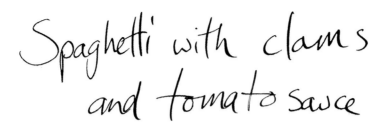

SPAGHETTI ALLE VONGOLE CON POMODORO

This may not be as popular as the version *in bianco*, but it's just as tasty. The fresh tomato sauce is heated separately from the clams so they don't overcook after they have opened. The tomato must not be overpowering or it will ruin the delicate flavour of the clams.

1 kg clams (vongole)
3 tablespoons white wine
100 ml extra virgin olive oil
400 g spaghetti
2 cloves garlic, peeled and lightly squashed
2 tablespoons chopped flat-leaf parsley
freshly ground black pepper, to taste
½ quantity tomato sauce I (see page 51), gently warmed

SERVES 4

Rinse the clams thoroughly under cold running water to remove any sand or grit from the grooves of their shells. Place them in a large frying pan over high heat with the white wine and 1 tablespoon of olive oil and let them pop open – this should take less than 5 minutes. As they are popping, stir them with a wooden spoon. When all the clams have opened, lift them out with a slotted spoon and put them in a large bowl. Boil the liquid remaining in the pan until it has reduced by half, then strain it into another bowl through a fine sieve to remove any grit and sand. Set it aside. Wash the pan thoroughly to remove any sediment.

When the clams are cool enough to handle, take most of them out of their shells and put them in the bowl with the strained liquid; leave the rest of the clams in their shells.

Cook the spaghetti in plenty of boiling salted water until very al dente (2 minutes less than the cooking time on the packet).

Meanwhile, heat the remaining olive oil in the cleaned frying pan over medium heat. Add the garlic and 2 teaspoons of the parsley and stir with a wooden spoon until the garlic is just golden, then remove and discard the garlic cloves. Add the shelled clams and their cooking liquid, grind over some black pepper and simmer for 2 minutes. Add the warm tomato sauce, stirring to combine.

Drain the spaghetti and add it to the frying pan. Sprinkle on the remaining parsley, then add the reserved clams in their shells. Toss over low heat for about 1 minute to allow the flavours to mingle, then serve immediately.

Spaghetti with capers, chilli and anchovies

SPAGHETTI ALLA PUTTANESCA

3 tablespoons extra virgin olive oil

1 clove garlic, finely chopped

6 anchovy fillets in oil, drained and
finely chopped

1 red chilli, finely chopped

400 g roma tomatoes, peeled and seeded
(see page 51) or 1 × 400 g tin peeled
tomatoes

150 g black olives, pitted and
roughly chopped

1 tablespoon capers in salt, rinsed and dried

sea salt

400 g spaghetti

SERVES 4

Here is another favourite from the streets of Rome – literally from the streets, since *puttanesca* means 'prostitute-style'. It's interesting to note that there are no herbs in any of the classic pasta dishes from Rome. I guess only geraniums grow on Roman balconies!

Heat the olive oil in a heavy-based frying pan over medium heat. Add the garlic and cook for about a minute until just golden, stirring with a wooden spoon. Add the anchovies and chilli and stir them through the oil for 1 minute.

Pass the tomatoes through a mouli or puree in a blender. Add to the pan with the olives and capers, season to taste with salt and mix well. Cook for 10–15 minutes, stirring regularly.

In the meantime, cook the spaghetti in plenty of boiling salted water until al dente. Drain, then add to the sauce and toss for 30 seconds. Serve immediately.

Spaghetti with bottarga

SPAGHETTI ALLA BOTTARGA

100 ml extra virgin olive oil

1 clove garlic, peeled and lightly squashed

1 red chilli, cut in half lengthways,
seeds removed

400 g spaghetti

60 g grated mullet bottarga

handful of flat-leaf parsley leaves,
finely chopped

SERVES 4

An ancient speciality from Sardinia, bottarga is mullet or tuna roe that has been pressed and then air-dried – it is available either grated or in one piece from specialist Italian delis. In Sicily, tuna bottarga is very popular, thinly sliced and served on freshly baked ciabatta. It has a particular taste and I find that people either love it or hate it, but you have to try it more than once, for it is not usually a case of 'love at first taste'. When you do fall in love with it, you should 'have the best and have a lot of it' – as Cipriani of Harry's Bar famously said about caviar.

This is a simple recipe. I do suggest you use the best mild olive oil you can find and the bottarga of mullet. And one more thing: a Sardinian friend once told me that the bottarga should never touch the pan when it is on the heat.

Heat the olive oil in a heavy-based frying pan over medium heat. Add the garlic and chilli and stir with a wooden spoon until just golden, then discard, setting aside the pan containing the infused oil.

Meanwhile cook the spaghetti in plenty of boiling salted water until al dente.

Return the frying pan to the heat to warm the oil through. Drain the spaghetti and add to the pan, then remove from the heat. Toss gently, adding the bottarga a little at a time so that it is evenly distributed. Serve very hot, sprinkled with the parsley.

Spaghetti with black olives and anchovies

SPAGHETTI ALLE OLIVE

This dish uses both olive paste and olives, so it's luscious enough without needing any parmesan, especially when walnuts are added for extra texture. You could even simplify the sauce by using just olive paste with some olive oil and parsley. Heat a little olive oil in a frying pan over medium heat with the parsley, then add the drained spaghetti and stir to coat thoroughly. Tip the spaghetti into a serving bowl and stir the olive paste through it, adding a bit of cooking water if you think it looks dry.

In Liguria, olive paste is called *il caviale dei poveri* – 'poor people's caviar' – and historically, a pot of it was often carried by sailors and pilgrims, ready to be spread on bread or crostini as a welcome taste of home. Nowadays it's handy for picnics, whether you are rich or poor, so I suggest you make more than you need for this pasta.

400 g spaghetti
large handful of basil leaves, shredded

OLIVE PASTE

2 anchovy fillets in oil, drained
4 walnuts
100 g black olives, pitted and
    roughly chopped
1 teaspoon capers in salt, rinsed and dried
1 tablespoon extra virgin olive oil

SAUCE

150 ml extra virgin olive oil
1 clove garlic, finely chopped
1 red chilli, finely chopped
large handful of flat-leaf parsley
    leaves, chopped
1 large tomato, peeled and seeded
    (see page 51), then diced
sea salt and freshly ground black pepper
50 g Sicilian green olives, pitted and sliced

SERVES 4

First make the olive paste. Place all the ingredients in a blender and pulse on a low speed until smooth. Transfer to a bowl and set aside.

To make the sauce, heat the olive oil in a heavy-based frying pan over low heat, add the garlic and chilli and stir with a wooden spoon for about a minute. Sprinkle in the parsley and mix thoroughly. Add the tomato and season lightly with salt and pepper. Increase the heat to medium–high and cook for 5 minutes, stirring often. Add the green olives and the olive paste, mix well and cook for another minute. Remove the pan from the heat.

Cook the spaghetti in plenty of boiling salted water until al dente. Drain, reserving some of the cooking water.

Place the sauce back over low heat. Add the spaghetti and basil to the pan and toss gently to combine. Add a tablespoon of the cooking water if it seems dry. Serve in a large bowl in the centre of the table, so everyone can help themselves.

Spaghetti with baby calamari

SPAGHETTI AI CALAMARETTI

This simple preparation is common in all the Mediterranean regions of Italy, though it changes from north to south. I remember having it often when I was growing up, cooked by my mother, my aunty Anna or my uncle Ciccio, and it varied even amongst them.

I've tried many times to re-create not only the taste of the dish, but the perfume of the sea near the rocks where the calamari were swimming, and the joy in my mother's eyes when the fishermen showed her the baby calamari still moving. I've incorporated my family's unique touches and the spirit of Liguria and the result, I think, is amazing. The main thing to remember is that you should only make this dish when you can get very fresh baby calamari.

50 g sultanas
400 g very fresh baby calamari
100 ml olive oil
1 clove garlic, finely chopped
1 tablespoon flat-leaf parsley leaves,
    finely chopped
50 g taggiasca or other small Ligurian olives,
    pitted and cut in half
30 g pine nuts
2 sprigs basil
3 large tomatoes, peeled and seeded
    (see page 51), then sliced
sea salt and freshly ground black pepper
400 g spaghetti

SERVES 4

Soak the sultanas in warm water for 10 minutes, then drain and pat dry with paper towels.

Over the sink, clean the calamari. Separate the tentacles from the body by holding the body in one hand and pulling away the tentacles with the other hand. Cut the tentacles straight across below the eyes and discard everything from the eyes up. Squeeze out and discard the bony beak. Remove and discard the quill and everything else from inside the body, then peel off the skin under running water and cut the body into thin rings. Wash the rings and the tentacles one more time under running water, then pat dry with paper towels.

Heat the olive oil in a heavy-based frying pan over low heat. Add the garlic and parsley and stir with a wooden spoon for 2 minutes. Add the calamari rings and tentacles and mix well, then add the olives, pine nuts, sultanas and basil sprigs. Mix thoroughly to blend all the flavours, then increase the heat to medium and cook for 5 minutes, stirring often. Stir in the tomato, season with salt and pepper and cook for another 5 minutes. Remove and discard the basil sprigs.

In the meantime, cook the spaghetti in plenty of boiling salted water until al dente. Drain and add to the sauce, then reduce the heat to low and toss the sauce through the spaghetti for about 1 minute. Serve immediately.

Maccheroni with fresh tuna

MACCHERONI AL TONNO FRESCO

A beautiful and fast swimmer, tuna is unpopular with Ligurian fishermen because during its migration it follows the coastline with its mouth wide open, eating up all the anchovies along the way. But Italian fishermen exact their revenge on tuna in the waters around Sicily, where they are circled and captured by the *tonnarotti* or tuna fishermen, usually after a long and difficult battle.

Tuna has vibrant red and strong-flavoured flesh that is often served as chargrilled tuna steaks pierced with mint and garlic, but here I am offering you tuna in a sauce complemented by some of the most beautiful Sicilian produce.

2 cloves garlic, very finely chopped
½ bunch flat-leaf parsley, leaves picked
3 tablespoons extra virgin olive oil
½ white onion, finely chopped
500 g fresh tuna, cut into 1 cm cubes
sea salt and freshly ground black pepper
3 tablespoons dry white wine
2 large ripe tomatoes, peeled and seeded
   (see page 51), then diced
60 g black olives, pitted
60 g blanched almonds, chopped
400 g maccheroni
1 tablespoon oregano leaves,
   roughly chopped

SERVES 4

Put the garlic and the parsley on a wooden board and use a mezzaluna or a large sharp knife to mince them very finely together. Set aside.

Heat the olive oil in a heavy-based frying pan over medium heat, add the onion and mix it around with a wooden spoon. Cook for 5 minutes or until soft and translucent.

Push the onion to one side of the pan and increase the heat to high. Add the tuna and sear on all sides for 1–2 minutes, mixing well with a wooden spoon. Stir the onion in with the tuna, add the garlic and parsley and mix well. Season with salt and pepper.

Pour in the wine and simmer for about 3 minutes until it has evaporated. Now add the tomato and olives to the pan and cook over low heat for 10 minutes, stirring gently but often. Mix in the almonds at the end.

Meanwhile, cook the maccheroni in plenty of boiling salted water until al dente. Drain, reserving 125 ml of the cooking water.

Add the pasta to the sauce and toss carefully, adding a little of the cooking water if it seems dry. Serve hot, sprinkled with oregano.

Linguine with swordfish

LINGUINE AL PESCE SPADA

In the seas around Sicily, June is the peak season for catching swordfish. One year I was lucky enough to visit Lipari (one of the Aeolian Islands, which lie to the north of Sicily) during that month, and the atmosphere in the village was amazing: there was optimism and serenity all around, just as there is before the harvest of a wonderful crop.

The people knew that after months of hard work and little income, they were finally going to see some money to help them through the next few months. The children would follow their fathers to the docks in the morning and watch them climb into their boats and disappear over the horizon. Then they'd be back in the afternoon, this time with their mothers, when the fishermen were returning like heroes with their boats full of huge flopping fish. The restaurateurs of the islands were also there, waiting to bid for the best fish, which they'd put on a table in the middle of their restaurant and slice to order.

I was staying with a family of fishermen who rented a room in their house to visitors, and that is where I first came across this way of serving linguine.

300 g mixed-colour cherry tomatoes
4 tablespoons extra virgin olive oil
2 cloves garlic, finely chopped
400 g swordfish, cut into 1 cm cubes
2 red chillies, thinly sliced
large handful of flat-leaf parsley leaves,
    finely chopped
small handful of basil leaves,
    roughly chopped
sea salt
400 g linguine

SERVES 4

Rinse the tomatoes, pat them dry and cut them into quarters. Set aside.

Heat the olive oil in a heavy-based frying pan over low heat, add the garlic and cook for 1 minute, stirring with a wooden spoon. Increase the heat to high and add the swordfish and chilli. Sear the fish on all sides for about 1 minute, stirring it through the oil and garlic with a wooden spoon.

Turn the heat down to medium, add the tomato and cook, stirring regularly, for about 8 minutes. Stir in the parsley and basil, season with salt and cook for 1 minute more, then take off the heat.

Cook the linguine in plenty of boiling salted water until al dente. Drain, reserving a little of the pasta cooking water.

Put the frying pan back over low heat and add the linguine. Toss well for about 1 minute, adding a tablespoon or two of the reserved cooking water if the sauce seems too dry. Serve immediately.

Bucatini with eggplant and anchovies

BUCATINI CON FILETTI DI MELANZANE

Here we combine the great products of the south – eggplant, anchovies, capers and olives – to make a very elegant and delicious dish.

3 eggplants (aubergines)
sea salt
450 g ripe tomatoes, peeled and seeded
   (see page 51)
1 tablespoon finely chopped basil
120 ml extra virgin olive oil
1 clove garlic, peeled and lightly squashed
6 anchovy fillets in oil, drained and
   roughly chopped
50 g capers in salt, rinsed and dried
50 g black olives
freshly ground black pepper
400 g bucatini

SERVES 4

Cut the ends off the eggplants, then peel and cut into thin strips. Place the strips in a colander over the sink, sprinkle with sea salt and leave for 40 minutes to sweat out any bitter juices.

In the meantime, pass the tomatoes through a mouli or puree in a blender. Stir in the basil and set aside.

Rinse the eggplant and pat dry with paper towel. Heat the olive oil in a non-stick frying pan over medium heat, add the eggplant in batches and cook for 3–4 minutes or until golden on all sides. Drain on paper towel.

Transfer the remaining eggplant oil to a heavy-based frying pan over low heat. Add the garlic and stir with a wooden spoon until just golden, then discard. Increase the heat to medium. Add the tomato, anchovies, capers and olives, and season with salt and pepper (remembering that both the anchovies and capers are salty). Mix thoroughly with a wooden spoon and simmer gently for 15 minutes. Salt the eggplant lightly and add it to the sauce, then reduce the heat to low and simmer for another 8 minutes.

Cook the bucatini in plenty of boiling salted water until al dente. Drain, then add to the sauce and toss well. Serve immediately.

Orecchiette with anchovies and capers

ORECCHIETTE ALLA SALSA DEL SOLE

I made this pasta at home one day to share with a friend who was recently back from Calabria. Being a Calabrese himself, he was talking proudly about the region's people and their food. 'Let's have some lunch,' I said. 'You've inspired me.' I chose orecchiette as the pasta, but any other kind of dried (non-egg) pasta would be fine here. My friend thoroughly enjoyed the dish, saying that it reminded him of the sun of Calabria.

8 anchovy fillets in oil, drained

handful of flat-leaf parsley leaves

1 clove garlic, peeled

1 tablespoon capers in salt, rinsed and dried

2 red chillies

4 tablespoons extra virgin olive oil

1 celery stalk, small and yellow,
   finely chopped

2 large ripe tomatoes, peeled and seeded
   (see page 51), then diced

sea salt and freshly ground pepper

large handful of basil leaves, shredded

400 g orecchiette

60 g freshly grated pecorino

SERVES 4

Place the anchovies, parsley, garlic, capers and chillies on a chopping board and, using a mezzaluna or a large sharp knife, finely chop everything together.

Heat the olive oil in a heavy-based frying pan over low heat. Add the parsley mixture and the celery and cook for 2 minutes until the garlic starts to colour, stirring constantly with a wooden spoon.

Stir in the tomato and season with salt and pepper, then cook for about 10 minutes, stirring regularly. Mix in the basil.

Meanwhile, cook the orecchiette in plenty of boiling salted water until al dente. Drain and toss in the sauce for 1 minute. Serve immediately, topped with grated pecorino.

Bucatini with prawns and artichokes

BUCATINI CON GAMBERI E CARCIOFI

During the artichoke season in spring, we always serve *gamberi e carciofi* (grilled prawns on a bed of thinly sliced raw artichokes dressed with lemon, olive oil and parmesan) as a special in my restaurant, Lucio's. It is such a lovely combination that I thought I'd turn it into a pasta dish, matched with bucatini, which can stand up to the big, meaty prawns I'm suggesting here. I also decided to start the sauce with a classic soffritto from my family restaurant in Liguria – garlic and parsley chopped together with a mezzaluna – plus a touch of tomato and chilli.

500 g large raw prawns

1 lemon, cut in half

5 large artichokes

3 cloves garlic, peeled

large handful of flat-leaf parsley leaves

45 ml extra virgin olive oil

1 small red chilli, finely sliced

sea salt

50 ml dry white wine

300 g ripe tomatoes, peeled and seeded
   (see page 51), then diced

400 g bucatini

10 basil leaves, chopped

SERVES 4

Peel and devein the prawns, but reserve the heads. Cut the prawns in half lengthways, then in half again, then cut each long slice in half across. Set aside.

Half-fill a bowl with cold water, and squeeze the juice of half a lemon into it. Pull away and discard the outer leaves of the artichoke until you reach the pale green and yellow leaves inside. Cut off and discard the stalk and the tops of the leaves to about a third of the way down. With a sharp knife, peel off any dark green bits from the base of the artichoke until you reach the yellow part. Rub the artichoke all over with a cut surface of the lemon, then cut the artichoke in half and rub the exposed interior surfaces with lemon as well. Scoop out and discard the hairy bits (the choke) until you get to the heart. Slice each half into thin segments and place the segments in the water.

Mix the garlic and parsley on a board and chop them together very finely with a mezzaluna or sharp knife.

Heat the olive oil in a heavy-based frying pan over high heat. Put the prawn heads in the pan, squashing them with a wooden spoon and mixing them around the pan to flavour the oil. When they change colour, take the pan off the heat, remove the prawn heads, and let the oil cool down for a minute so it won't burn the garlic.

Add the garlic and parsley mixture to the oil and put the pan back over low heat. Cook for 2 minutes, stirring constantly, then add the chilli and the artichokes and cook for 5 minutes, stirring often. Season with a little salt.

Pour in the wine, turn up the heat to medium and continue stirring until the alcohol has evaporated. Add the prawns and tomato, mix them through the sauce and season with a little more salt. Cook for about 5 minutes until the artichokes are tender, stirring often. Take off the heat.

Cook the bucatini in plenty of boiling salted water until al dente. Drain, reserving a little of the cooking water.

Sprinkle the basil into the sauce, put the pan back over low heat and add the bucatini. Toss well for 1 minute, adding a tablespoon or two of the reserved cooking water if the sauce seems too dry. Serve immediately.

Linguine with preserved tuna

LINGUINE AL TONNO

**The art of preparing dishes only with products kept in the *cambusa*
('ship's pantry') was mastered by the sailors, but we don't mind making it
ours too. After all, turning a tin of tuna into something respectable is always
an achievement. Try to find capers grown on Pantelleria, one of the Aeolian
islands off the coast of Sicily, if you can – their flavour is incomparable.**

200 g tuna in oil
75 ml extra virgin olive oil
6 anchovy fillets in oil, drained
1 clove garlic, peeled and lightly squashed
1 small onion, thinly sliced
100 g black olives, pitted
40 g capers in salt, rinsed and dried
sea salt and freshly ground black pepper
500 g ripe tomatoes, peeled and seeded
   (see page 51), then diced
400 g linguine
50 g breadcrumbs

SERVES 4

Remove the tuna from the tin, discarding the oil, and break up the tuna with a fork.

Heat the olive oil in a heavy-based frying pan over low heat. Add the anchovies
and melt them into the oil by squashing them with a fork. Add the garlic and stir
with a wooden spoon until just golden, then discard. Add the onion and sauté
gently for 3–4 minutes until soft and translucent. Turn up the heat to medium,
add the olives, tuna and capers and season to taste with salt and pepper.
Stir in the tomato and continue cooking for another 10 minutes, stirring from
time to time.

Meanwhile, cook the linguine in plenty of boiling salted water until al dente.
Toast the breadcrumbs in a small non-stick frying pan until just golden.

Drain the linguine. Quickly add to the pan and toss in the sauce until well coated.
Sprinkle with the breadcrumbs and serve immediately.

Penne with capsicum and anchovies

PENNE AI PEPERONI E ACCIUGHE

One of my mother's specialities was roasted yellow capsicums (from our vegetable garden). She would fold them over anchovies and capers, pinning them together with a toothpick and preserving them under oil. The problem was that I thought I didn't like capsicums so I wouldn't eat them, which upset my mother. Then one day she made a pasta dish with the same three ingredients, and I became an instant convert – I hope you will be too. I like to add some fresh tomato and basil at the end to enhance the flavours. I don't recommend serving cheese with this, but if you insist, I'd suggest a mild pecorino rather than parmesan.

On a hot summer's day, this sauce works well as a cold dressing for hot pasta: instead of using chopped garlic, just cut one garlic clove in half and rub the cut surfaces around the inside of a large ceramic bowl. Add all the other sauce ingredients to the bowl and allow them to macerate for 10 minutes, then cook the pasta until al dente and toss through the sauce in the bowl. Serve warm.

4 capsicums (peppers) – a mixture of
    yellow and red is pleasing
3 tablespoons extra virgin olive oil
4 anchovy fillets in oil, drained
2 cloves garlic, finely chopped
handful of flat-leaf parsley leaves,
    finely chopped
1 teaspoon capers in salt, rinsed and dried
2 large ripe tomatoes, peeled and seeded
    (see page 51), then diced
sea salt and freshly ground black pepper
large handful of basil leaves, finely chopped
400 g penne

SERVES 4

First prepare the capsicums. Place them on an open flame, or under the grill. When one side is black, turn them over with a pair of tongs and blacken the other side. Place them in a plastic bag, close it tightly and set aside for 15 minutes. Take the capsicums out of the bag and peel off the skin, then remove and discard the stalk and the seeds. Cut the flesh into 5 mm wide strips.

Heat the olive oil in a heavy-based frying pan over medium heat and, with the help of a fork, melt the anchovies into the oil. Add the garlic and parsley and cook for 2 minutes, stirring constantly with a wooden spoon. Add the capers, tomato and capsicum strips. Sprinkle on a little salt and pepper, mix thoroughly and cook for 3 minutes. Stir in the basil, then take the pan off the heat.

Cook the penne in plenty of boiling salted water until al dente. Drain and add it to the sauce. Put the pan back over low heat and toss for about 1 minute, then serve hot.

Orecchiette with broccoli and anchovies

ORECCHIETTE AI BROCCOLI

Although orecchiette ('little ears') is a form of pasta that originated in the south of Italy, this dish has long been associated with Rome. The ancient Romans were addicted to a salty fish sauce called *garum*, which they used the way Chinese now use soy sauce and Australians use tomato sauce – to boost the flavour of other ingredients, especially broccoli, which they regarded (rightly) as a health food. Modern Romans use anchovies and chillies to the same effect.

½ head broccoli
400 g orecchiette
100 ml extra virgin olive oil
2 cloves garlic, peeled and lightly squashed
2 red chillies, finely sliced
5 anchovy fillets in oil, drained
sea salt and freshly ground black pepper
freshly grated parmesan, to serve (optional)

SERVES 4

Prepare the broccoli by removing the florets, and discarding any larger woody parts of the stems; thinly slice the remaining stems.

Bring a large pan of salted water to the boil. Blanch the broccoli florets and stems for about 4 minutes, then remove with a slotted spoon and plunge into ice-cold water. Drain and set aside.

Throw the orecchiette into the still-boiling water and cook until al dente.

Meanwhile, heat the olive oil in a large non-stick frying pan over low heat. Add the garlic, chilli and anchovies and sauté for 3 minutes, being very careful not to let the garlic burn, then remove and discard the garlic cloves. Add the broccoli, stirring delicately with a wooden spoon, then season to taste with salt and pepper.

Drain the orecchiette, reserving a little of the cooking water. Add to the frying pan and stir well to coat, adding a tablespoon or two of the reserved cooking water to make a nice creamy sauce.

Serve immediately. Parmesan may be grated on top, if desired.

Penne with anchovies, sultanas and breadcrumbs

PENNE ALLE ACCIUGHE E PANGRATTATO

Are breadcrumbs the parmesan cheese of the south? Probably. They are used in many pasta sauces that hail from the southern regions of Italy, which have historically been poorer than the north, as an alternative to expensive cheese.

This is another pasta dish that can be put together from a moderately well-stocked pantry – wonderful if friends drop by unexpectedly, or if you come home late from a party and find yourself too hungry to go to sleep.

25 g sultanas

100 ml extra virgin olive oil

1 clove garlic, finely chopped

10 anchovy fillets in oil, drained and
    roughly chopped

2 teaspoons capers in salt, rinsed and dried

25 g pine nuts

2 large red chillies, thinly sliced

2 tablespoons flat-leaf parsley leaves,
    finely chopped

sea salt and freshly ground black pepper

400 g penne rigate

150 g breadcrumbs

SERVES 4

Revive the sultanas by soaking them in warm water for 10 minutes. Drain them and pat dry with paper towels, then roughly chop and set aside.

Heat the olive oil in a frying pan big enough to hold the pasta over medium heat and sauté the garlic for 1 minute until it just starts to change colour. Add the anchovies, capers, pine nuts and sultanas. Mix with a wooden spoon and heat gently for 2–3 minutes, to let all the flavours combine. Sprinkle in the chilli and parsley, season with salt and pepper and mix well. Remove from the heat.

Cook the penne rigate in plenty of boiling salted water until al dente.

Meanwhile, toast the breadcrumbs in a small non-stick frying pan until just golden.

Put the sauce back on the heat. Drain the pasta and add to the pan, tossing to mix thoroughly. Sprinkle in the breadcrumbs, toss again and serve hot.

Penne with mussels and potatoes

PENNE ALLE PATATE E COZZE

I love mussels, not only for their wonderful flavour of the sea, but also because they are a great social equaliser. They are so cheap that anybody can go to a restaurant or trattoria, order a bowl of mussels with toasted bread and a glass of chilled white wine, and have as good a time as those eating lobster at the next table. As a kid, I used to carry a short knife when I went for a swim near my home so that I could pick the mussels from the rocks, open them and eat them raw.

This is a quick and simple recipe, but very satisfying. It is also an example of how versatile mussels can be.

1.5 kg mussels, scrubbed and debearded
120 ml extra virgin olive oil
2 cloves garlic, 1 clove finely chopped,
    1 peeled and lightly squashed
400 g penne
300 g potatoes, peeled and cut into
    1 cm cubes
2 tablespoons flat-leaf parsley leaves,
    finely chopped
freshly ground black pepper

SERVES 4

Put the mussels in a large saucepan with 2 tablespoons of the olive oil and the chopped garlic clove and place over medium heat. After a minute or two the mussels will start to open. As soon as they do, remove them from the pan with tongs and put on a plate to cool – this way the mussels will not be overcooked.

Once the mussels have all been removed, simmer the cooking liquid left in the pan over medium heat until it has reduced to about half its initial volume. Strain the liquid into a bowl through a fine sieve to remove any bits of grit or shell and set it aside.

When the mussels are cool enough to handle, remove all but eight of them from their shells and roughly chop them. The remaining eight will be used later for presentation.

Cook the penne and potato in plenty of boiling salted water until the pasta is al dente and the potato is tender.

Meanwhile, heat the remaining olive oil in a heavy-based frying pan over low heat, add the squashed garlic clove and stir with a wooden spoon until the garlic just changes colour, then discard. Add the chopped mussels and 4 tablespoons of their reduced cooking liquid and sprinkle the parsley over the top. Mix thoroughly, then increase the heat to medium and cook for 3 minutes.

Drain the pasta and potato, add to the mussels and gently toss for about 1 minute. If it seems a bit dry, add a bit more of the reduced cooking liquid. Divide among four pasta bowls, top each bowl with two of the reserved mussels, then sprinkle with pepper and serve immediately.

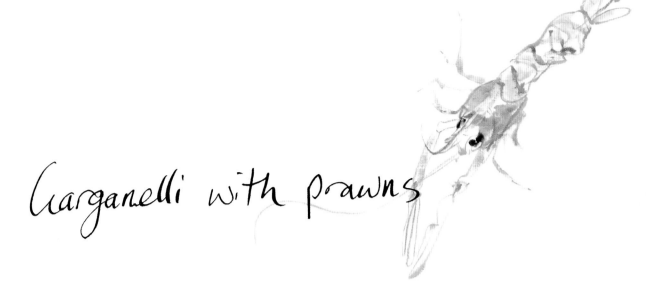

Garganelli with prawns

GARGANELLI AI GAMBERI

This dish is well worth a try: the sauce somehow retains each individual flavour, and the loosely rolled form of the garganelli holds the sauce very well. Don't be put off by the lengthy preparation: it's very easy, and the dried tomatoes can be done the night before. For visual effect, I suggest you leave the heads on some of the prawns, but it's not essential.

600 g ripe tomatoes

sea salt

4 cloves garlic, peeled – 2 sliced, 1 left
    whole and 1 chopped

large handful of basil leaves

100 ml extra virgin olive oil

400 g medium-sized raw prawns,
    peeled and deveined (heads reserved)

65 ml dry white wine

freshly ground black pepper

400 g garganelli

SERVES 4

Preheat the oven to 80°C. Remove the stalks from the tomatoes and cut them in half horizontally. Using a teaspoon, remove the seeds, then place the tomato halves cut-side up in a baking dish. Sprinkle with salt and place a few slices of garlic on each half. Dry them in the oven for 3 hours. Remove and, when cool enough to handle, discard the pieces of garlic. Gently peel the skin off the tomatoes then slice them lengthways.

Next make the basil oil. Place the basil in a blender with the whole garlic clove, 3 tablespoons of the olive oil and a pinch of salt. Pulse until it has a creamy consistency – you may have to scrape down the sides a couple of times. Set aside.

Heat the remaining olive oil in a heavy-based frying pan over medium heat, add the chopped garlic and cook for 2 minutes, stirring with a wooden spoon. Add the reserved prawn heads, pressing them down with the wooden spoon to release the flavours, then stir in the wine and simmer until the alcohol has evaporated. Remove and discard the prawn heads. Add the prawns to the pan and cook for 2 minutes, stirring and seasoning with salt and pepper. Finally, add the slices of tomato and toss for 1 minute, then take the pan off the heat and stir in the basil oil.

Cook the garganelli in plenty of boiling salted water until al dente. Drain and add to the pan, toss well, then serve immediately.

Conchiglie with mussels

CONCHIGLIE CON MUSCOLI

I am very fond of this dish – in fact, it is one of my all-time favourites. Even though they are amongst the cheapest seafood available, I have the highest respect for mussels. If you know how to treat them, they will give you a lot of pleasure. Make sure you buy them very fresh, then scrub and debeard them, discarding any that are open and won't close when you tap them. Do not overcook them and use their cooking liquid (sieved to remove any grit and fragments of shell) in moderation; the right amount of this liquid will make a dish unforgettable and imbued with the taste of the sea, but too much will make it inedible! Here I pair the mussels with a wonderfully fresh-tasting sauce made from cherry tomatoes, and I serve them with conchiglie pasta because I like the way the mussels get trapped inside the shells.

3 tablespoons extra virgin olive oil
1 small onion, very finely chopped
1 celery stalk, very finely chopped
350 g cherry tomatoes, cut in half
sea salt and freshly ground black pepper
1 kg black mussels, scrubbed and debearded
1 clove garlic, peeled and lightly squashed
3 teaspoons dry white wine
a few thyme and marjoram leaves
400 g conchiglie
handful of flat-leaf parsley leaves, chopped

SERVES 4

Heat half the olive oil in a heavy-based frying pan over low heat and sauté the onion and celery for about 5 minutes until the onion starts to colour. Add the cherry tomatoes, season with salt and pepper and cook for another 8 minutes (or longer if the tomatoes are not very ripe), stirring every now and then.

At this stage you can leave the sauce as it is or, for a smoother result, pass it through a mouli or coarse sieve. Either way, set it aside in a bowl.

Place the mussels in a large frying pan over high heat (the larger the pan, the more even the opening process). As soon as each mussel opens, remove it to a bowl. Once they are all opened, strain the mussel liquid into a separate container and keep to one side.

Remove the mussels from the now-cooled shells and roughly chop half of them, keeping the rest whole.

Heat the remaining olive oil in the mussel pan over low heat. Add the garlic and stir with a wooden spoon until just golden, then discard. Add all the mussels, sprinkle with the white wine and let it evaporate. Add the tomato mixture and about 3 tablespoons of the mussel liquid (more or less as you see fit). Stir in the thyme and marjoram and season to taste.

Meanwhile cook the conchiglie in plenty of boiling salted water until al dente. Drain and add to the mussel mixture in the pan, stirring gently for 1 minute. Sprinkle with the parsley and serve immediately.

Farfalle with prawns and prawn butter

FARFALLE AI PEPERONI E GAMBERI

100 ml extra virgin olive oil
6 golden shallots, chopped
1 bunch thyme
4 cloves garlic, chopped
450 g large raw prawns, peeled and
   deveined (heads reserved)
250 g unsalted butter, diced
1 red capsicum (pepper)
200 g snowpeas (mange-tout),
   topped and tailed, sliced
200 ml fish stock (see page 30)
sea salt and freshly ground black pepper
400 g farfalle

SERVES 4

The subtle flavours of prawns and summertime vegetables in this dish are given a welcome lift by the prawn butter, which also adds a rich glossy sheen to the sauce.

To make the prawn butter, heat half the olive oil in a medium-sized saucepan over low heat, add the shallot, thyme and half the garlic and cook gently for about 3 minutes – do not allow to colour. Add the prawn heads and cook for 8–10 minutes, crushing them with a potato masher to extract as much juice as possible. Add the butter and allow it to melt but do not boil. Remove the pan from the heat when the butter is completely melted. Set aside to cool for 15 minutes, then strain the prawn butter into a bowl and chill until firm.

Place the capsicum on an open flame, or under the grill. When one side is black, turn it over with a pair of tongs and blacken the other side. Place it in a plastic bag, close it tightly and set aside for 5 minutes. Peel off the skin, then remove and discard the stalk and the seeds. Cut the flesh into small dice.

Chop the prawn meat and place in a small bowl with the remaining garlic. Set aside to marinate.

Heat the remaining olive oil in a large frying pan to just below smoking point (when the oil starts to shimmer) and quickly fry the prawn and garlic mixture for 30–60 seconds. Remove to a bowl. Add the capsicum, snowpeas, stock, salt and pepper to the pan, stir briefly and put to one side.

Cook the farfalle in plenty of boiling salted water until al dente.

Drain the pasta, reserving a little of the cooking water, and add to the pan with the capsicum mixture. Add the prawns and stir gently to combine. If it seems too dry, add a little of the reserved cooking water. Turn off the heat, add the prawn butter and stir until rich and glossy. Serve immediately.

Fusilli with cuttlefish and peas

FUSILLI ALLE SEPPIE E PISELLI

As a kid, I loved summertime in Bocca di Magra, the fishing village where my family had their restaurant. We got almost four months of school holiday over the summer, so it was like a different life.

Most of all I loved going to the mouth of the river with my mother, late in the morning, to wait for the fishermen returning with their catch. The boat we awaited with the greatest anticipation was Vené's. He specialised in calamari, octopus and cuttlefish, and these were my mother's specialities too. She would fry them or turn them into seafood salad. But when Vené had some small cuttlefish, my mother used to keep some to make a spaghetti sauce for her family. If it happened to be pea season, then her sauce would include peas as well.

If you cannot buy the cuttlefish already cleaned, it is easy to do at home – messy, but easy. Over the sink, pull the tentacles away from the body. With a pair of scissors, cut the body open lengthways, and discard everything that is inside. Peel off the skin and rinse the body and tentacles thoroughly under running cold water. Pat dry and cut the white flesh into 1 cm strips. For the tentacles, cut off the eye at the base, leaving just enough flesh to hold them together. Rinse and pat dry, but leave them whole, because they will look fantastic in the sauce.

Heat the olive oil in a terracotta dish if you have one (or a heavy-based frying pan if you don't) over medium heat. Add the onion and garlic and cook for about 5 minutes, stirring constantly with a wooden spoon, until the onion is soft and translucent. Discard the garlic as soon as it starts to change colour.

Add the cuttlefish – body and tentacles – and sprinkle with 1 tablespoon of the parsley. Stir and cook for about 5 minutes until the cuttlefish becomes ivory white. Stir in the white wine and simmer until the alcohol has evaporated.

Add the tomato and season with salt and pepper. Mix well, then turn the heat down to low–medium and simmer for 15 minutes, checking and stirring regularly. Add the peas and cook for another 10 minutes (5 minutes if using frozen peas), adding a little warm water, a tablespoon at a time, if the sauce seems too dry.

Cook the fusilli in plenty of boiling salted water until al dente. Drain and add to the sauce. Sprinkle with the remaining parsley, toss for about a minute then serve immediately.

400 g small cuttlefish, cleaned
120 ml extra virgin olive oil
½ white onion, finely chopped
2 cloves garlic, peeled and lightly squashed
2 tablespoons chopped flat-leaf parsley
4 tablespoons dry white wine
5 large ripe tomatoes, peeled and seeded
   (see page 51), then diced
sea salt and freshly ground black pepper
320 g fresh or frozen peas
400 g fusilli

SERVES 4

Risotto-style pasta with tomato

PASTA RISOTTATA AL POMODORO

In the past few years Italy has seen a new trend, mainly in restaurants, to cook pasta like a risotto. The resulting sauce is creamier because the starch from the pasta is released into it, instead of being drained away with the cooking water. The pasta will be a little heavier as well, as it will have absorbed all that water or stock, but the result is a natural and exceptionally tasty dish. Because it is also easy and fun to make, *pasta risottata* is getting more popular at home as well, especially as there are two less implements to wash: the pasta cooking pot and the colander! I do suggest using a short pasta for this method of cooking – and a heavy-based pan with high sides.

60 ml extra virgin olive oil
½ onion, finely chopped
1 × 400 g tin peeled tomatoes, passed through a mouli or squished with your hands
sea salt and freshly ground black pepper
400 g small maccheroni or other short pasta
handful of basil leaves, chopped
60 g freshly grated parmesan

SERVES 4

Heat the olive oil in a heavy-based pan over a medium heat and add the onion. Mix with a wooden spoon and sauté for about 6–7 minutes or until the onion is translucent. Now stir in the tomatoes, season with salt and pepper and immediately add the pasta. Mix the pasta and tomato together for a minute, then add enough water to just cover the pasta, mix well again, and cook for about 6 minutes, keeping an eye on it and stirring from time to time so it does not stick.

At this point it will start to look a little dry, so add some more water, but not enough to cover the pasta this time, just enough to loosen the mix – probably half of what you put in the first time. You want a nice reduced sauce, and if you put in too much water, the pasta will overcook. Keep stirring and tasting until the pasta is al dente, about another 5 minutes, lowering the heat if necessary to stop it catching.

The *pasta risottata* is ready when the pasta is cooked, and you have a beautiful light red and creamy sauce. At this point, add the basil, mix well and serve immediately, sprinkled with the parmesan.

Risotto-style penne with zucchini and prawns

PASTA RISOTTATA CON ZUCCHINE E GAMBERI

The trend of serving *pasta risottata* in restaurants may be new, but the method is quite ancient, dating from a time when olive pickers and other seasonal workers, away from home all day and having little or no water in which to cook their pasta, would simply add it to the sauce. This version of risotto-style pasta gets a flavour boost from a quick stock made from the reserved prawn heads, and the freshness of the zucchini is a perfect foil.

120 ml extra virgin olive oil
2 cloves garlic, peeled and lightly squashed
400 g raw prawns, peeled and deveined but
     with tails left intact (heads reserved)
½ onion, finely chopped
400 g small zucchini (courgettes),
     ideally a mixture of yellow and green,
     trimmed and sliced
1 tablespoon thyme leaves
400 g penne rigate
60 ml dry white wine
sea salt and freshly ground black pepper
1 tablespoon flat-leaf parsley leaves,
     chopped

STOCK

1 carrot, peeled and cut in half
½ onion, peeled and cut in half
1 celery stalk, cut in half
1 bay leaf
prawn heads
sea salt

SERVES 4

First make the stock. Place the carrot, onion, celery and bay leaf in a stockpot or large saucepan and add about 2 litres of cold water. Squash the prawn heads a little in a bowl to release their juices then add to the pan. Bring to the boil, season with a little salt and simmer gently for about 20 minutes. Pass through a sieve into a bowl, discarding the solids. Return the stock to the rinsed-out pan and keep warm.

Heat the olive oil in a large heavy-based pan over medium heat. Add the garlic and stir with a wooden spoon until it just starts to change colour, then discard. Add the prawns and quickly sear them on both sides – this should not take more than 3 minutes in total – then remove and set aside. Add the chopped onion and sauté for about 5 minutes until soft and translucent; do not allow it to colour. Add the zucchini and thyme, mix thoroughly and sauté until the zucchini is just starting to turn light golden.

Now add the penne rigate and the wine, season with salt and pepper to taste, and mix thoroughly. When the wine has evaporated (about 3 minutes), add enough hot stock to cover the pasta. Mix well to prevent the pasta from sticking and cook for about 5–7 minutes, stirring regularly. As the sauce starts to dry, add more stock, just as you would when making risotto, and mix gently. Keep stirring and tasting until the pasta is al dente, about another 5 minutes, lowering the heat if necessary to stop it catching (the pasta will probably take 3–5 minutes longer than the time suggested on the packet). When the pasta is ready, you should have a wonderfully shiny and creamy sauce.

Add the prawns, mix well and turn the heat down to low. Cook for a minute or so, just until the prawns are warmed through. Sprinkle with parsley and serve immediately.

Fresh pasta

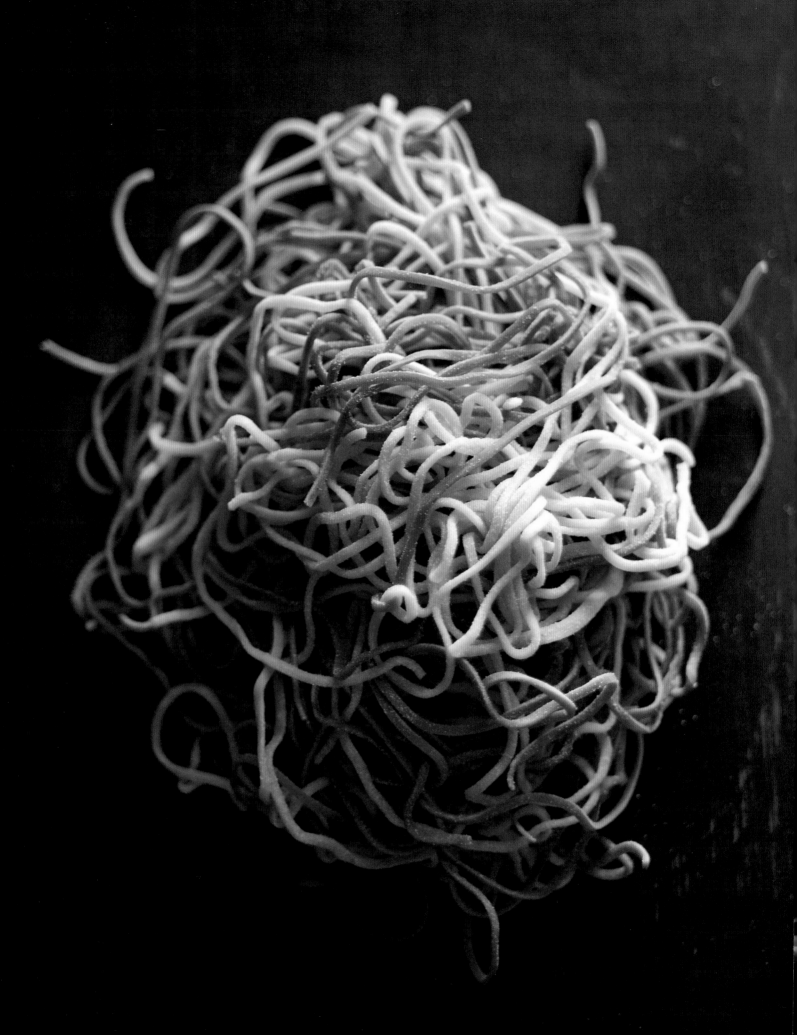

Fresh pasta (*pasta fresca*) hails mainly from the north and centre of Italy, where the sun does not shine as strongly as it does in the south, so the pasta is made to be eaten straight away rather than being slowly dried.

There are many regional variations when it comes to making pasta dough. In Emilia Romagna, particularly in Bologna, they like to use a lot of eggs, which results in a very yellow, rich pasta. Ligurians use fewer eggs – sometimes only one to each half kilo of flour – to produce a lighter pasta, in terms of both colour and density. Sometimes an almost white pasta is made, without any eggs at all.

Once you have mastered the art of making fresh pasta – and this might take a few attempts – I hope you will enjoy making it and find it a very satisfying experience. But of course, if time is an issue and you can find some good-quality fresh pasta from a shop, by all means buy it!

As for the choice of sauce, fettuccine, tagliatelle, pappardelle, lasagnette and maltagliati all go well with rich sauces – particularly ragùs, thick tomato sauces and thick cream sauces – while tagliolini and other narrow ribbon pastas are best served with lighter sauces, such as tomato sauces, light cream sauces and those based on butter or oil.

Parmesan farfalle with mushrooms

GASSE CON SALSA AL FUNGHETTO

In Liguria, any vegetable sliced and pan-fried with garlic, oil and parsley is called *al funghetto*, which means 'mushroom-style'. I pair this sauce with farfalle, known as *gasse* in Liguria (*farfalle* means butterfly; *gasse* means bowtie), because the hint of oregano and the frisson of garlic brings to mind a flying butterfly as it reaches your palate. I don't suggest sprinkling parmesan on the finished dish, but I do like to flavour the pasta itself with a mild parmesan. As for the olive oil, I suggest a Ligurian-style oil with a subtle presence.

400 g plain flour
30 g freshly grated mild parmesan
4 eggs
pinch of sea salt

SAUCE

2 small eggplants (aubergines)
sea salt
100 ml extra virgin olive oil
2 cloves garlic, peeled and lightly squashed
2 tablespoons flat-leaf parsley leaves,
    finely chopped
300 g mixed mushrooms, thinly sliced
3 zucchini (courgettes), thinly sliced
freshly ground black pepper
2 tablespoons oregano leaves,
    roughly chopped

SERVES 4

First make the pasta dough (see page 11), mixing the grated parmesan into the flour before you shape it into a mound.

While the pasta dough is resting, cut the ends off the eggplants and slice the eggplants thinly. Place the slices in a colander over the sink, sprinkle with sea salt and leave for 40 minutes so that they sweat out any bitter juices. Rinse the eggplant slices, pat dry with paper towels and cut into strips.

Roll out the pasta dough and make the farfalle (see page 23), setting them aside on lightly floured tea towels while you make the sauce.

Heat the olive oil in a heavy-based frying pan over low heat. Add the garlic and the parsley and stir with a wooden spoon for about 3 minutes or until the garlic is just starting to turn golden, then remove and discard the garlic.

Add the mushrooms, zucchini and eggplant to the pan, season with salt and pepper and sprinkle on the oregano. Increase the heat to medium, mix thoroughly and cook for about 15 minutes.

In the meantime, cook the farfalle in plenty of boiling salted water until just cooked, about 3–4 minutes. Drain and toss gently in the sauce for about 30 seconds to coat the pasta completely. Serve immediately.

Tagliatelle with raw mushrooms

TAGLIATELLE AI FUNGHI CRUDI

The original version of this dish is made with fresh truffles: the pasta is tossed with butter and parmesan, then fresh truffles are shaved on top . . . and it's amazing! But mushrooms belong to the same family as truffles, so I thought why not? The result is fantastic, a different sensation on the palate. It is very important that you slice the mushrooms very thinly and toss them really well but quickly through the pasta while it is still hot.

I suggest you use king brown mushrooms, if available, because of their firmness and flavour. Otherwise, shiitake or button mushrooms are fine – just make sure they are very fresh, clean, firm and not bruised.

400 g basic pasta dough (see page 11)
120 g unsalted butter
80 g freshly grated parmesan
sea salt and freshly ground black pepper
200 g king brown mushrooms,
  very thinly sliced

SERVES 4

Roll out the pasta and cut into tagliatelle (see page 20). Cook the pasta in plenty of boiling salted water until just cooked, about 2–3 minutes.

Meanwhile, melt the butter in a large non-stick frying pan over low heat, then stir in a couple of tablespoons of the parmesan.

Drain the tagliatelle, reserving a little of the cooking water. Add the pasta to the frying pan and give it a toss, seasoning with a little salt, a generous amount of black pepper and some more parmesan.

Remove from the heat, then add the mushrooms and the rest of the parmesan and toss well. If it seems too dry, add a little of the reserved pasta cooking water. Serve immediately on hot plates.

Saffron tagliatelle with zucchini flowers, tomatoes and basil

TAGLIATELLE AI FIORI DI ZUCCHINI, POMODORO E BASILICO

Saffron, the dried stigma of crocus flowers, adds an invigorating sharpness, as well as a golden colour. In Italy, saffron is mostly produced in the Abruzzo region of southern Italy, being taken up by other Italians when workers from Abruzzo went to Milan and started using it to flavour and colour rice. With saffron doing such wonders for risotto alla Milanese, it seemed logical to try it with pasta. This is one of the signature dishes at Lucio's, celebrating the start of the zucchini flower season.

400 g saffron pasta dough (see page 15)
16 zucchini (courgette) flowers
3 ripe tomatoes, peeled and seeded
    (see page 51), then diced
120 ml extra virgin olive oil
sea salt and freshly ground black pepper
3 teaspoons chopped basil

SERVES 4

Roll out the pasta dough and cut into tagliatelle (see page 20). Lay the pasta on lightly floured tea towels while you make the sauce.

Remove and discard the stigma from each zucchini flower and check them carefully for any stray insects. Place the flowers, tomato and olive oil in a frying pan and simmer for 3 minutes, then season with salt and pepper.

Meanwhile, cook the tagliatelle in boiling salted water until just cooked, about 2 minutes. Drain well, then add to the pan with the zucchini flowers and tomato. Add the basil, toss gently and serve.

Maltagliati with vegetables

MALTAGLIATI DEL CONTADINO

What's going on here: adding breadcrumbs to the flour when making pasta? What may seem like an unusual combination is a classic example of peasant frugality, where nothing is wasted and luxury can come out of poverty. The breadcrumbs need to be quite fine, so the texture of the pasta isn't too rough. Either buy the finest you can, or make your own by grating toasted stale bread or whizzing it briefly in a food processor. The result looks elegant on the plate and feels smooth on the palate. The sauce is also a matter of making do with what you have – in the vegetable garden.

200 g fine breadcrumbs
200 g plain flour
3 eggs
60 ml white wine
pinch of sea salt

SAUCE

1 small eggplant (aubergine)
200 g small zucchini (courgettes)
100 g snow peas (mange-tout), trimmed
60 ml extra virgin olive oil
3 spring onions, finely sliced
100 g fresh or frozen peas
400 g ripe tomatoes, peeled and seeded
   (see page 51), then diced
8 basil leaves
sea salt and freshly ground black pepper
1 tablespoon chopped flat-leaf parsley
60 g freshly grated parmesan

SERVES 4

First make the pasta dough (see page 11), mixing the breadcrumbs into the flour before you shape it into a mound and adding the wine with the eggs. Roll the rested dough into sheets, then cut into maltagliati (see page 23). Let them dry on lightly floured tea towels while you make the sauce.

Cut the ends off the eggplant, then peel the eggplant and cut into 1 cm cubes. Trim the zucchini and cut them into cubes the same size as the eggplant. Cut each snow pea crosswise into about three pieces.

Heat the olive oil in a large non-stick frying pan over medium heat, then add the spring onion and cook for about 3 minutes, stirring with a wooden spoon. Add the peas, eggplant, zucchini and snow peas, stir and let them cook for 3 minutes.

Add the tomato and basil and mix thoroughly, then cover the pan and cook over low heat for 30 minutes, stirring often, until the vegetables are tender. Taste and add a little salt and pepper if necessary.

Cook the maltagliati in plenty of boiling salted water with a few drops of olive oil until just cooked, about 3 minutes. When they are ready, scoop them out with a slotted spoon and place in the sauce. Sprinkle with the parsley and parmesan, toss delicately and serve.

'Silk handkerchiefs' with mushrooms

MANDILLI DE SAEA AI FUNGHI E BASTA

Mandilli di saea, the name for this pasta from the Italian Riviera, means 'silk handkerchiefs', which is what these squares should look like. You cannot buy them – you must make them yourself, and take pride in the silky texture you've achieved by repeatedly stretching the dough through the pasta machine or under the rolling pin. The addition of a couple of tablespoons of semolina to the dough helps to make it more elastic, so it's easier to make it as fine as silk.

In my area of Liguria, this pasta is usually eaten with pesto, but I think this simple mushroom sauce is a great homage to autumn.

400 g plain flour
2 tablespoons semolina
4 eggs
pinch of sea salt

SAUCE

450 g mixed mushrooms
80 ml extra virgin olive oil
2 golden shallots, thinly sliced
60 ml white wine
sea salt and freshly ground black pepper
2 tablespoons finely chopped flat-leaf
   parsley leaves
80 g freshly grated parmesan

SERVES 4

First make the pasta dough (see page 11), mixing the semolina into the flour before you shape it into a mound.

Once the dough has rested, roll it repeatedly to make very thin pasta sheets (see pages 17–18), then cut it into 10 cm squares. Let the mandilli dry on lightly floured tea towels while you make the sauce.

Wipe the mushrooms clean with a damp cloth, then slice them roughly, leaving the smallest ones whole. Heat the olive oil in a heavy-based frying pan over low heat, then add the shallot and sauté, stirring with a wooden spoon, for about 4 minutes. Turn up the heat to medium–high, add the mushrooms, and cook for about 4 minutes or until they start to soften, stirring every so often.

Pour in the wine and let the alcohol evaporate for about 3 minutes. Season with a little salt and pepper and continue to cook for 20 minutes, stirring regularly with the wooden spoon. The mushrooms should be nicely moist – if they give off too much liquid, discard some of the excess by carefully tipping the pan and scooping it out. Sprinkle the mushrooms with the parsley, mix thoroughly and turn off the heat.

Cook the mandilli in plenty of boiling salted water with a few drops of olive oil until just cooked, about 3 minutes.

When the mandilli are ready, scoop them out with a slotted spoon. Place a layer of mandilli in the bottom of a warmed serving dish, then spoon on a layer of mushrooms, followed by a sprinkling of parmesan. Repeat these layers until everything is used, finishing with mushrooms and parmesan. Shake the dish a few times to distribute the sauce evenly. Serve immediately.

Rag Pasta with tomato, herbs and goat's cheese

STRACCI AL CAPRINO E POMODORO

In my region of Italy, this kind of spontaneous and improvised dish is called *fuori dall' uscio*, or 'outside the door', because the farmer's wife is supposedly able to step out the back door and grab a handful of herbs, a few ripe tomatoes and the family goat (for milking to make fresh cheese). She can then tear a square of pasta dough into *stracci* ('rags') and throw everything together to make a rough and ready meal in minutes. I've refined the process a little: you can slice the dough instead of tearing it, and you can peel and seed the tomatoes instead of just squashing them in your hands – but you'll still end up with the same sort of big, rustic flavours that a farmer's family would appreciate.

400 g basic pasta dough (see page 11)
4 vine-ripened tomatoes, peeled and seeded
   (see page 51), then diced
150 ml extra virgin olive oil
2 teaspoons chopped tarragon
2 teaspoons chopped chervil
2 teaspoons chopped basil
2 teaspoons chopped flat-leaf parsley
sea salt and freshly ground black pepper
250 g goat's cheese, crumbled
chervil leaves, to garnish

SERVES 4

Roll the pasta dough into very thin sheets (see pages 17–18). Using a sharp knife, cut into irregular shapes, trying to keep them similar in size.

Cook the pasta in plenty of boiling salted water until just cooked, about 2 minutes.

Meanwhile, place the tomato, olive oil and the chopped herbs in a large bowl. Season with salt and pepper. Drain the pasta, then add to the bowl and toss well.

Arrange layers of the pasta in a warmed serving dish, alternating with the goat's cheese. Serve immediately, garnished with chervil.

Lasagnette with a ragù of mushrooms

LASAGNETTE AL TOCCO DI FUNGHI

Tocco is a Ligurian word for sauce – in this case, one made with mushrooms that became a seasonal favourite with our family. My mother used to make this sauce in autumn with the fresh porcini mushrooms that my brother would collect in the forest. It never took him long, because he knew exactly where to go, often bringing back so many porcini that we would have whole dinners based around them. My brother was so proud of his mushrooms that, with the excuse of having a coffee, he would stop at the local bar on his way back from the forest to show them to everybody and accept all the compliments that came his way.

Rosemary is rarely used in pasta sauce, but its clean taste works well with the earthiness of the mushrooms here, and its distinctive aroma takes me right back to our family kitchen, where my mother and Aunty Anna always seemed to be bustling in front of a battery of pans large and small. Although there are no fresh porcini in Australia, you can approximate their flavour in this sauce by using firm mushrooms, such as shiitake or Swiss brown, together with a few of the best-quality dried porcini imported from Italy.

400 g basic pasta dough (see page 11)
15 g dried porcini mushrooms
1 × 400 g tin peeled tomatoes
80 g unsalted butter
60 ml extra virgin olive oil
2 cloves garlic, finely chopped
1 tablespoon chopped flat-leaf parsley
1 tablespoon chopped rosemary
300 g firm fresh mushrooms, thinly sliced
sea salt and freshly ground black pepper
80 g freshly grated parmesan

SERVES 4

Roll out the pasta dough into thin sheets (see pages 17–18), then cut into rectangles about 15 cm × 10 cm. Lay the pasta on lightly floured tea towels while you make the sauce.

Soak the dried porcini mushrooms in warm water for 15 minutes. Discard the water, then pat the mushrooms dry and chop them roughly. Place the tomatoes in a bowl and squash them with your hands or a potato masher.

Melt 60 g of the butter with the olive oil in a heavy-based frying pan over low heat. Add the garlic, parsley, rosemary and porcini and cook for about 3 minutes, stirring constantly with a wooden spoon, until the garlic starts to turn golden. Stir in the fresh mushrooms, then add the tomato and season with a little salt and pepper. Simmer over low–medium heat for 20 minutes, checking and stirring regularly. Add a little water if it seems to be drying out.

Meanwhile, cook the lasagnette in plenty of boiling salted water until just cooked, about 4 minutes.

Pour half the sauce into a serving bowl, then drain the pasta and add it to the bowl. Pour over the rest of the sauce and dot with the remaining butter. Toss gently but quickly, sprinkling with the parmesan. Serve immediately.

Trofie with basil and walnut pesto

TROFIE AL PESTO DI CASTELNUOVO

My primary school was in Castelnuovo Magra, an ancient hilltop village in Liguria, near the border with Tuscany. A local writer describes the people of Castelnuovo as *strampalati* – eccentric, with a mind of their own – so no one should be surprised that their way of making pesto is quite different from that which prevails in the rest of Liguria. Probably this distinctive pesto arose to make good use of the walnut trees that pepper the hillsides around the village and the beautiful herbs grown in the area.

Trofie, a typical Ligurian pasta, is made without eggs, often using a mixture of chestnut flour and wheat flour in areas where wheat is scarce. (Chestnut flour can be found at Italian delis and some specialist food stores.) This pasta is often called *pasta bastarda* ('bastard pasta'), but the flavour is legitimate!

200 g chestnut flour
200 g plain flour, plus extra for dusting
pinch of sea salt
100 ml warm water
1 tablespoon extra virgin olive oil
freshly grated parmesan, to serve
handful of roughly chopped walnuts,
    to serve

BASIL AND WALNUT PESTO

25 g raw walnuts, roughly chopped
1 clove garlic, peeled
pinch of sea salt
handful of basil leaves
handful of flat-leaf parsley leaves,
    finely chopped
1 tablespoon marjoram leaves
75 g freshly grated pecorino
90 ml extra virgin olive oil

SERVES 4

First make the trofie. Sieve the two flours into a bowl, add a pinch of salt and mix thoroughly. Place the flour in a mound on your workbench, make a well in the centre and add the water. Mix with your hands, kneading, pressing and folding the dough for about 8 minutes. You should end up with a ball of dough that is firm, uniform and smooth.

When the dough has rested for an hour, lightly flour your work surface and start making the trofie. Tear off small pieces of dough about the size of an olive and, using the palms of your hands, quickly roll them backwards and forwards so that they develop a spiral shape. Allow the trofie to drop onto the floured work surface, then leave to rest while you make the pesto.

If using a mortar and pestle to make the pesto, place the walnuts in the mortar and start pounding. After a minute or so, add the garlic, salt, basil, parsley and marjoram. Pound everything really well, adding the pecorino a little at a time. When you have a smooth paste, add the olive oil and mix well to amalgamate all the ingredients.

If using a blender for the pesto, pulse all the ingredients together on the lowest speed until the sauce is creamy.

Add 1 tablespoon of olive oil to a large saucepan of boiling salted water and cook the trofie for 3–4 minutes: they are ready when they float to the surface. Drain, reserving a little of the cooking water.

Place the pesto in a serving bowl big enough to hold the pasta, add a couple of tablespoons of the reserved cooking water and mix well. Add the pasta, sprinkle with some grated parmesan and a handful of chopped walnuts, and mix thoroughly but gently. Serve immediately.

Curly fettuccine with zucchini

PICCAGGE CON ZUCCHINE

When I opened my first restaurant in 1981, I used to cook one day a week – every Thursday – because that was the chef's day off. I am not a professional chef, so I needed a repertoire of simple dishes that I could throw together easily. One day, when we had bought some fantastic zucchini from the market, I decided to slice them, pan-fry them in olive oil infused with garlic and toss some fettuccine through them. In just a few weeks, this simple pasta became a favourite with my Thursday clientele.

Of course, it had to happen – one day that was not a Thursday, a waiter went into the kitchen and said to the chef, 'Somebody is asking for the fettuccine with zucchini. Can you do it?' And the chef replied, 'What fettuccine with zucchini?'

Nowadays I make this with piccage, a Ligurian version of fettuccine with a crinkly edge, but regular fettuccine is fine too.

400 g basic pasta dough (see page 11)
60 ml extra virgin olive oil
2 cloves garlic, peeled and lightly squashed
400 g small zucchini (courgettes),
    cut into discs
sea salt and freshly ground black pepper
small handful of flat-leaf parsley leaves,
    chopped
1 tablespoon pine nuts, roughly chopped
handful of basil leaves, shredded
60 g freshly grated parmesan

SERVES 4

Roll out the pasta dough and cut it into fettuccine (see page 20), using a fluted ravioli cutter or pastry wheel if you want to make the edges crinkly. Lay the pasta on lightly floured tea towels while you make the sauce.

Heat the olive oil in a large non-stick frying pan over medium heat. Add the garlic and stir it around the pan with a wooden spoon to flavour the oil. As soon as the garlic starts to change colour (about 2 minutes), remove and discard it.

Add the zucchini to the pan, season with salt and pepper and sprinkle with the parsley. Mix thoroughly and cook for 5 minutes, stirring frequently. Stir in the pine nuts and cook for another 5 minutes.

Meanwhile, cook the fettuccine in plenty of boiling salted water until just cooked, about 3–4 minutes. Drain, reserving a little of the cooking water, and add the pasta to the frying pan. Toss delicately, sprinkling first with the basil and then with the parmesan. If the sauce seems too dry, add a tablespoon of the cooking water. Serve immediately.

Fettuccine with cream sauce

FETTUCCINE ALL'ALFREDO

The origins of most pasta dishes are shrouded in myth and mystery, but this one comes with a specific history. It was invented in 1914 in a Roman restaurant called Alfredo alla Scrofa, by Alfredo di Lelio. Alfredo's pregnant wife was off her food, so he decided to try a variation on a classic Roman dish called *fettuccine al doppio burro* ('double butter') by substituting cream for the extra butter. It worked. She loved it, and so did the customers to whom Alfredo started serving it. Oddly, this dish is more famous in the English-speaking world than in Italy, and it has been bastardised in America and England with the addition of ingredients such as ham and mushrooms that would have shocked its creator. Let's try the original – very rich, but also very simple.

Roll out the pasta dough and cut it into fettuccine (see page 20). Lay the pasta on lightly floured tea towels while you make the sauce.

Melt the butter in a heavy-based frying pan over low heat. Add the cream, then increase the heat to medium and simmer for 5 minutes, stirring often. Add 2 tablespoons of the parmesan and season with salt and pepper. Mix thoroughly and take the pan off the heat. Keep the sauce warm while you cook the pasta.

Cook the fettuccine in plenty of boiling salted water until just cooked, about 3 minutes. Drain, then add to the pan with the sauce and toss gently, adding the rest of the parmesan. Serve hot.

400 g basic pasta dough (see page 11)
125 g unsalted butter
300 ml cream
80 g freshly grated parmesan
sea salt and freshly ground black pepper

SERVES 4

Buckwheat fazzoletti with sweet cabbage

FAZZOLETTI DI GRANO SARACENO AI CAVOLI

This dish is a creation of the chef at Lucio's, Logan Campbell. It is based on the classic dish of *pizzoccheri* from the Lombardy region that lies to the north of Milan. Traditionally this dish is made with buckwheat tagliatelle, but I'll let Logan explain his choice of pasta here: 'I have kept many of the original components of the dish, with the exception of the cut of pasta. Buckwheat flour is notoriously difficult to make into a dough as it contains no gluten, so a percentage of durum wheat flour is added to compensate. To make the pasta a little easier to manage at home I went for fazzoletti ('handkerchiefs') instead of tagliatelle, on the grounds that there would be less broken strands of pasta and less swearing.'

200 g plain flour
200 g buckwheat flour
4 eggs

SAUCE

¼ savoy cabbage
200 g butter, diced
8 sage leaves, roughly chopped
2 tablespoons balsamic vinegar
sea salt and freshly ground black pepper
250 g stracchino cheese, broken into
    small pieces
100 g freshly grated parmesan

SERVES 4

Make the pasta dough following the instructions on page 11, but using the ingredients and quantities given here. Rest the dough, then roll it into sheets (see pages 17–18) and cut into 8 cm squares. Lay the pasta on lightly floured tea towels while you make the sauce.

Preheat the oven to 180°C.

Cut the cabbage into 5–6 cm rough squares and blanch in boiling salted water for 2 minutes, then plunge into iced water to refresh. Drain and set aside.

Have all your ingredients ready and to hand. Heat the butter in a medium-sized frying pan until it starts to melt and foam. Use a metal spoon to push the foam aside and check the butter underneath: when it is a light brown colour, quickly add the sage, then the balsamic and immediately turn the heat off. Quickly add the cabbage, season to taste with salt and pepper and stir gently.

Cook the fazzoletti in plenty of boiling salted water until just cooked, about 3 minutes, then drain, reserving a little of the cooking water. Add the pasta to the cabbage pan, along with about 50 ml of the pasta cooking water.

Place a square of pasta on each of four individual ovenproof plates, followed by some of the cabbage, stracchino, parmesan and a little of the sage-infused butter. Repeat these layers until everything is used up, finishing with a sprinkling of parmesan. Bake in the oven for 4 minutes or just long enough to melt the cheese. Serve immediately – but remember the plates will be very hot!

Priest stranglers with sage butter

STRANGOLAPRETI

There are a few versions of this dish, all from the north of Italy and using moulded bread rather than flour for the pasta. Legend gives various origins to the name. One is that the consistency is so substantial it could cause delicately mannered priests to choke. Other versions still have the priest choking, but perhaps have more to do with wishful thinking on the part of the poor tenant farmer watching the priest – representing the farmer's landlord, the Catholic Church – stuffing himself on the peasant's good wife's cooking.

This particular recipe is a classic from Trentino Alto Adige. In other regions it is sometimes called *ravioli nudi* ('naked ravioli') and calls for the addition of nutmeg; I prefer not to add nutmeg, as I find it breaks the harmony of the other ingredients. In southern regions of Italy, the name changes from *strangolapreti* to *strozzapreti*. The meaning is the same, but the dish is a type of homemade pasta without eggs. The pasta sheet is rolled out a little thicker than usual and then cut into long rectangular shapes that are either bent around a stick or quickly rubbed in the middle, and left to dry. This pasta is now commercially produced and available in packets.

650 g stale Italian bread, crusts removed
250 ml milk
1 kg silverbeet (Swiss chard)
2 eggs
sea salt and freshly ground black pepper
1–2 tablespoons breadcrumbs
plain flour, for dusting
100 g butter
handful of sage leaves
60 g freshly grated parmesan

SERVES 4

Tear the bread into small pieces and place in a large bowl. Pour in the milk and set aside.

Remove and discard the white stalks from the silverbeet. Wash and drain the leaves, then cook in boiling salted water for 3 minutes. Drain and refresh in cold water. When the silverbeet is cool enough to handle, squeeze it firmly to dry as much as possible. Chop roughly, then add to the bread and milk in the bowl, mixing well. Add the eggs, season with salt and pepper and mix thoroughly. Pass the mixture through a mouli or puree in a blender, then return to the bowl. Slowly add enough of the breadcrumbs to make a homogenous and firm, yet soft, mixture.

Lightly flour your work surface. Divide the mixture into three or four smaller pieces and, working lightly and quickly, shape each one into a roll about 1.5 cm in diameter, then cut into 4 cm lengths to make your strangolapreti.

Cook the strangolapreti in plenty of boiling salted water for about 5 minutes – they will float when they are ready. As they rise to the surface, remove them from the water using a slotted spoon and place in a large serving bowl.

Meanwhile, gently melt the butter in a small frying pan and add the sage. Sizzle for a few minutes until the sage leaves are crisp, then pour the butter and sage over the strangolapreti to coat them well. Sprinkle with the parmesan and mix delicately using two large spoons. Serve immediately.

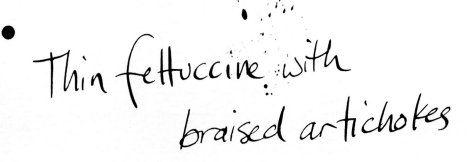

Thin fettuccine with braised artichokes

PICCAGGE AI CARCIOFI

Piccagge ('thin ribbons') from Liguria are a good match for artichokes – so rough on the outside, so tender at heart. I like to use whole braised artichokes and treat the dish as a *piatto unico* (a meal in itself). The sauce is full of flavour, particularly with the addition of the pancetta and chilli to the *soffritto*. Once you've tried it, you'll await the artichoke season each year with a sense of great anticipation.

400 g basic pasta dough (see page 11)

BRAISED ARTICHOKES

8 baby artichokes
½ lemon
2 cloves garlic, finely chopped
2 tablespoons chopped flat-leaf parsley
2 tablespoons chopped basil
90 ml extra virgin olive oil
sea salt and freshly ground black pepper

SAUCE

4 baby artichokes
½ lemon
120 ml extra virgin olive oil
½ white onion, finely chopped
50 g pancetta, cut into small pieces
1 clove garlic, peeled and lightly squashed
1 tablespoon chopped flat-leaf parsley
2 small red chillies, chopped
sea salt and freshly ground black pepper
90 ml white wine
80 g freshly grated parmesan

SERVES 4

Roll out the pasta dough (see pages 17–18), then cut into 1–2 cm wide ribbons. Lay the pasta on lightly floured tea towels while you make the braised artichokes and the sauce.

For the braised artichokes, peel off and discard the outer leaves of the artichokes until you reach the tender yellow leaves inside. Cut off and discard the top two-thirds of the leaves. Cut off and discard most of the stem and lightly peel the outer layer of what is left of the stem. Rub all the cut surfaces of the artichokes with the lemon half to prevent discoloration. Hold each artichoke in your hand and, using a sharp knife, scrape out the hairy choke from the inside.

Combine the garlic, parsley and basil and sprinkle most of the mixture inside the artichokes. Pour a little olive oil into each artichoke, season with a little salt and pepper, and place in a non-stick saucepan, stems up. Pour over the rest of the olive oil and sprinkle over the rest of the garlic and herb mixture. Pour about 100 ml of water around the artichokes and place the pan over low heat. Cover and cook for about 45 minutes, shaking the pan regularly and adding more water if it seems to be drying out.

While the artichokes are cooking, make the sauce. Trim the artichokes as above, but this time cut off and discard all of the stems. Slice the trimmed artichokes very thinly, then place in a bowl of cold water acidulated with lemon juice.

Heat the olive oil in a large heavy-based frying pan over medium heat then add the onion, pancetta, garlic and parsley. Stir with a wooden spoon and cook for about 5 minutes, then remove and discard the garlic. Add the sliced artichokes and the chilli and sprinkle on a little salt. Cook, stirring frequently, for 8 minutes. Add the wine and mix well, then reduce the heat to low–medium and cook for 20 minutes, stirring regularly.

Meanwhile, cook the fettuccine in plenty of boiling salted water until just cooked, about 3–4 minutes. Drain, then add to the pan with the sauce. Mix the sauce and pasta together for 1 minute, then sprinkle with the parmesan.

To serve, place the braised artichokes in the middle of a large serving dish with some of their braising liquid, and arrange the pasta around them. Pour the rest of the braising liquid into a jug and pass it around the table for guests to help themselves. It's best to eat the pasta first while it is hot, and then the braised artichokes – which taste better at room temperature.

Tagliatelle with baby asparagus

TAGLIATELLE AGLI ASPARAGI SOTTILI

When you see those thin asparagus at your local fruit and veg shop, first check that their tips are intact – if they are, think about making a plate of tagliatelle with them. Those thin spears remind me of the wild asparagus that my mother and the other women of our village would pick in spring, scouring the countryside and riverbanks for them. Mum used to come back looking very pleased with herself and carrying a basket full of the tender little wonders (mind you, she had that same pleased look when she came back with huge bunches of fresh grass for the rabbits!). Of all the dishes she made with wild asparagus, this was my favourite.

400 g basic pasta dough (see page 11)

300 g baby or wild asparagus

80 ml extra virgin olive oil

2 small golden shallots, finely chopped

80 g pancetta or bacon, finely diced

2 sprigs flat-leaf parsley

2 sprigs basil

4 large ripe tomatoes, peeled and seeded
  (see page 51), then diced

sea salt and freshly ground black pepper

80 g freshly grated parmesan

SERVES 4

Roll out the pasta dough and cut it into tagliatelle (see page 20). Lay the pasta on lightly floured tea towels while you make the sauce.

Wash the asparagus under cold running water. Add to a saucepan of boiling salted water and boil for about 2 minutes. Drain then plunge into iced water and drain again. Cut off and discard the bottom third of each stalk. Save a few whole spears for garnish. With the rest of the asparagus, cut off and reserve the tips then cut the remaining stalks in half lengthways and then into 1 cm pieces.

Heat the olive oil in a heavy-based frying pan over medium heat. Cook the shallot and pancetta for about 5 minutes, stirring often with a wooden spoon, until the shallot is soft and the pancetta is crisp. Add the whole sprigs of parsley and basil and stir briefly just to flavour the oil. Add the asparagus tips and stalks and toss delicately, then add the tomato and a little salt and pepper. Cook for 5 minutes, stirring gently every so often with a wooden spoon. Remove and discard the wilted herbs.

Cook the tagliatelle in plenty of boiling salted water until just cooked, about 2–3 minutes, then drain. Take the sauce off the heat and add the pasta. Toss gently, garnish with the whole asparagus spears and sprinkle with the parmesan. Serve immediately.

Lasagnette with a tomato ragù

LASAGNETTE AL RAGÙ DI POMODORO

I call this tomato sauce a ragù even though it contains no meat, because it's cooked in the style of a ragù and so becomes beautifully rich. It is good with any kind of pasta really, but with these curly-edged lasagnette I think it takes on a certain identity – a soul, if you will. I love the sound lasagnette make when you move them with a fork – it's as if they are talking to you. In Italy we say, 'The pasta was so good, it was talking' (*parlanti*). You can of course find factory-made dried lasagnette, and they are good too, but not as good as homemade. Either way, I hope you will hear your lasagnette talking to you . . .

15 g dried porcini mushrooms

60 g unsalted butter

60 ml extra virgin olive oil

30 g pine nuts

1 white onion, finely chopped

2 cloves garlic, finely chopped

1 tablespoon rosemary leaves,
   finely chopped

6 anchovy fillets in oil, drained

6 large tomatoes, peeled and seeded
   (see page 51), then diced

sea salt and freshly ground black pepper

400 g basic pasta dough (see page 11)

80 g freshly grated parmesan

SERVES 4

Soak the porcini mushrooms in warm water for 15 minutes, then pat dry and dice. Discard the soaking water.

Melt the butter with the olive oil in a heavy-based frying pan over medium heat. Add the pine nuts and toast them for a couple of minutes until golden brown, then remove with a slotted spoon and set aside. Add the onion, garlic and rosemary to the pan and sauté, stirring with a wooden spoon, until the onion is soft, about 5 minutes. Add the anchovies, squashing them so that they melt into the oil and butter. Add the mushrooms and stir for a minute, then add the tomato and season with salt and pepper.

Using a mortar and pestle, pound the pine nuts to a paste and add to the sauce. Simmer for 20 minutes, stirring regularly. If the sauce seems to be drying out, add a little water.

Meanwhile, roll out the pasta dough into very thin sheets (see pages 17–18). With a fluted ravioli cutter or pastry wheel, cut the pasta sheets into rectangles about 8 cm × 2.5 cm. Cook the pasta in plenty of boiling salted water until just cooked, about 3–5 minutes. Drain and place in a large ceramic serving bowl. Pour the sauce over, toss well and sprinkle with the parmesan. Serve immediately.

Green and white tagliolini with cream and mushrooms

PAGLIA E FIENO ALLA BOSCAIOLA

Aaah, the mighty '80s, when *paglia e fieno*, the white and green pasta resembling hay (*fieno*) and straw (*paglia*), was as famous as Armani. Every Italian restaurant had its own version, some really excellent but others never to be forgotten . . . never to order again. But the version here will fill you up with joy.

When you see the word *boscaiola*, it means that something is cooked with mushrooms and tomatoes or mushrooms and cream. Too often I see *paglia e fieno* made with tagliatelle, but I much prefer elegant tagliolini for this delicate dish.

200 g basic pasta dough (see page 11)
200 g green pasta dough (see page 14)
20 g butter
2 golden shallots, finely chopped
80 g pancetta, finely diced
300 g mixed mushrooms – shiitake,
    Swiss brown, chanterelle – thickly sliced
200 ml cream or crème fraîche
sea salt and freshly ground black pepper
80 g freshly grated parmesan

SERVES 4

Roll out both of the pasta doughs and cut into tagliolini (see page 20), then gently mix together and set aside on lightly floured tea towels while you make the sauce.

Melt the butter in a large heavy-based non-stick frying pan over medium heat. Add the shallot and pancetta and cook for about 5 minutes, stirring with a wooden spoon, until the shallot is soft. Add the mushrooms and cook for about 15 minutes or until they are soft and tender. Turn the heat to high and mix with a wooden spoon, allowing any excess moisture to evaporate. Lower the heat, then add the cream and allow the sauce to return to the boil. Season to taste with salt and pepper.

Cook the tagliolini in plenty of boiling salted water until just cooked, about 2–3 minutes, then drain and immediately add to the sauce. Toss gently, sprinkle with the parmesan and serve immediately.

Fettuccine with egg and prosciutto

FETTUCCINE ALLA PAPALINA

This dish is called *alla Papalina* because it was invented in the 1930s for Cardinal Pacelli, who went on to become Pope Pius XII ('Il Papa'). When the cardinal asked the Roman restaurant that supplied meals to the Vatican to make a lighter version of carbonara, the chef decided to use prosciutto instead of pancetta, and mild parmesan in place of sharp pecorino. Years later, cooks began to add an extra element: peas. If you want to do the same, cook the peas separately then add them to the sauce just before the fettuccine.

400 g basic pasta dough (see page 11)
3 eggs
sea salt
80 g freshly grated parmesan
20 g butter
½ white onion, thinly sliced
150 g prosciutto, cut into small pieces
200 g fresh or frozen peas (optional)
freshly ground black pepper

SERVES 4

Roll out the pasta dough and cut it into fettuccine (see page 20). Lay the pasta on lightly floured tea towels while you make the sauce.

Break the eggs into a bowl and whisk them with a little salt and 2 tablespoons of the parmesan. Set aside.

Melt the butter in a large heavy-based frying pan over medium heat. Add the onion and cook for 3 minutes, stirring with a wooden spoon, until the onion is translucent. Stir in the prosciutto and cook for 5 minutes until the prosciutto is becoming crispy.

If using peas, cook them in lightly salted boiling water for 5–6 minutes if fresh or 3 minutes if frozen, then drain and add to the frying pan.

Cook the fettuccine in plenty of boiling salted water until just cooked, about 3 minutes. Drain the fettuccine and add it to the frying pan, then pour in the egg and parmesan mixture and stir gently for 1 minute over low heat. Serve hot, sprinkled with pepper and the remaining parmesan.

Fettuccine with Sausage Sauce

STRANGOZZI ALLA NORCINA

Norcina means 'in the style of Norcia', Norcia being a town in Umbria whose inhabitants are so skilled at making salami and sausages that they are summoned to other parts of Italy to perform pork butchery. Back in Umbria, strangozzi is the most popular form of pasta – it resembles fettuccine with tiny holes in it. If you want to reproduce it at home, just make normal fettuccine then prick the ribbons with a fork. In autumn, black truffle is sometimes added to the sauce just before serving.

20 g dried porcini mushrooms
400 g basic pasta dough (see page 11)
60 ml extra virgin olive oil
1 clove garlic, finely chopped
20 g butter
200 g pork sausages, roughly chopped
sea salt and freshly ground black pepper
100 ml cream
40 g freshly grated parmesan

SERVES 4

Soak the dried porcini in warm water for 15 minutes. Rinse, then squeeze very dry and chop roughly. Discard the soaking water.

Roll out the pasta dough and cut it into fettuccine (see page 20); if you want to turn your fettuccine into strangozzi, gently prick them with a fork. Lay the pasta on lightly floured tea towels while you make the sauce.

Heat the olive oil in a large heavy-based frying pan over low heat and add the garlic. Cook for 1 minute, stirring with a wooden spoon, until the garlic just starts to change colour. Stir in the mushrooms, then add the butter. When the butter has melted, add the sausages and turn the heat up to medium. Season with salt and pepper and cook for about 5 minutes, stirring, until the sausages are browned all over. Add the cream and 1 tablespoon of the parmesan. Cook for another 10 minutes, stirring often.

Meanwhile, cook the fettuccine in plenty of boiling salted water until just cooked, about 4 minutes.

Drain the pasta, reserving a little of its cooking water, then tip into the pan with the sauce and toss gently for a minute to mix well. If the sauce seems dry, add some of the reserved pasta cooking water, a tablespoon at a time. Serve hot, sprinkled with the rest of the parmesan.

Parmesan farfalle with prosciutto and peas

GASSE AI PISELLI

Gassa is the Ligurian word for farfalla (bowtie or butterfly-shaped pasta), although it actually refers to a bow you would tie on the ribbon round a gift. Here the pasta dough is boosted with a little parmesan, creating a perfect flavour blend with the prosciutto, chicken stock and peas. And of course, you'll add more parmesan after you've tossed your bows in the sauce, to make the gift complete.

400 g plain flour
30 g freshly grated parmesan
2 eggs
pinch of salt

SAUCE

30 ml extra virgin olive oil
60 g butter
1 onion, chopped
100 g prosciutto, finely chopped
400 g fresh or frozen peas
sea salt and freshly ground black pepper
500 ml chicken stock
45 g freshly grated parmesan

SERVES 4

First make the pasta dough (see page 11), mixing the grated parmesan into the flour before you shape it into a mound.

When the pasta dough has rested, roll it out into thin sheets and cut into farfalle (see page 23). Set the pasta aside on lightly floured tea towels while you make the sauce.

Heat the olive oil and butter in a heavy-based frying pan over low heat and add the onion. Fry for about 5 minutes until softened, then add the prosciutto and mix well. Sauté for 5 minutes. Add the peas, then season with salt and pepper (keeping in mind that the prosciutto is quite salty) and pour in half the stock. Stir well and cook for about 4–6 minutes until the peas are tender, adding more stock as necessary. Keep the sauce warm while you cook the pasta.

Cook the farfalle in plenty of boiling salted water until just cooked, about 3–4 minutes. Drain and place in a large serving bowl.

Pour the sauce over the pasta, add two-thirds of the parmesan and a little more pepper. Toss gently but thoroughly, then sprinkle the remaining parmesan on top and serve immediately.

Pici with pheasant and porcini ragù

PICI AL RAGÙ DI FAGIANO E PORCINI

This is another impressive creation from Logan Campbell, the chef at Lucio's. It uses pheasant meat, but if you can't find that, you could use quail meat instead. Logan explains the pasta: 'Pici are irregular-shaped noodles made by hand from flour and water. As simple as that sounds, this is not a task for the faint-hearted. Much attention must be paid to the kneading of the dough and the rolling of the pasta. Traditionally this kind of pasta is served with simple sauces, probably because of the time it takes to roll out the pasta. But this ragù can be made beforehand then tossed with the freshly cooked pici and finished with fresh herbs. All that hard work seems worth it in the end!'

200 ml extra virgin olive oil

100 g plain flour

2 pheasants, jointed – ask your butcher
   to do this

100 ml sherry or brandy

3 litres chicken stock

20 g dried porcini mushrooms

150 g pancetta, finely chopped

2 cloves garlic, chopped

6 golden shallots, finely chopped

1 carrot, finely chopped

2 roma (plum) tomatoes, roughly chopped

100 ml tomato sauce II (see page 52)

100 g green garlic shoots or chives

1 tablespoon chopped flat-leaf parsley

sea salt and freshly ground black pepper

PICI DOUGH

350 g strong white flour, plus extra
   for dusting

190 ml cold water

1 tablespoon extra virgin olive oil

SERVES 4

To make the pici dough, put the flour in a bowl, make a well in the centre and add the water and olive oil. Knead the dough briefly to amalgamate (do not work the dough too much or the pici will be tough), then cover in plastic film and leave to rest for 30 minutes. Dust the dough with flour and form into a ball. Cut the ball into 10–12 smaller pieces then roll these with your palm and fingers to make noodle shapes. Place the pici on a lightly floured tray or large plate in a single layer, cover with plastic film and refrigerate while you make the ragù.

Heat half the olive oil in a large saucepan or stockpot. Lightly flour the pheasant pieces and, working in batches, fry until brown all over, then remove from the pan. Add the sherry, followed by the stock, then return all the pheasant pieces to the pan. Cover and simmer for 40 minutes or until the pheasant is tender. Remove the pheasant and set aside to cool, but keep the stock on the heat and simmer it until it is reduced to 1.5 litres, about 40 minutes. When the pheasant is cool enough to handle, strip the meat from the bones and set aside. Discard the bones.

Soak the dried porcini in warm water for 15 minutes. Rinse, then squeeze very dry and chop roughly. Discard the soaking water.

Heat the remaining olive oil in a heavy-based frying pan and sauté the pancetta until brown. Add the garlic, shallot, carrot and porcini and cook for 3 minutes. Add the chopped tomato, tomato sauce and reduced stock and simmer until reduced by half, about 25 minutes. Add the pheasant meat and continue to cook the ragù until somewhat thick. Finally, stir through the green garlic shoots and parsley and season to taste with salt and pepper.

Cook the pici in plenty of boiling salted water until just cooked, about 7 minutes. Drain and toss with the ragù, then serve immediately.

'Guitar' maccheroni with lamb ragù

MACCHERONI ALLA CHITARRA AL RAGÙ D'AGNELLO

In this recipe, *maccheroni* refers to the ancient name for pasta (which is still used in some regions in the south of Italy) and not the tube-shaped pasta we know as maccheroni today. The word *maccheroni* comes from the Latin *maccare*, which means to press to make a mixture, and this maccheroni is a type of thick spaghetti that is cut using a special instrument called a *chitarra* ('guitar'). The *chitarra* has a rectangular wooden frame and is strung with wires that resemble the strings on a guitar. The dough sheet is rolled out a little thicker than usual and then placed on top of the strings and pressed through with a rolling pin. If you don't have a *chitarra*, just use the thinnest cutter on your pasta machine.

The pasta is a speciality of the Abruzzo region and is sometimes called *tonnarelli* or *tondarelli*. It contains semolina flour to give the strands strength and thus the ability to hold up well with heavier sauces, such as this classic lamb ragù with yellow capsicums. It's perfect for wintry weekends, when it is cold outside and the kitchen becomes the heart of the house, filled with family and friends and reassuring smells! In other seasons, this pasta is excellent with a vegetable sauce scented with thyme, a simple dressing of mushrooms, or even just a robust southern Italian olive oil and a scattering of capers and olives.

300 g plain flour
100 g semolina flour
4 eggs
pinch of sea salt

SAUCE

120 ml extra virgin olive oil
2 cloves garlic, peeled and lightly squashed
½ small carrot, finely chopped
½ young celery stalk, finely chopped
½ small white onion, finely chopped
3 bay leaves
50 g pancetta, diced
400 g boneless lamb shoulder, trimmed
    and cut into 2 cm cubes
1 tablespoon rosemary leaves,
    finely chopped
1 tablespoon sage leaves, finely chopped
150 ml dry white wine
2 yellow capsicums (peppers), seeds and
    membranes removed, cut into strips
2 red chillies, chopped
1 × 400 g tin peeled tomatoes
1 tablespoon tomato paste
sea salt and freshly ground black pepper
100 g freshly grated pecorino

SERVES 4

First make the ragù. Heat the olive oil in a large heavy-based frying pan over medium heat. Add the garlic and stir with a wooden spoon until it just starts to change colour, then discard. Add the carrot, celery, onion, bay leaves and pancetta. Mix well and sauté for about 5 minutes until the vegetables are soft.

Turn up the heat and add the lamb in small batches. Cook each batch until browned all over, then remove from the pan. When all the lamb is browned, return it to the pan with the rosemary and sage. Add the wine and boil to let it evaporate (5–6 minutes). Add the capsicum, chilli, tomatoes and tomato paste. Season with salt and pepper, then mix well and bring to the boil. Cover and turn the heat down to low. Cook gently for 2 hours until the lamb is very tender, stirring regularly to make sure that nothing sticks to the pan and adding a little water if it seems too dry. The sauce should become wonderfully thick and rich.

Meanwhile, make the pasta. Combine the flours and make the pasta dough (see page 11). Divide the dough into four, then roll out each piece into a sheet about 3 mm thick. Cut the pasta sheet to fit the length of the *chitarra*, then place the pasta on top of the wires and roll a rolling pin back and forth to cut the pasta. Alternatively, use the thinnest cutter on your pasta machine. Sprinkle the maccheroni with a little flour and lay them on lightly floured tea towels to dry for about 1 hour.

Cook the maccheroni in plenty of boiling salted water until just cooked, about 3–4 minutes. Drain the pasta and place in a large serving dish. Pour over the sauce and toss delicately, then sprinkle with the pecorino and serve immediately.

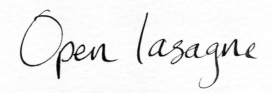

LASAGNE TORDELLATE

Ligurian cuisine is generally simple and family orientated, but every now and then you come across a refined dish like this lasagne, which is served with a sauce that normally functions as the filling for ravioli or tordelli – hence the name *tordellate*, which means 'tordelli-style'. You can use relatively cheap cuts of beef and pork for this, because they are slow-cooked – just be sure to trim off the fat first.

500 g plain flour
2 eggs
pinch of salt

SAUCE

30 ml extra virgin olive oil
30 g butter
1 white onion, finely chopped
1 carrot, chopped
1 celery stalk, chopped
1 handful flat-leaf parsley leaves,
    finely chopped
300 g boneless lean beef, roughly chopped
300 g boneless lean pork, roughly chopped
sea salt and freshly ground black pepper
3 bay leaves
a few gratings of nutmeg
30 ml dry white wine
500 g tomatoes, peeled and seeded
    (see page 51), then diced
1 bunch silverbeet (Swiss chard)
1 white bread roll, crust removed and
    inside torn into small pieces
about 200 ml milk
2 eggs
60 g freshly grated parmesan

SERVES 4

Make the pasta dough following the instructions on page 11, but using the ingredients given here. While the pasta dough is resting, make the sauce.

Heat the olive oil and butter in a heavy-based frying pan over low heat. Add the onion, carrot, celery and parsley, mix with a wooden spoon and cook for a few minutes until the vegetables are soft and the onion is translucent. Stir in the beef and pork and turn up the heat to medium–high. Season with salt and pepper, then add the bay leaves and nutmeg. Mix thoroughly and cook for 8–10 minutes. Add the wine and let it evaporate, then turn the heat to low and stir in the tomato. Cook for 30 minutes, stirring regularly and adding a little water if the mixture becomes too dry – the sauce should be fairly thick.

Remove and discard the white stalks from the silverbeet. Wash and drain the leaves, then place in a frying pan over low heat and cook with just the water clinging to the leaves until the leaves are wilted. When the silverbeet is cool enough to handle, squeeze dry and chop finely, then set aside in a large bowl. Place the bread in a small saucepan and add just enough milk to cover. Cook over low heat for 3–4 minutes, stirring constantly. Transfer the contents of the pan to the bowl with the silverbeet.

Take the sauce off the heat and transfer the pieces of meat to a chopping board. With a mezzaluna or sharp knife, chop the meat finely. Add to the silverbeet and bread mixture, along with the eggs, half the parmesan and some pepper. Mix thoroughly.

Put the sauce back over low heat and add the meat and silverbeet mixture. Stir gently and cook for another 30 minutes.

Roll out the pasta dough into very thin sheets (see pages 17–18), then cut into 8 cm squares. Cook the pasta squares a few at a time in plenty of boiling salted water with a little olive oil added until just cooked, about 5 minutes. Drain them one by one using a slotted spoon and place on a warm plate, keeping the sheets separate so they don't stick together. Then, working very quickly, build the lasagne on individual plates, using 4–5 sheets of pasta for each. Start with a little sauce on the plate, then place a square of pasta on it, followed by some more sauce, then some parmesan, another square of pasta, and so on, ending with sauce and parmesan. Serve immediately.

Capsicum pappardelle with oxtail

PAPPARDELLE DI PEPERONI AL RAGÙ DI CODA

Rich, gelatinous, fantastic. This sauce was inspired by the famous Roman dish *coda alla vaccinara* (which is often served with fettuccine) – *vaccinara* means cattle butcher, and the custom in the nineteenth century was for farmers to pay the men who cut up their cattle with parts of the animal. So the butcher would take home the tail and cook it for a very long time until it was falling off the bone. It was always sweetened with sultanas, which suggests an Arab influence.

Here the oxtail pairs very well with the sharpness of the capsicum in the pasta. The sauce is also excellent served with dried large rigatoni. In that case, though, I suggest you add a couple of roasted red capsicums, cut into thin strips, to the sauce at the same time as the celery.

400 g capsicum pasta dough (see page 15)
80 ml extra virgin olive oil
80 g pancetta, cut into small cubes
1 small white onion, finely chopped
1 carrot, finely chopped
3 bay leaves
1 tablespoon freshly chopped flat-leaf
    parsley leaves
1 oxtail, washed and cut into pieces
sea salt and freshly ground black pepper
60 ml dry white wine
1 × 400 g tin peeled tomatoes, passed
    through a mouli or squished with
    your hands
5 sprigs marjoram
2 celery stalks
2 tablespoons pine nuts
1 tablespoon sultanas, roughly chopped
50 g freshly grated parmesan
50 g freshly grated pecorino

SERVES 4

Roll out the pasta dough and cut into pappardelle (see page 20). Lay the pasta on lightly floured tea towels while you make the sauce.

Heat the olive oil in a deep heavy-based frying pan over medium heat. Add the pancetta, onion, carrot, bay leaves and parsley. Mix well with a wooden spoon and cook for 6–8 minutes, stirring often. Add the oxtail and brown on all sides – if it produces any liquid, let it evaporate. Season with salt and pepper, then pour in the wine. Cook until the wine has evaporated (until you don't smell it any more). Add the tomato and marjoram and mix thoroughly. Turn the heat down to low and cook for about 2 hours until the meat is falling off the bone. Stir and check regularly, adding a little water if the sauce dries out too much.

Cook the celery in boiling water until very soft, about 8–10 minutes. Drain, then cut into 1–2 cm pieces and set aside.

Take the pan with the sauce off the heat. Remove and discard the marjoram. Transfer the pieces of oxtail to a bowl and, when they are cool enough to handle, debone them. Discard the bones and return the meat to the pan. Put the pan back over low–medium heat and add the celery, pine nuts and sultanas. Mix thoroughly, breaking up any pieces of meat that are too big and simmer for 15 minutes. The sauce is now ready.

Cook the pappardelle in plenty of boiling salted water until just cooked, about 3 minutes. Drain, reserving a little of the pasta cooking water, and place the pappardelle in a large serving dish. Pour the sauce over and toss gently, adding a tablespoon or two of the reserved pasta cooking water if it seems too dry. Sprinkle over the parmesan and pecorino and serve immediately.

Lasagnette with rabbit sauce

LASAGNETTE AL SUGO DI CONIGLIO

This beautifully satisfying and energising dish is a favourite in both Liguria and Tuscany. Rabbit sauce is always accompanied by silky ribbons of fresh pasta – tagliatelle, lasagnette, pappardelle or maltagliati – it's as if we want the softness of the pasta to meld with the softness of the rabbit meat. Sometimes tomato is added to the sauce and that's very good too. However, being a rabbit lover, I like mine without, just as my mother used to make it. The rabbit, then, is what you taste, complemented by the herbs. I hope you like it.

The sauce can also be made with hare, if you like a stronger flavour. The procedure is the same, except you begin by rinsing the hare with the white wine to moderate its gaminess.

400 g basic pasta dough (see page 11)
1 onion
1 celery stalk
1 clove garlic, peeled
100 ml extra virgin olive oil
50 g butter
1 × 1.5 kg rabbit, cut into about ten pieces
1 tablespoon chopped flat-leaf parsley
sea salt and freshly ground black pepper
125 ml dry white wine
40 g freshly grated parmesan

SERVES 4

First make the pasta dough and, while it is resting, make the sauce.

Chop the onion, celery and garlic together to make a soffritto. Heat the olive oil and butter in a large heavy-based saucepan, then add the soffritto and sauté over medium heat for about 3 minutes. Add the rabbit and parsley and season to taste with salt and pepper. Cook over a low heat for about 15 minutes, stirring regularly so the rabbit takes on all the flavours.

Add the wine and stir well, then cover and cook over low heat for about 90 minutes or until the meat is so tender it easily separates from the bone. Add water if necessary to stop the pan from drying out, and stir from time to time so that the meat does not stick to the bottom of the pan.

Remove the rabbit pieces from the sauce. When they are cool enough to handle, debone them and shred the meat. Return the meat to the sauce and mix well. The sauce is now ready to use.

Roll out the pasta dough into very thin sheets (see pages 17–18) then, using a fluted ravioli cutter or pastry wheel, cut the dough into rectangles about 8 cm × 2.5 cm. Cook the pasta in plenty of boiling salted water until just cooked, about 3–5 minutes, then drain carefully.

Spread a little of the sauce on the bottom of a serving dish and add a layer of pasta. Add more sauce and sprinkle over some parmesan. Continue layering until you have used all the ingredients, finishing with parmesan. Shake the dish a little so that the sauce covers all the pasta. Serve immediately.

Tagliatelle with prosciutto and figs

TAGLIATELLE AL PROSCIUTTO E FICHI

Prosciutto and figs are a match made in heaven. At my restaurant during the fig season, we marinate the fruit quickly with olive oil, balsamic vinegar and garlic, then grill them and serve them with prosciutto. One day I thought it would be interesting to try those same grilled figs and prosciutto with pasta. We added leeks to the soffritto and cut the prosciutto thick and diced it (like bacon), and the result was *squisito*!

400 g basic pasta dough (see page 11)
800 g figs
160 ml extra virgin olive oil
80 ml balsamic vinegar
sea salt and freshly ground black pepper
leaves from 5 sprigs marjoram
3 cloves garlic, lightly crushed
3 slices prosciutto, cut as thick as bacon
2 small leeks
30 ml dry white wine
2 tablespoons freshly grated parmesan

SERVES 4

Roll out the pasta dough and cut into tagliatelle (see page 20). Lay the pasta on lightly floured tea towels while you make the sauce.

Wipe the figs clean with a wet cloth, then cut off and discard the stems. Cut the figs into quarters. Place in a bowl and pour over half of the olive oil. Add the balsamic vinegar, then season with salt and pepper. Sprinkle over the marjoram leaves and add the garlic. Mix delicately to coat the figs with the marinade and set aside for 30 minutes.

Meanwhile, cut the prosciutto into small cubes. Trim the ends of the leeks, keeping only the white part. Strip off the outer leaves and chop the inner parts finely.

Heat the remaining olive oil in a heavy-based frying pan over medium heat. Add the prosciutto and leek and cook for about 8 minutes, stirring regularly with a wooden spoon, until the leek is very soft and the prosciutto is crunchy.

Remove the figs from the marinade, then add to the pan with the wine and 3 tablespoons of the marinade. Season with a little salt and pepper and cook for about 5 minutes, stirring delicately every so often.

Cook the tagliatelle in plenty of boiling salted water until just cooked, about 3 minutes, then drain and add to the pan with the sauce. Toss gently, sprinkle with the parmesan and serve immediately.

Corzetti with pork and fennel Sausage

CORZETTI DI VALPOLCEVERA

Corzetti pasta is unique to Liguria. There are two distinct types, one for each Riviera: the *corzetti stampati* ('stamped' corzetti, see page 193) of the Riviera di Levante resemble large medallions; while the *corzetti di Valpolcevera*, from the valley of the Riviera di Ponente (west of Genoa), are small, orecchiette-like pasta resembling the figure 8.

In addition to the suggestion here, both types of corzetti are excellent simply tossed with butter and parmesan, chopped pine nuts and marjoram. They can also be served with a ragù of meat or tomato, a rather runny pesto, or a walnut sauce with mushrooms.

400 g basic pasta dough (see page 11)
20 g dried porcini mushrooms
1 clove garlic, peeled
handful of flat-leaf parsley leaves
90 ml extra virgin olive oil
2 golden shallots, finely chopped
3 pork and fennel sausages, skins removed
sea salt and freshly ground black pepper
4 large ripe tomatoes, peeled and seeded
   (see page 51), then diced
60 g freshly grated parmesan

SERVES 4

When the pasta dough has rested, tear off a piece the size of a chickpea and roll it into a ball. Rest it on your left palm and flatten it with your right index finger. Now, with your index and middle finger together, press on to the flattened disc to leave the impression of a figure 8. You have made your first corzetti! Repeat until all the dough is shaped. Sprinkle the corzetti with a little flour and lay on lightly floured tea towels to dry for about 1 hour.

To make the sauce, soak the porcini mushrooms in warm water for 10–15 minutes. Drain, discarding the water, then pat the mushrooms dry and place on a chopping board with the garlic and parsley. Using a mezzaluna or a sharp knife, mince them all together to make your soffritto.

Heat the olive oil in a heavy-based frying pan over medium heat and add the shallot. Sauté until it softens, about 5 minutes, stirring with a wooden spoon. Break up the sausage meat, then add it to the pan and cook until brown all over (about 4 minutes), breaking up any large pieces with the wooden spoon. Add the porcini soffritto, season with salt and pepper, then stir for a couple of minutes before adding the tomato. Mix well, cover the pan and simmer over low heat for 30 minutes, stirring regularly and adding a little water if necessary.

Meanwhile, cook the corzetti in plenty of boiling salted water until just cooked, about 6–8 minutes. Drain. Add to the sauce in the pan and toss gently, sprinkling with the parmesan. Serve immediately.

Chocolate tagliatelle with wild boar

TAGLIATELLE DI CIOCCOLATO CON RAGÙ DI CINGHIALE

It's a very unusual combination, chocolate and meat, but it works – the strong flavour of the wild boar ragù marries perfectly with the bitterness of the chocolate. I first tried this dish when I was young and brave at the Latin restaurant in Melbourne. The Latin had no doubt been inspired by recipes from Tuscany, which is where chocolate first took off as a flavouring for the wealthy after its arrival from the Americas in the sixteenth century.

400 g chocolate pasta dough (see page 15)
90 ml extra virgin olive oil
60 g butter
1 small onion, finely chopped
1 small carrot, finely chopped
1 celery stalk, finely chopped
4 sprigs sage
4 sprigs rosemary
200 g boneless wild boar meat, finely diced
120 ml white wine
200 ml chicken stock
sea salt and freshly ground black pepper
120 g Swiss brown mushrooms, finely sliced
2 tablespoons pine nuts, toasted
freshly grated parmesan, to serve

SERVES 4

Roll out the pasta dough and cut into tagliatelle (see page 20). Lay the pasta on lightly floured tea towels while you make the sauce.

Heat the olive oil and half the butter in a large heavy-based frying pan over low heat. Add the onion, carrot and celery and cook for 6–8 minutes, stirring regularly with a wooden spoon, until the vegetables are soft. Tie the herb sprigs together and add to the pan, along with the wild boar meat. Mix well and cook until the meat is browned all over, about 8 minutes. Stir in the wine and let it evaporate. Add half of the stock, season to taste with salt and pepper, and cook over a low heat for about 1 hour or until the meat is tender, stirring regularly and gradually adding the rest of the stock. Remove and discard the herbs.

Meanwhile, heat the remaining butter in a non-stick frying pan. Add the mushrooms and sauté for about 8 minutes. Transfer the mushrooms to the pan with the sauce, add the pine nuts and mix thoroughly. Check the seasoning and cook for another 2 minutes, then take the pan off the heat.

Cook the chocolate tagliatelle in plenty of boiling salted water until just cooked, about 2–3 minutes. Drain and add to the pan with the sauce. Toss gently with the beautiful ragù until all the flavours are combined, then sprinkle with parmesan and serve.

Tagliolini with red mullet Sauce and zucchini flowers

TAGLIOLINI AL RAGÙ DI TRIGLIE E FIORI DI ZUCCHINI

Red mullet, called *triglia* (pronounced 'trilya') in Italian, is one of my favourite fish because of its sweet, pink flesh. I'm pairing it here with the thin tagliolini known in my local dialect as *tajarin*. If you don't have a pasta machine, you can easily cut tagliolini the way my grandmother did: make a sheet of fine pasta dough, then roll it up like a newspaper and slice thin discs off the end of the roll. When you unravel the discs, you'll have your noodles!

400 g basic pasta dough (see page 11)
8 zucchini (courgette) flowers, cleaned
    and finely sliced lengthways
2 tablespoons extra virgin olive oil
1 golden shallot, finely chopped
1 clove garlic, finely chopped
2 small red chillies, seeded and
    finely chopped
500 g red mullet fillets
125 ml dry white wine
150 g cherry tomatoes, quartered
1 tablespoon marjoram leaves, chopped
sea salt and freshly ground black pepper
6 basil leaves, roughly chopped
1 tablespoon pine nuts

SERVES 4

Roll out the pasta dough and cut into tagliolini (see page 20). Lay the pasta on lightly floured tea towels while you make the sauce.

Remove and discard the stigma from each zucchini flower, checking them carefully for any stray insects. Finely slice the zucchini flowers lengthways.

Heat the olive oil in a heavy-based frying pan over medium heat and add the shallot, garlic and chilli. Sauté for 3–4 minutes, stirring with a wooden spoon. Add the red mullet fillets, breaking them up with a fork. Add the white wine and let the alcohol evaporate for about 5 minutes, then add the tomatoes and marjoram. Season to taste with salt and pepper and cook for about 6 minutes, stirring regularly. Stir in the zucchini flowers, basil and pine nuts, then cook for another 3 minutes.

Meanwhile, cook the tagliolini in plenty of boiling salted water until just cooked, about 2–3 minutes. Drain the pasta, then add to the frying pan with the sauce. Toss delicately and serve immediately.

Corzetti with pine nuts, anchovies and almonds

CORZETTI STAMPATI ALLA FRANTOIANA

Hailing from Liguria's Riviera di Levante (east of Genoa), *corzetti stampati* look like large medallions stamped (*stampati*) on both sides – the grooves of the stamped pattern help to hold the sauce. As they are very labour intensive, they were originally served only in noble families as a sign of wealth and power, having been made by the servants in the kitchen. Called *croxetti* in the Genoese dialect (from *croxe*, meaning 'cross'), it is thought that corzetti were stamped with a simple cross during the Crusades. Although it is difficult to find genuine corzetti stamps (which are made of beechwood, since it does not leave any odour), you can imprint your corzetti with a cross, use a biscuit stamp or your fingers to make a pattern on them, or even just leave them plain.

400 g basic pasta dough (see page 11)
100 g pine nuts, roughly chopped
50 g blanched almonds, roughly chopped
2 tablespoons marjoram leaves,
    roughly chopped
45 ml extra virgin olive oil
30 g butter
2 anchovy fillets
2 cloves garlic, peeled and lightly squashed
3 sprigs basil
60 g freshly grated parmesan

SERVES 4

Roll the pasta dough into sheets about 2–3 mm thick (the sheets need to be quite robust for corzetti, so the discs won't break when they are stamped). Dust your work surface with flour and lay out a sheet of pasta dough. Cut the dough into 5 cm discs, using either the sharp cutter on the bottom part of a corzetti stamp or a glass or a cookie cutter. When they are all cut, you can start stamping. If you have a corzetti stamp, simply pick up the pasta discs one by one and place them on the bottom part of the stamp, then press with the top part. Your corzetti are now stamped on both sides. Otherwise, you can leave them plain, or use a biscuit stamp or your fingers to make an impression on the surface. Sprinkle the corzetti with a little flour and lay on lightly floured tea towels to dry for about 1 hour.

Combine the pine nuts, almonds and marjoram in a small bowl and set aside.

Cook the corzetti in plenty of boiling salted water until just cooked, about 6–8 minutes.

While the pasta is cooking, place the olive oil and butter in a heavy-based frying pan over low heat and melt the butter. Add the anchovies, pressing with a fork to melt them into the oil and butter, then stir well with a wooden spoon. Add the garlic and basil and sauté until the garlic just starts to change colour, then discard both of them (you only want to scent the oil and butter). Add the nut mixture to the pan, stir for about 1 minute, then take the pan off the heat.

Place 1 tablespoon of the parmesan in the bottom of a large serving bowl. Drain the corzetti and add half of it to the bowl, followed by another spoonful of parmesan and the sauce. Add the rest of the corzetti, toss gently to combine well and serve, sprinkled with the remaining parmesan.

Green pappardelle with Balmain bugs

PAPPARDELLE VERDI AI BATTIBA

This creation of Logan Campbell, Lucio's executive chef, uses what Sydney people call Balmain bugs, and Brisbane people call Moreton Bay bugs. In Italy, the crustaceans used in this sort of dish are called *cicale di mare* ('cicadas of the sea') or, in Ligurian dialect, *battiba* (for the sound they make as they clatter around on the bottom of the fishing boat). Logan has this to say about the pappardelle: 'This cut of pasta is by far my favourite. There's something very satisfying about eating wide ribbons of pasta that I just can't put my finger on. Marrying these ribbons with sweet bug meat, cherry tomatoes and zucchini flowers makes this a quick dish to make, as well as a delicious one.'

400 g green pasta dough (see page 14)

80 ml extra virgin olive oil

200 g raw Balmain bug meat (from about 600–750 g Balmain bugs), chopped

3 cloves garlic, chopped

½ punnet cherry tomatoes (about 12), peeled (see page 51)

sea salt and freshly ground black pepper

1 tablespoon thyme leaves

6 zucchini (courgette) flowers, stalks cut into rounds and flowers roughly chopped

SERVES 4

Roll out the pasta dough and cut into pappardelle (see page 20). Lay the pasta on lightly floured tea towels while you make the sauce.

Heat the olive oil in a large heavy-based frying pan over medium–high heat. Add the bug meat and garlic and sauté for 1 minute, then remove from the pan. Add the cherry tomatoes to the pan, lightly crushing them with a wooden spoon, then season to taste with salt and pepper and add the thyme. Turn the heat down to low and keep warm while you cook the pasta.

Cook the pappardelle in plenty of boiling salted water until just cooked, about 3–4 minutes. Drain, reserving a little of the cooking water. Add the pasta to the frying pan and toss well, adding some of the reserved pasta cooking water if it seems too dry. Add the sautéed bug meat and the zucchini stalks and toss gently. Serve hot, topped with the zucchini flowers.

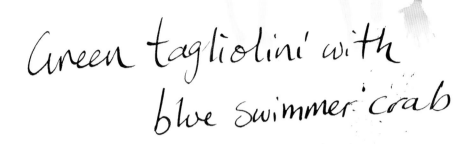
Green tagliolini with
blue swimmer crab

TAGLIOLINI ALLA GRANSEOLA

I started serving this nearly 30 years ago, and it soon became one of my first signature dishes. Soon after, my cousin Mario came from Italy to visit me, and he liked the idea so much that he started serving the dish in the family restaurant back in Liguria. That made me very proud, because Mario had been my mentor in the hospitality business. If you can't find blue swimmers, you can use any other kind of crabmeat, as long as it is fresh and not already cooked.

400 g green pasta dough (see page 14)
3 large raw blue swimmer crabs
80 ml extra virgin olive oil
1 clove garlic, finely diced
1 quantity tomato sauce II (see page 52)
1 teaspoon butter

SERVES 4

Roll out the pasta dough and cut into tagliolini (see page 20). Lay the pasta on lightly floured tea towels while you make the sauce.

To clean the crabs, remove the claws from the bodies. Break the claws and remove the meat. Remove the heads and discard the grey, feathery lungs. Break the bodies in half lengthways and squeeze the meat out. Place all the crabmeat in a colander over the sink and let it drain for 10 minutes.

Place the olive oil and the drained crabmeat in a large heavy-based frying pan big enough to hold the pasta over low–medium heat. Cook gently for 2–3 minutes. Add the garlic and cook for a further 2 minutes, but do not let the crab or the garlic brown. Add the tomato sauce, bring to the boil and simmer for a further 2 minutes.

Meanwhile, cook the tagliolini in plenty of boiling salted water until just cooked, about 2 minutes. Drain well and add to the frying pan, along with the butter. Toss well and serve immediately.

Mussel testaroli with anchovy sauce

TESTAROLI ALLE COZZE

Testaroli are so called because they were originally made in a special terracotta utensil called a *testo*, which resembles a tagine but is dome shaped. A speciality of the mountains of Lunigiana, where Liguria meets Tuscany, testaroli are hardly known outside this region. Effectively thick crepes made with flour and water, which are then cut into diamond shapes and cooked like pasta, they are probably one of the most ancient types of pasta, having served as portable food for Ligurian shepherds for at least 2000 years. Testaroli are often served simply with pesto or olive oil and parmesan, but I thought it was about time they went down to the sea!

300 g mussels
2 tablespoons chopped marjoram
1 tablespoon chopped chives
800 g plain flour
extra virgin olive oil, for drizzling
60 g freshly grated pecorino

SAUCE

100 ml extra virgin olive oil
6 anchovy fillets
3 cloves garlic, peeled and lightly squashed
8 cherry tomatoes, quartered
sea salt and freshly ground black pepper
10 basil leaves, roughly torn

SERVES 4

Scrub and debeard the mussels, then carefully extract the mussel meat by inserting a small knife and sliding it along inside the shell until you reach the hinge and it pops open. Save the water the mussels let out and chop the mussel meat very finely. Place the mussel meat in a bowl and add 100 ml of the reserved mussel water, 130 ml water, the marjoram and chives and mix well. Now add the flour a little at a time, whisking well to obtain a smooth batter.

Heat a 20 cm non-stick frying pan over medium heat. When hot, brush with olive oil and pour in the testaroli batter to a depth of 3–4 mm and cook until set and lightly browned, then flip it over and cook on the other side for 1–2 minutes. Remove from the pan and repeat until all the batter is used, then cut the testaroli into diamond shapes and set aside.

For the sauce, heat the olive oil in a heavy-based frying pan with the anchovies, pressing with a fork to melt them into the oil. Add the garlic and stir with a wooden spoon to flavour the oil, discarding the garlic just as it starts to change colour. Stir in the tomatoes, together with a little salt and pepper, and cook for 5 minutes. Add the basil and stir well, then take the pan off the heat.

Meanwhile, cook the testaroli in plenty of boiling water (it doesn't need to be salted) until just cooked, about 3 minutes. Drain the pasta, reserving a little of the cooking water, then place in a bowl. Drizzle generously with olive oil and sprinkle with pecorino and stir with a wooden spoon. Pour in the anchovy sauce and a tablespoon or two of the reserved pasta cooking water, mix well and serve immediately.

Tagliolini with whitebait

TAGLIOLINI CON BIANCHETTI

My cousin Mario made this dish for a group of friends one night while he was waiting for his sister Rosi to give birth to the beautiful Roberta. They were in the family restaurant in the early hours of the morning, still opening bottles of wine hours after the last customer had left, and wondering what to eat next. It was the season of whitebait (actually baby sardines in my area, although we call them *bianchetti* – little whites – because that is the colour they turn when they are boiled) and the fishermen were coming back to the docks in their boats after fishing all night, their bright beams playing across the water. One fisherman saw the light still on in the restaurant and came in with a box of whitebait and small red mullet. Mario said, 'I'll make pasta with them.' Everyone, including the fisherman, joined him in the kitchen . . . and so this recipe was born, along with baby Roberta.

400 g basic pasta dough (see page 11)
90 ml extra virgin olive oil
1 clove garlic, peeled and lightly squashed
½ white onion, finely chopped
2 red mullets, cleaned and filleted
300 g very small whitebait, washed
leaves from 3 sprigs oregano,
  roughly chopped
120 ml dry white wine
1 large ripe tomato, peeled and seeded
  (see page 51), then diced
sea salt and freshly ground black pepper
2 tablespoons chopped flat-leaf parsley

SERVES 4

Roll out the pasta dough and cut into tagliolini (see page 20). Lay the pasta on lightly floured tea towels while you make the sauce.

Heat the olive oil in a heavy-based frying pan over low heat. Add the garlic and onion and stir with a wooden spoon just until the garlic starts to change colour, then remove and discard the garlic. Keep cooking for a few more minutes until the onion is soft, then add the red mullet fillets and cook for 1 minute. Add the whitebait and oregano and mix thoroughly but gently for 1 minute, trying not to break up the fish too much. Turn up the heat to medium, add the wine and cook until the alcohol has evaporated completely. Add the tomato and sprinkle on a little salt and pepper. Mix carefully and cook for 5 minutes. Sprinkle with the parsley, mix again and remove from the heat.

In the meantime, cook the tagliolini in plenty of boiling salted water until just cooked, about 2–3 minutes. Drain, retaining a little of the cooking water.

Place half the sauce in a large serving bowl. Put the tagliolini on top and pour the rest of the sauce on top of the pasta. Toss well, adding a tablespoon or two of the cooking water if it seems too dry. Serve hot.

Black tagliatelle with grilled scampi and leeks

TAGLIATELLE NERE AI PORRI CON SCAMPI ALLA GRIGLIA

One day some years ago, when I was having a chat with my good friend, the great Australian artist John Olsen, after one of his many lunches at my restaurant, he asked me, 'Why don't you have black sauce on your menu?' He was referring to the sauce made from cuttlefish ink that is used in a Spanish dish called arroz negro, a kind of black paella. Well, a request from the maestro can't be ignored, so I said, 'Maestro, it will be on my menu from tomorrow.'

I decided not to put cuttlefish ink in a sauce, though, because I think it can taste too strong, and it leaves your mouth very black – you can't smile at your bella or bello after eating that! So I put the ink in pasta, where the flavour subtly complements the sauce without overpowering it. Since then I have always had some kind of black pasta on my menu, and this is one of the most loved, using leek – a favourite Ligurian ingredient.

400 g black pasta dough (see page 14)
150 ml extra virgin olive oil
2 leeks, washed and diced
1 clove garlic, finely chopped
sea salt and freshly ground black pepper
6 scampi
olive oil, for grilling

SERVES 4

Roll out the pasta dough and cut into tagliatelle (see page 20). Lay the pasta on lightly floured tea towels while you make the sauce.

Place the olive oil in a frying pan over medium heat, add the leek and garlic and sauté for 4 minutes or until soft. Season to taste with salt and pepper.

Cut the scampi in half lengthways, rinse and place on a lightly oiled hot barbecue grillplate or chargrill pan for 2 minutes each side. (If you prefer, you can pan-fry the scampi in a little olive oil for 2 minutes each side.)

Meanwhile, cook the tagliatelle in plenty of boiling salted water until just cooked, about 3 minutes. Drain well, add to the frying pan with the leek and toss well. Serve the pasta in bowls with the scampi on top.

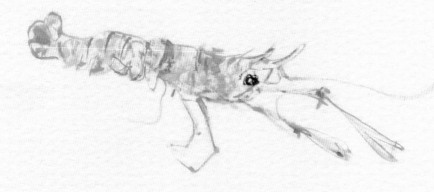

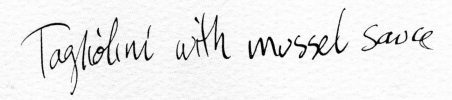

TAGLIOLINI AL SUGO DI COZZE

When I opened my restaurant in Paddington in 1983, I put this tagliolini on the menu in honour of my family's restaurant in Italy, where the dish had been on the menu since the restaurant opened in 1950. My mother and Aunty Anna would make the pasta, and my uncle Ciccio would make the sauce. It was one of their signature dishes and people travelled from far and wide to eat it. In Sydney I thought of the dish as a good-luck charm, because it had contributed to the success of my family in Italy in doing what they loved.

There is no need to roll the dough very thin for this pasta – thicker noodles work better with the heaviness of the mussels. If you don't have time to make the pasta yourself, you can serve any type of long pasta with this sauce.

400 g basic pasta dough (see page 11)
1.2 kg mussels
90 ml dry white wine
120 ml extra virgin olive oil
3 cloves garlic
1 × 400 g tin peeled tomatoes
3 sprigs basil
sea salt
large handful of flat-leaf parsley leaves,
    finely chopped
12 basil leaves, chopped

SERVES 4

Roll out the pasta dough into sheets, then cut into tagliolini (see page 20). Lay the pasta on lightly floured tea towels while you make the sauce.

Wash the mussels under cold running water, scrubbing and debearding them. Place them in a large frying pan over medium–high heat and add the wine and about a tablespoon of the olive oil. Take the mussels out of the pan as soon as they open, and set them aside. (Discard any mussels that won't open.) Reduce the liquid in the pan to about half, then strain it through a fine sieve into a bowl.

When the mussels are cool enough to handle, take them out of their shells. Roughly chop two-thirds of them and leave the remaining third whole. Place them all in a bowl and cover with some of the reduced cooking liquid. Set aside.

Finely chop 2 of the garlic cloves and leave the third one whole. Pass the tomatoes through a mouli or puree in a blender. Place 2 tablespoons of the olive oil in a saucepan over medium heat, add the whole garlic clove and stir with a wooden spoon until it just starts to change colour, then discard the garlic. Add the tomato puree to the oil, along with the sprigs of basil and a little salt (remembering that the mussel cooking liquid will already be salty). Cook for 10 minutes, stirring regularly.

Heat the remaining olive oil in a heavy-based frying pan over low heat. Add the chopped garlic and parsley and cook for 2 minutes, stirring constantly with a wooden spoon. Add the mussels together with the reduced cooking liquid they were resting in. Stir for 2 minutes, then add the tomato sauce. Mix thoroughly and cook for 3 minutes. Remove and discard the basil sprigs.

Cook the tagliolini in plenty of boiling salted water until just cooked, about 3 minutes. Drain and add to the pan with the sauce, then toss for about 1 minute to combine the flavours. Sprinkle on the chopped basil and serve immediately.

Black tagliolini with whitebait

TAGLIOLINI NERI AI BIANCHETTI

This is another of chef Logan Campbell's dishes, so I'll let him introduce it to you: 'Coming from a New Zealand background, I just can't help myself when it comes to these little gems. Available fresh for only two weeks in September, these fish larvae are delicate and unfortunately very expensive. However, the fishing industry here in Australia is showing signs of interest and may soon start harvesting whitebait locally – at a sustainable level, we hope.'

400 g black pasta dough (see page 14)
150 ml extra virgin olive oil
3 cloves garlic, finely chopped
2 red chillies, finely chopped
300 g New Zealand whitebait
600 ml fish stock
½ bunch chervil, leaves picked
sea salt and freshly ground black pepper
2 tablespoons salmon roe

SERVES 4

Roll out the pasta dough and cut into tagliolini (see page 20). Lay the pasta on lightly floured tea towels while you make the sauce.

Place the olive oil in a hot frying pan and quickly fry the garlic, chilli and whitebait until the garlic and chilli are aromatic and the whitebait is just cooked. Tip it all into a bowl and set aside.

Pour the fish stock into the pan and bring it to a simmer.

Meanwhile, cook the tagliolini in plenty of boiling salted water until just cooked, about 3 minutes. Drain and add to the stock, along with the garlic, chilli, whitebait and oil. Add the chervil, season to taste with salt and pepper and toss everything together gently until the oil and stock emulsify and the sauce looks creamy. Serve immediately, with the roe scattered on top.

PIZZOCCHERI AL SUGO DI OSTRICHE

Pizzoccheri is a type of tagliatelle made with buckwheat flour. A speciality from the mountains of Lombardy, it is usually eaten with a substantial sauce made from savoy cabbage, potatoes and parmesan, or simply with butter, sage and melted fontina cheese – but, I thought, let's take the *pizzoccheri* to the sea . . .

Just a word of warning: oysters are not usually used in pasta sauces, and it is all too easy to overcook them – they need only the couple of minutes it will take for the alcohol to evaporate from the white wine.

20 oysters
90 ml extra virgin olive oil
3 golden shallots, finely chopped
zest of 1 small lemon, cut into thin strips
2 tablespoons dry white wine
freshly ground black pepper
16 small basil leaves, fried in a little
   olive oil until crisp (optional)

BUCKWHEAT PASTA

200 g plain flour
200 g buckwheat flour
4 eggs
2 tablespoons marjoram leaves,
   finely chopped

SERVES 4

Make the pasta following the instructions on page 11, but using the ingredients and quantities given here. Roll out the pasta dough and cut into tagliatelle (see page 20). Lay the pasta on lightly floured tea towels while you make the sauce.

Carefully shuck the oysters, saving the liquor from half of them. Heat the olive oil in a large heavy-based frying pan over medium heat, then add the shallots and lemon zest and sauté for about 5 minutes, stirring with a wooden spoon. Sprinkle with half the white wine, then add the oysters and their reserved liquor. Mix thoroughly and simmer for 1 minute, then add the rest of the wine and let it evaporate for 2–3 minutes.

Meanwhile, cook the tagliatelle in plenty of boiling salted water until just cooked, about 5 minutes. Drain, then add to the sauce, season with pepper and toss gently. Serve immediately, topped with the fried basil, if using.

Filled pasta

Ravioli originated as a way to use chopped-up leftovers to feed workers quickly. The earliest form of raviolo was a kind of miniature pie that was boiled instead of baked, but it has since evolved into the jewel of Italian cooking. Over the centuries, it has grown more refined, with the pasta being stretched so thinly that it becomes translucent, letting you glimpse the colours inside.

Regional variations on ravioli (the generic name I use for all sorts of filled pasta parcels) have since multiplied all over Italy, but it is in the northwest, particularly Liguria and Piedmont, that they have reached their peak — made in dazzling variety for all sorts of special occasions. As a child, I remember that whenever there was a birthday in our family, my mother would say, '*Ti faccio i ravioli*' (I'll make ravioli for you). She'd chop the ingredients for the filling, put on the ragù for the sauce, sprinkle the board with flour and start rolling out the two layers of pasta dough. We always knew that these parcels would be much better than any presents, because she was making something with her own hands for us.

A FEW BASIC FILLINGS

The most important thing in ravioli is the filling, which must not be too soft or too wet. Below are some ideas for a few basic fillings: I leave the shape of the ravioli and the choice of sauce to your creativity. But if you run out of ideas or time one day, just remember that in my region of Liguria, where simplicity is a virtue, we say, 'Ravioli are very good, but with olive oil and parmesan they are even better'.

POTATO

This ravioli filling was created, according to legend, in the mountains that serve as border for the regions of Liguria, Emilia-Romagna and Tuscany. In the beginning only potatoes were used, and the ravioli were eaten with just olive oil and pecorino cheese, because that is what was available. I remember my father telling me when a particular season had not gone well, the family would fill up on potato ravioli. But I think these ravioli are not only substantial, they are also delicious. Try them with olive oil and pecorino: infuse about 100 ml extra virgin olive oil with some chopped thyme and chives over low heat for a few minutes. Pour the herb-infused oil over the ravioli, sprinkle with some freshly grated mild pecorino and serve.

20 g butter
1 clove garlic, finely chopped
handful of flat-leaf parsley leaves, chopped
1 pork and fennel sausage, skin removed
1 teaspoon tomato paste
200 g potatoes, boiled and mashed
50 g ricotta
1 tablespoon rosemary leaves, finely chopped
1 egg
40 g freshly grated parmesan
a few gratings of nutmeg
sea salt and freshly ground black pepper

Melt the butter in a non-stick frying pan over low heat, add the garlic and parsley and cook for about 1 minute, stirring with a wooden spoon. Add the sausage, break it up with the wooden spoon and cook until browned all over. Stir in the tomato paste, then transfer to a bowl. Add the mashed potatoes and remaining ingredients to the bowl, season to taste with salt and pepper and mix thoroughly.

RICOTTA, PROSCIUTTO AND MOZZARELLA

A fresh tomato and basil sauce (see page 51) will bring out the sunshine of Naples in this ravioli *alla moda di Napoli*.

200 g ricotta
1 egg
50 g freshly grated parmesan
handful of flat-leaf parsley leaves, finely chopped
100 g prosciutto, finely diced
200 g fior di latte mozzarella, cubed
sea salt and freshly ground black pepper

Place the ricotta and egg in a bowl and mix well. Add the remaining ingredients, season to taste with salt and pepper and mix thoroughly.

ZUCCHINI

A simple tomato and basil sauce (see page 51) goes well with zucchini ravioli.

20 g butter
a few drops of extra virgin olive oil
200 g zucchini (courgettes), thinly sliced
sea salt and freshly ground black pepper
150 g ricotta
60 g freshly grated parmesan
a few gratings of nutmeg
1 tablespoon marjoram leaves, finely chopped

Heat the butter and the olive oil in a non-stick frying pan over medium heat and sauté the zucchini until soft, seasoning with salt and pepper to taste. Place the zucchini in a bowl and mash, then add the ricotta, parmesan, nutmeg and marjoram. Mix thoroughly.

MUSHROOM

For extra flavour, use porcini pasta (see page 14) to make your mushroom ravioli.

100 ml extra virgin olive oil
2 cloves garlic, peeled and lightly squashed
600 g mixed mushrooms, chopped
sea salt and freshly ground black pepper
80 g freshly grated parmesan
100 g bechamel sauce (see page 62)
1 egg

Heat the olive oil in a heavy-based frying pan over medium heat, add the garlic and stir with a wooden spoon until it just starts to colour. Add the mushrooms, turn up the heat to medium–high and sauté for 2 minutes, then remove and discard the garlic.

Season the mushrooms with salt and pepper to taste and cook over low–medium heat for about 10 minutes, stirring often. Allow the mushrooms to cool a little, then transfer to a bowl and add the parmesan, bechamel sauce and egg. Mix thoroughly with a wooden spoon to amalgamate.

ASPARAGUS

This delicate filling makes lovely small ravioli – serve in a light chicken broth scented with saffron, perhaps with a few whole asparagus spears as a garnish. You can use the rest of the asparagus spears in a soup or risotto.

200 g asparagus tips
100 g ricotta
150 g freshly grated parmesan
1 egg
1 tablespoon marjoram leaves, finely chopped
sea salt and freshly ground black pepper

Blanch the asparagus tips in boiling water until tender. Refresh in iced water, then drain and place in a bowl. Mash the asparagus with a fork. Add the ricotta, parmesan, egg and marjoram, season to taste with salt and pepper, then mix thoroughly.

ARTICHOKE

Artichoke ravioli are lovely with melted butter, thinly sliced sautéed leeks and parmesan, or served the Ligurian way, with walnut sauce (see page 221). They also go with seafood, prawns or cuttlefish.

4 artichokes
½ lemon
20 ml extra virgin olive oil
sea salt and freshly ground black pepper
1 tablespoon mint leaves, chopped
100 g ricotta
2 eggs
60 g freshly grated parmesan
2 tablespoons breadcrumbs

To prepare the artichokes, peel off and discard the outer leaves until you reach the tender yellow leaves inside. Cut off and discard the top two-thirds of the leaves and the stems. Hold each artichoke in your hand and, using a sharp knife, scrape out the hairy choke from the inside. Cut each artichoke into quarters then place in a bowl of cold water acidulated with lemon juice.

Bring a saucepan of salted water to the boil and cook the artichokes until tender, about 10–15 minutes, then drain well. Heat the olive oil in a non-stick frying pan over medium heat, add the artichokes and season with salt and pepper. Pan-fry the artichokes for about 1 minute, then remove and chop finely. Place in a bowl, add the remaining ingredients and mix thoroughly with a wooden spoon.

MAKING FILLED PASTA

The shape of your pasta parcels really comes down to your own personal preference: they can be square, round, rectangular, crescent, oval, triangular, diamond-shaped or even shaped like hats, rings or moneybags. Their names vary according to the type of filling, their region of origin and their size, such that it would be almost impossible to classify all the filled pastas available around Italy. Sometimes it seems to me that some of the shapes were invented by mothers-in-law purely to make life difficult for the wives of their sons!

When making any filled pasta, the dough must be as thin and elastic as possible. Roll out the pasta dough into very thin sheets (see pages 17–18), then place the filling on the pasta in evenly spaced mounds. Brush the exposed edges of the pasta with a little water or beaten egg to help it stick together. Use your fingers to gently push out any air around the filling (air bubbles will expand during cooking and can cause the pasta parcels to explode), then seal all the edges securely. Lay the filled pasta on floured tea towels, making sure they do not touch each other, and sprinkle lightly with more flour.

FAZZOLETTI PIEGATI

The name means 'handkerchiefs', and these are one of the simplest forms of filled pasta. Roll out the pasta dough into very thin sheets (see pages 17–18). Lay out a pasta sheet on a lightly floured work surface. Cut the pasta into 7.5 cm squares and then diagonally into two triangles. Liberally sprinkle your freshly chopped herb of choice and parmesan over one half of each triangle and then fold it over on itself, sealing the edges well with a fork.

FAGOTTINI

Roll out the pasta dough into very thin sheets (see pages 17–18). Lay out a pasta sheet on a lightly floured work surface and cut it into 4 cm squares. Place a teaspoon of filling in the centre of each square. Brush a little water on the exposed pasta and, using the fingers of both hands, gather up the sides around the filling to create a little purse or moneybag. Squeeze the sides together well, so that the filling is totally enclosed. You may have to experiment a couple of times to get just the right amount of filling in proportion to the pasta squares.

RAVIOLI

Although there is a special tool called a ravioli maker or plaque that you can use to make uniform ravioli (it looks rather like an ice tray), I think it's quicker and easier to make them by hand, once you get the hang of it. Roll out the pasta dough into two very thin sheets (see pages 17–18), each roughly the same size and shape. Lay out one of the pasta sheets on a lightly floured work surface. Place teaspoons of the filling 3–4 cm apart in rows on the pasta, leaving 2 cm at the edge of the pasta sheet. Carefully brush a little water or beaten egg onto the pasta around each mound of filling. Lay the second sheet of pasta over the first and gently, using your fingers, press down on the sheet around the mounds of filling, pushing out any air that may have been trapped. Cut out the ravioli using a ravioli cutter or sharp knife (or the rim of a glass for round ravioli) and finish each one with a final press of your fingers to seal it around the edges.

TORTELLI

Roll out the pasta dough into very thin sheets (see pages 17–18). Lay out a pasta sheet on a lightly floured work surface. Using a round ravioli cutter or a glass, cut the pasta sheet into circles about 7.5 cm in diameter. Place a teaspoon of the filling on one side of each pasta circle, lightly brush the edges with water, then fold over to make a half-moon shape, pushing out any trapped air and crimping the edges with a fork.

TORTELLINI

Roll out the pasta dough into very thin sheets (see pages 17–18). Lay out a pasta sheet on a lightly floured work surface and cut it into 6 cm squares. Place a teaspoon of filling in the centre of each square. Carefully brush a little water onto the pasta around the filling, then take one corner of each square and fold it over the filling to form a triangle. Seal the edges with your fingers, making sure to expel any trapped air. Fold the tip of each triangle back over, so that the point extends slightly past the base of the triangle. Now fold the other two points behind the filling and around your finger so that they overlap each other. Squish them together to make a ring around the filling.

FAGOTTINI AL FORMAGGIO

The word *fagottino* means 'a little bundle' – of the kind ancient travellers might have carried with them, having wrapped a few possessions in a scarf, knotted it on a stick and put the stick over their shoulder. In this case we're making bundles of cheese and herbs, pinching each parcel together at the top. The use of ricotta, gorgonzola and butter marks this dish as one from the far north of Italy, close to the border with Switzerland, and its richness makes it ideally suited to the harsh Alpine winters.

400 g basic pasta dough (see page 11)
80 g butter
handful of basil leaves, chopped
1 clove garlic, finely chopped
80 g freshly grated parmesan
freshly ground black pepper

FILLING

1 egg
100 g ricotta
100 g freshly grated parmesan
100 g gorgonzola dolcelatte, diced
1 teaspoon each of finely chopped thyme,
    basil and flat-leaf parsley

SERVES 4

To make the filling, whisk the egg in a bowl, then add the cheeses and mix well. When you have a homogenous mixture, stir in the herbs. Set aside.

Roll out the pasta dough into very thin sheets (see pages 17–18). Lay out a pasta sheet on a lightly floured work surface and cut into 4 cm squares. Place a teaspoon of filling in the centre of each square. Brush a little water on the exposed pasta and, using the fingers of both hands, gather up the sides around the filling to create a little purse or moneybag. Squeeze the sides together well, so that the filling is totally enclosed. You may have to experiment a couple of times to get just the right amount of filling in proportion to the pasta squares. Leave the fagottini to rest on floured tea towels for 30 minutes, making sure they do not touch each other.

When you are almost ready to serve, melt the butter in a non-stick frying pan, then add the basil and garlic. Cook over medium heat until the butter is very, very hot and foaming, and the garlic is about to change colour, but do not let it burn. Remove from the heat.

Place four serving plates near your stovetop and sprinkle 1 tablespoon of the parmesan over each plate. Cook the pasta parcels in plenty of boiling salted water for 5 minutes, then lift out using a slotted spoon and divide among the plates. Pour some of the butter over each one, then sprinkle with pepper and the remaining parmesan. Serve these little wonders hot.

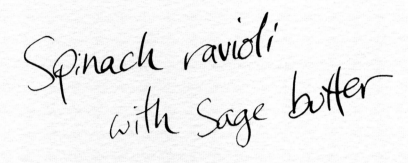
Spinach ravioli with Sage butter

RAVIOLI DI MAGRO AL BURRO E SALVIA

The use of aromatic herbs (in this case, sage) is attributed to the fact that sailors returning home after long stints at sea craved the perfume of the Ligurian hillsides, as well as fresh vegetables (in this case, spinach).

400 g basic pasta dough (see page 11)
60 g butter
20 sage leaves
3–4 tablespoons freshly grated parmesan

FILLING

500 g spinach leaves
3 eggs
4 tablespoons freshly grated parmesan
100 g ricotta
a few gratings of nutmeg
sea salt and freshly ground black pepper

SERVES 4

To make the filling, wash the spinach, then toss in a large pan over medium heat and wilt in only the water left clinging to the leaves – this should only take a few minutes. Squeeze dry and chop finely. Break the eggs into a bowl and beat lightly. Add the spinach, parmesan, ricotta and nutmeg. Season with salt and pepper and mix with a wooden spoon until everything is properly amalgamated.

Make the ravioli following the instructions on page 217, using the filling you have just made. Leave the ravioli to rest on floured tea towels for 30 minutes, making sure they do not touch each other.

When you are nearly ready to serve, melt the butter in a large non-stick frying pan over low heat with about half of the sage leaves. Meanwhile, cook the ravioli a few at a time in plenty of boiling salted water for 3–4 minutes. Lift out using a slotted spoon and transfer to the frying pan. When all the ravioli are cooked, add the rest of the sage leaves and the parmesan, then toss gently for a minute or so. The sauce should not be too dry – if you think it needs a little more butter, add it to the pan now. (You can also add more parmesan, if you like.) Place the ravioli on a platter and serve immediately.

Pansotti with walnut sauce

PANSOTTI ALLA SALSA DI NOCI

The word pansotti is derived from *pancia*, which means 'belly' – and these pasta parcels live up to the name, being plump and well-rounded. They come in many different shapes, from square to round to rectangular, from tortellini parcels to half-moons; as long as they honour the name and are fat, they may be called pansotti. The traditional filling was *preboggion*, a selection of wild greens that is also called *erbi*. Because it can be difficult, even in Italy, to get hold of these greens, and because they have a short season, the version given here is made with silverbeet. The walnut sauce is an ancient recipe that has become gentler over the years, losing some of the strength of its garlic flavour – but, in true Ligurian style, it is still thickened with white bread.

400 g basic pasta dough (see page 11)
1 egg, lightly beaten
60 g butter
freshly grated parmesan, to serve
marjoram leaves, to garnish (optional)

SAUCE

20 walnut kernels (about 250 g),
    from about 1 kg walnuts in the shell
2 slices Italian bread (about 50 g),
    crusts removed
3 tablespoons milk
30 g pine nuts
1 clove garlic
75 g ricotta
45 ml extra virgin olive oil
1 tablespoon marjoram leaves,
    finely chopped
sea salt

FILLING

800 g silverbeet
60 g freshly grated parmesan
100 g ricotta
2 eggs
1 tablespoon chopped marjoram
3 teaspoons extra virgin olive oil
freshly grated nutmeg
sea salt and freshly ground black pepper

SERVES 4

To prepare the sauce, blanch the walnut kernels in a small saucepan of boiling water for a few seconds, then drain and peel off the papery skins. Using a mortar and pestle, pound the walnut kernels a few at a time to a coarse paste. Briefly soak the bread in the milk and squeeze it out, then add it to the mortar with the walnuts and pound. Add the pine nuts and garlic and keep pounding until you achieve a homogenous paste. Transfer the paste to a bowl, add the ricotta and mix with a spoon to amalgamate. Add the olive oil and the marjoram, season to taste with salt and pepper and mix well. Set aside.

Next, prepare the filling. Remove the white stalks from the silverbeet and wash the leaves. Place the silverbeet in a large pan and cook with only the water clinging to the leaves until soft and wilted, about 3 minutes. When the silverbeet is cool enough to handle, squeeze it dry and chop finely. Transfer to a bowl and add the parmesan, ricotta, eggs, marjoram, olive oil, a few gratings of nutmeg and a generous pinch of salt. Mix thoroughly.

Now make the pansotti. Roll out the pasta dough into two very thin sheets (see pages 17–18), each roughly the same size and shape. Lay one pasta sheet on a lightly floured work surface and brush with the beaten egg. Place tablespoons of the filling 3–4 cm apart in rows on the pasta, leaving 2 cm at the edge of the pasta sheet. Place the second sheet of pasta on top of the first and, using your fingers, press gently around each mound of filling, taking care not to leave any air bubbles inside. Use a glass to press over each mound and cut out round pansotti, finishing each one with a final press of your fingers to seal the edges well. Leave the pansottti to rest on floured tea towels for 30 minutes, making sure they do not touch each other.

Cook the pansotti in plenty of boiling water for 3–4 minutes. Meanwhile, melt the butter and transfer it to a large bowl. When the pansotti are ready, lift them out using a slotted spoon and transfer them to the bowl with the melted butter. Sprinkle with some of the parmesan and toss delicately. Add the walnut sauce and toss again. (Never heat the walnut sauce, or its fragrance will be lost.)

Place the pansotti on a platter or individual plates and sprinkle with some more parmesan before serving. Garnish with fresh marjoram leaves, if you like.

Beetroot ravioli

CASUNZIEI

Casunziei are half-moon-shaped ravioli which come from the beautiful town of Cortina d'Ampezzo in the Dolomite mountains of northern Italy. We've made them round here, because we like the way the pink shows through the fine pasta in a sort of . . . full moon. They are simply dressed with butter, poppy seeds and pecorino. This way of serving ravioli is sometimes called *a culo nudo* ('with naked bottom'), because there is no sauce underneath them.

80 g butter
1 tablespoon poppy seeds,
    lightly crushed in a mortar
60 g freshly grated aged pecorino

PASTA

400 g plain flour
2 eggs
125 ml milk
pinch of salt

FILLING

600 g beetroot
40 g butter
1–2 tablespoons breadcrumbs
100 g smoked or baked ricotta
1 egg
a few gratings of nutmeg
sea salt and freshly ground black pepper

SERVES 4

Prepare the pasta dough following the instructions on page 11, but using the quantities and ingredients given here. While the pasta dough is resting, prepare the filling.

For the filling, peel and roughly dice the beetroot. Boil in salted water for about 10–15 minutes until very soft, then drain and mash with a fork. Melt the butter in a non-stick frying pan over medium heat. Add 1 tablespoon of the breadcrumbs and let them colour a little, then add the beetroot and cook for about 5 minutes to reduce any excess moisture, stirring with a wooden spoon. Place the beetroot in a bowl with the ricotta, the egg and a generous amount of nutmeg, and season with salt and pepper. Mix thoroughly – if the filling seems too soft, add some more breadcrumbs. Let the filling rest and firm up while you roll out the pasta.

Roll out the pasta dough into very thin sheets (see pages 17–18). Lay out a sheet of pasta on a lightly floured work surface, then cut into circles about 5 cm in diameter using a fluted ravioli cutter or biscuit cutter. Place 2 teaspoons of filling in the centre of half of the circles, brush the edges of the pasta with a little water and place another pasta circle on top. Be sure to expel any air, then seal by pressing the edges together. Leave the ravioli to rest on floured tea towels for 30 minutes, making sure they do not touch each other.

Cook the casunziei in plenty of boiling salted water for 3–5 minutes – they're ready when they rise to the surface. Meanwhile, melt the butter with the poppy seeds in a non-stick frying pan over medium heat until the butter is very hot and foaming, but do not let it burn. Lift out the casunziei using a slotted spoon and place on warm serving plates. Sprinkle with the pecorino and dress with the melted butter and poppy seeds. Serve immediately.

Pumpkin tortelli

TORTELLI DI ZUCCA

From the region of Lombardy in northern Italy, and particularly from the plains south of Milano towards Emilia-Romagna, come the most unusual tortelli filled with pumpkin, amaretti and mustard fruits (fruits preserved in sugar and mustard). The result is a fantastic flavour somewhere between sweet, salty and spicy (but not sweet and sour), where the sweetness is balanced by the saltiness of the parmesan and the spiciness of the nutmeg, not by sour ingredients such as lemon or vinegar. For the sauce we use only butter and parmesan, not even sage, so that the flavours of the filling are not contaminated.

100 g freshly grated parmesan
80 g butter

PASTA

400 g plain flour
4 eggs
1 tablespoon milk
pinch of salt

FILLING

1 kg pumpkin
1 tablespoon extra virgin olive oil
sea salt
100 g amaretti biscuits, coarsely crushed
100 g mustard apple (if unavailable, use
    mixed mustard fruits), chopped
100 g sultanas, finely chopped
100 g freshly grated parmesan
freshly grated nutmeg

SERVES 4

Start by making the pasta dough (see page 11), but use the quantities given here. While the dough is resting, prepare the filling.

Preheat the oven to 180°C. Cut the pumpkin into wedges, leaving the skin on and removing the seeds. Rub with a little olive oil and sprinkle with salt and place on a baking tray. Roast for 30–40 minutes until tender. When the pumpkin is cool enough to handle, scrape the flesh into a bowl and mash it. Add the amaretti biscuits, mustard apple, sultanas, parmesan and a few gratings of nutmeg. Mix well, then set aside to cool.

Make the tortelli following the instructions on page 217, using the filling you have just made. Leave them to rest on floured tea towels for 30 minutes, making sure they do not touch each other.

Sprinkle a ceramic serving dish with half the parmesan, and place it near the stovetop. Cook the tortelli in plenty of boiling salted water for about 4 minutes.

Meanwhile, melt the butter in a non-stick frying pan over medium heat until very hot, being careful not to burn it. Lift out the tortelli using a slotted spoon and place in the serving dish. Sprinkle with the rest of the parmesan and pour the melted butter on top. If you have more than one layer of tortelli in the dish, make sure each layer is sprinkled with parmesan and dressed with the butter. Serve immediately.

CULINGIONES

Culingiones are an ancient dish that is present all over the island of Sardinia, although with different names and shapes. Unlike ravioli from the north of Italy, Mediterranean ravioli are not a winter dish. Different types of vegetables (zucchini, eggplant, capsicum) or spicy salami are used for the filling, always with a ricotta or other soft cheese. The flour used is semolina, not the plain flour of the north, and the ravioli are often eaten with a heavy and spicy meat ragù.

The pecorino used in this filling must be very fresh; you may have some difficulty finding one soft enough – if so, you can always grate the pecorino for the filling. In some parts of Sardinia fresh mint is added to the filling, which I think is very appropriate.

400 g basic pasta dough (see page 11)
1 quantity tomato sauce I (see page 51)
60 g freshly grated pecorino

FILLING

300 g silverbeet
1 teaspoon butter
400 g very fresh pecorino cheese at room
    temperature, crust removed
3 eggs
pinch of saffron threads, lightly crushed
    in a mortar
5 mint leaves, finely chopped
freshly grated nutmeg
sea salt and freshly ground black pepper
1 small boiled potato, crushed with a fork

SERVES 4

To make the filling, remove and discard the white stalks from the silverbeet. Wash the leaves and chop them finely, then transfer to a saucepan and let them wilt over low heat in just the water clinging to the leaves – this should only take a few minutes. Squeeze dry and place in a non-stick frying pan over medium heat with the butter. Cook for a few minutes to get rid of any excess moisture.

Using your hands, work the pecorino in a bowl until creamy, then add the silverbeet, eggs, saffron, mint, a few gratings of nutmeg and some salt and pepper. Mix thoroughly. If the filling seems too moist and soft, work in some of the potato.

Roll out the pasta dough into thin sheets (see pages 17–18), then cut into 8 cm × 4 cm rectangles. Place a generous teaspoon of filling in the middle of each rectangle, lightly brush the edges with water, then fold it like a book, pushing out any trapped air and sealing well by pressing with a fork. Leave the ravioli to rest on floured tea towels for 30 minutes, making sure they do not touch each other.

Gently heat the tomato sauce over low heat. Cook the ravioli in plenty of boiling salted water for 4 minutes. Lift out using a slotted spoon and place on a flat serving dish. Sprinkle with the grated pecorino and dress with the tomato sauce. If you have more than one layer of ravioli in the serving dish, make sure each layer is sprinkled with pecorino and dressed with tomato sauce.

Duck egg ravioli

RAVIOLI CON UOVA D'ANATRA

This is a spectacular creation from Logan Campbell, executive chef at Lucio's. Here's what he says about it: 'This dish is a play on some classic flavours – eggs, asparagus and truffles. The wild mushrooms are there to augment the truffle's earthy flavour, but any kind of cultivated mushrooms will do the trick.'

It's an exhilarating experience to cut into the top of the ravioli and see the runny egg yolk ooze out. Although this recipe uses only the tender tips of the asparagus, you can use the rest of the asparagus spears in a soup or risotto. And if you can't find truffles, you could try replacing them with dried porcini that have been soaked in warm water for 20 minutes, then sliced.

100 ml extra virgin olive oil, plus extra
    to serve
1 onion, finely diced
2 cloves garlic, finely diced
1 bunch thyme, leaves picked
500 g pine mushrooms, chopped
500 g slippery jacks, chopped
250 g chestnut mushrooms, chopped
sea salt and freshly ground black pepper
4 duck eggs
400 g basic pasta dough (see page 11)
12 asparagus spears, tips only
100 g freshly shaved parmesan
1 black truffle (optional)

SERVES 4

In a large frying pan, heat the olive oil until it shimmers. Add the onion, garlic and thyme, and sauté for 3 minutes. Add all the mushrooms, season with salt and pepper to taste and cook for 20–30 minutes, stirring regularly, until all the moisture has evaporated. Remove from the heat and allow to cool.

Separate the duck eggs, being careful not to break the yolks. Lightly whisk the egg whites, just to break them up.

Roll out the pasta dough into two very thin sheets (see pages 17–18), each roughly the same size and shape. Lay one pasta sheet on a lightly floured work surface and brush with egg white. Divide the mushroom filling into quarters, then place each quarter in a mound on the pasta sheet, spacing them evenly. Make a well in each mound of mushroom filling, then carefully place an egg yolk in each well. Gently cover with the other sheet of pasta, pressing around the edges to seal, and cut out the four large round ravioli with a ravioli cutter or a sharp knife. Leave the ravioli to rest on floured tea towels for 30 minutes, making sure they do not touch each other.

Cook the ravioli in plenty of boiling salted water for 3 minutes, adding the asparagus after 2 minutes. Carefully drain the ravioli and asparagus, then toss gently in a bowl with a little olive oil and seasoning. Finish with the shaved parmesan and truffle, if using.

RAVIOLI DI PATATE E PANCETTA

This may seem like an exotic dish, with the sweet warmth and fragrance of cinnamon, but this spice has been a part of Italian cooking for more than 2000 years. Originally native to Sri Lanka, cinnamon was brought to Rome by Phoenician spice traders, who in turn had been introduced to it by Indonesian spice traders. It became highly esteemed: the Emperor Nero is said to have shown how much he loved his wife Poppaea by burning a year's worth of Rome's cinnamon supplies at her funeral. By the fourteenth century, Venice had the monopoly on the cinnamon trade in Europe, with Venetian traders travelling to Alexandria and buying up all the supplies coming from the Middle East. Nowadays, of course, you can simply pick it up in the supermarket.

400 g basic pasta dough (see page 11)
100 g butter
½ teaspoon ground cinnamon
1 teaspoon poppy seeds
60 g freshly shaved parmesan

FILLING

400 g potatoes, peeled and cut into chunks
40 ml extra virgin olive oil
1 onion, finely diced
100 g pancetta or bacon, finely diced
2 egg yolks
50 g freshly grated parmesan
large handful of flat-leaf parsley
    leaves, chopped

SERVES 4

To make the filling, place the potato in a saucepan, cover with water and boil until cooked, about 10–15 minutes. Drain and mash. Wipe out the saucepan, then add the olive oil and place over medium heat. Add the onion and pancetta and sauté for about 10 minutes. Tip into the bowl with the mashed potato, mix well then leave to cool completely before stirring in the egg yolks, parmesan and parsley.

Make the ravioli following the instructions on page 217, using the filling you have just made. Leave the ravioli to rest on floured tea towels for 30 minutes, making sure they do not touch each other.

Cook the ravioli in plenty of boiling salted water for 3–4 minutes, slipping them gently into the water.

Meanwhile, place a large frying pan over low heat and melt the butter, then add the cinnamon and poppy seeds. Lift out the ravioli using a slotted spoon and add to the frying pan, tossing gently. Serve immediately with the shaved parmesan.

Sausage ravioli

CASONSEI

Typical of the north-east of Italy, close to the Austrian border, casonsei come in different shapes and have different fillings and different names, even though they are all basically very similar. Most of the names come from dialects and some are not even in Italian. We've included a couple of these: casunziei (see page 222) and this one, from the town of Brescia in Lombardy. Traditionally, these ravioli are considered so important that they are never missing from the menu for an important occasion. The filling is very simple – just sausages, stale bread and parmesan (not even an egg) – but of course every family has their own recipe.

400 g basic pasta dough (see page 11)
80 g butter
10–15 sage leaves
80 g freshly grated parmesan

FILLING

100 g stale Italian bread, crusts removed
60 ml milk
200 g pork and fennel sausages,
    skin removed
100 g freshly grated parmesan
sea salt

SERVES 4

To make the filling, soak the bread in the milk for a few minutes and then, using your hands, squeeze it dry and break it up. Place the bread in a bowl and add the sausage and parmesan. Mix thoroughly with your hands, then season to taste with salt and set aside.

Roll out the pasta dough into very thin sheets (see pages 17–18). Lay out a pasta sheet on a lightly floured work surface then, using a fluted ravioli cutter or pastry wheel, cut into 10 cm × 6 cm rectangles. Place a teaspoon of the filling in the centre of each rectangle and fold the pasta over to the longer side so it measures 10 cm × 3 cm. Press the open sides together to seal, being careful to expel any air around the filling. Now, to form the classic casonsei shape, very carefully stretch the two ends towards the centre to form a semi-circle or horseshoe. Leave the casonsei to rest on floured tea towels for 30 minutes, making sure they do not touch each other.

Cook the casonsei in plenty of boiling salted water for 6 minutes.

Meanwhile, melt the butter with the sage leaves in a small frying pan until the butter is very hot, but be careful not to burn it. Have a large, flat serving dish ready. Sprinkle the bottom of the dish with 2 tablespoons of the parmesan.

Lift out the pasta using a slotted spoon and place in the dish. Dress with the hot melted butter and the sage, then sprinkle with the rest of the parmesan and serve hot.

Beef and pork ravioli

TORDEI

Tordei is dialect in my neighbourhood in Italy for round ravioli, which the rest of Italy calls tortelli. Here's a brief language lesson: the base word is *torta* (a kind of savoury pie), and from this we derive *tortello* for a small pie that you'd toss in a sauce, and *tortellino* for an even smaller pie served in broth. Over time, these same words came to be applied to filled pasta. Tortelli pasta parcels were first described in Italian food writing of the Middle Ages, usually stuffed with vegetables. This recipe is for feast days, extravagantly stuffing the tortelli with meat and serving them with a meat sauce.

400 g basic pasta dough (see page 11)
80 g freshly grated parmesan

SAUCE

1 small onion
1 clove garlic
5 sage leaves
few sprigs of rosemary, leaves picked
100 ml extra virgin olive oil
300 g minced beef
250 g tomatoes, peeled and seeded
   (see page 51), then diced
250 ml stock

FILLING

1 bunch silverbeet (Swiss chard)
200 g spinach leaves
3 tablespoons extra virgin olive oil
sea salt and freshly ground black pepper
handful of breadcrumbs
5 eggs, lightly beaten
200 g freshly grated parmesan
few gratings of nutmeg
1 tablespoon thyme leaves
1 clove garlic
handful each of chopped parsley, sage
   and rosemary
150 g minced beef
150 g minced pork or veal
100 g tomatoes, peeled and seeded
   (see page 51), then diced
125 ml stock

SERVES 4

For the sauce, chop the onion, garlic, sage and rosemary together finely. Heat the olive oil in a deep pan over medium heat and fry the onion and herb mixture until the garlic starts to colour. Add the beef and fry for 10 minutes until the meat is browned. Stir in the tomato and stock, then reduce the heat and simmer for 1½ hours, adding water as necessary.

For the filling, remove and discard the white stalks from the silverbeet. Wash the silverbeet and spinach and blanch in boiling water for 2 minutes. Drain, squeeze dry and chop finely. Heat 1 tablespoon of the olive oil in a large frying pan and sauté the greens with a little salt and pepper for 3 minutes. Transfer to a bowl and add the breadcrumbs, eggs, parmesan, nutmeg, a pinch of salt and the thyme. Mix well and set aside. Wipe out the frying pan. Chop the garlic, parsley, sage and rosemary and add to the pan with the remaining oil over medium heat. When the garlic starts to change colour, add the meats and cook for 10 minutes, stirring often to make sure all the meat is browned. Add the tomato and stock and simmer for 15 minutes. Remove from the heat and leave to cool, then add to the spinach mixture and mix well.

Make the tortelli following the instructions on page 217, using the filling you have just made. Leave them to rest on floured tea towels for 30 minutes, making sure they do not touch each other.

Cook the tortelli in plenty of boiling salted water for 7–8 minutes, slipping them into the water very delicately. Carefully lift out using a slotted spoon and arrange in a serving dish, dressing each layer with the sauce and plenty of parmesan. Serve immediately.

RAVIOLI DI CARNE AL TOCCO DI CARNE

What a plate of ravioli! This dish is the pride of the countryside and hills of Liguria – and a favourite of our family when I was growing up. My mother made these ravioli often, but particularly for special events in the fields, such as the wheat harvest or the cutting of the hay, when all my father's older brothers would come to lend a hand. My mother knew she had a critical audience, and she always delighted in watching the surprised faces of her brothers-in-law as they tasted just how good her ravioli were. So, do try them, and you will know what I mean.

1 quantity Ligurian meat sauce
   (see page 55)

PASTA

300 g plain flour
2 eggs at room temperature
45 ml warm water

FILLING

45 ml extra virgin olive oil
1 clove garlic, finely chopped
1 tablespoon finely chopped flat-leaf parsley
200 g minced beef
200 g minced pork (or minced pork sausage)
sea salt
200 g silverbeet (Swiss chard)
2 thick slices Italian bread (about 50–60 g),
   crusts removed, torn into pieces
50 g mortadella, finely chopped
4 eggs
a few gratings of nutmeg
freshly ground black pepper
120 g freshly grated parmesan

SERVES 4

Make the pasta dough following the instructions on page 11, but using the ingredients given here.

For the filling, heat the olive oil in a heavy-based frying pan over low heat and fry the garlic and parsley for 3 minutes, mixing with a wooden spoon. Add the minced meats and sprinkle with salt. Mix thoroughly and brown for 10 minutes, stirring frequently.

Remove and discard the white stalks from the silverbeet leaves. Wash the leaves and chop them finely, then transfer to a hot saucepan and let them wilt over low heat in just the water clinging to them – this should only take a few minutes. Wrap the silverbeet in a tea towel and squeeze out the moisture, then chop finely.

Dip the bread in the Ligurian meat sauce then transfer to a large bowl. Add the silverbeet, mortadella, eggs and nutmeg and mix thoroughly. Season with salt and pepper, then add the meat and 45 g of the parmesan. Mix well to amalgamate and set aside.

Make the ravioli following the instructions on page 217, using the filling you have just made. Leave the ravioli to rest on floured tea towels for 30 minutes, making sure they do not touch each other.

If you've made the Ligurian meat sauce in advance, gently reheat it, then spread some sauce over the bottom of a serving dish. Cook the ravioli in plenty of boiling salted water for 4–5 minutes. Lift out using a slotted spoon and transfer to the serving dish. Cover with the rest of the sauce, sprinkle the remaining parmesan on top, and serve immediately.

Tortellini with peas, ham and cream

TORTELLINI TRE P

200 g fresh or frozen peas
30 g butter
100 g ham, cut into 1 cm cubes
½ white onion, very finely chopped
200 ml cream or crème fraîche
sea salt and freshly ground black pepper
400 g tortellini
80 g freshly grated parmesan

SERVES 4

Tortellini with cream and cheese is an Italian classic that is known all over the world. This version, with ham and peas, featured on the first menu at my Paddington restaurant in 1983. We called it *tortellini tre p* because, in Italian, peas (*piselli*), ham (*prosciutto*) and cream (*panna*) all start with the letter 'p', and it was a big seller – a sign of the times.

For this dish, bought tortellini generally stands up better to being tossed with the sauce. If you decide to make your own tortellini (see page 217), be sure to handle it very delicately.

Cook the peas in a small saucepan of boiling salted water until tender, about 3–5 minutes. Drain and set aside.

Melt the butter in a non-stick frying pan over medium heat, then add the ham and cook for 2–3 minutes. Add the onion and cook until soft and translucent (about 5–6 minutes), stirring with a wooden spoon. Add the peas and cream, season with salt and pepper, mix thoroughly and simmer for about 5–7 minutes or until reduced to a coating consistency.

Meanwhile, cook the tortellini in plenty of boiling salted water for 4 minutes or as directed on the packet. Drain, then add to the sauce and toss gently. Serve hot, sprinkled with the parmesan.

Black ravioli filled with snapper and prawns

RAVIOLI NERI DI GAMBERI E PESCE

400 g black pasta dough (see page 14)

FILLING

200 g raw prawns, peeled and deveined
200 g snapper fillets, cleaned
50 ml cream
sea salt and freshly ground black pepper

SAUCE

100 ml fish stock
50 g butter
3 tomatoes, peeled and seeded
    (see page 51), then diced

SERVES 4

Technology buffs tell me that 'black ravioli' has been adopted as the name of a kind of padding that enhances the sound of a stereo system. But for me, the name conjures up only a vision of glistening pasta parcels. They are best stuffed with a mixture of fresh snapper and prawns that has not been cooked beforehand, so you get a burst of flavour when you bite into the parcels. That's all the music I need.

For the filling, mince the prawns and snapper together. Add the cream, season with salt and pepper to taste, and mix well.

Make the ravioli following the instructions on page 217, using the filling you have just made. Leave the ravioli to rest on floured tea towels for 30 minutes, making sure they do not touch each other.

Cook the ravioli in plenty of boiling salted water for 3–4 minutes, slipping them into the water very delicately.

While the ravioli are cooking, make the sauce. Combine the fish stock, butter and tomato in a frying pan and cook over high heat until reduced by half.

Carefully lift out the ravioli using a slotted spoon and place in the frying pan. Toss well to coat, then serve immediately.

Baked pasta

In Italy, baked pasta (*pasta al forno*) does not mean only lasagne or cannelloni. There are many dishes, made with dried or fresh pasta, that can be finished in the oven, and every region has its specialities.

In fact, baked pasta seems to have been the first kind of pasta made in Italy. The Romans (the rich ones, at least) liked to roll out sheets of dough, cut them into wide strips, then layer them with meat sauce and cheese, and bake them in the oven. They called these dishes *lagana*, and we can see how little the word – and the recipe – has changed over time.

Nowadays baked pastas are usually made on festive days or special occasions such as weddings. They range from a very simple *pasta gratinata*, where pasta is tossed, placed in a baking dish with or without bechamel, sprinkled with parmesan and placed under the grill. Then there is the *timballo*, where pasta and sauces are layered in an oven dish, each layer being finished with cheese (parmesan or mozzarella), and then baked. But the ultimate baked pasta dish would have to be *timpano*, where a large baking dish is first layered with pastry or grilled eggplant, then filled with pasta and very substantial sauces containing meatballs, sausages, salami and cheeses, which are then covered with more layers of pastry or eggplant and baked. The result is a wonderful cake-style layered dish, which is carefully sliced and eaten with as much passion as it takes to make it.

TAGLIATELLE AL FORNO CON ASPARAGI BIANCHI

Simple and delicious, this plate of pasta is complemented by the addition of ricotta and the few minutes' baking, which infuses the beautiful white asparagus with the flavours of all the other ingredients. It's like that extra cuddle!

400 g basic pasta dough (see page 11)
40 ml extra virgin olive oil
300 g white asparagus
200 g ricotta
2 eggs
a few gratings of nutmeg
sea salt and freshly ground black pepper
50 g butter
1 small white onion, finely chopped
leaves from 3 sprigs marjoram
80 g freshly grated parmesan

SERVES 4

Cut the pasta dough into tagliatelle following the instructions on page 20. Lay the pasta on lightly floured tea towels while you make the sauce.

Preheat the oven to 180°C. Brush the bottom and sides of a baking dish with a little of the olive oil.

Wash the asparagus under cold running water, then transfer to a pan of boiling water and cook for 4 minutes. Refresh in iced water and drain. Cut off and discard the woody bottom halves of the asparagus stalks. Cut off the tips and slice the remaining stalks into thin strips. Set the tips and sliced stalks aside.

Place the ricotta in a bowl and work it with a spoon, adding the eggs, nutmeg and a little salt and pepper, until you obtain a smooth cream.

Melt the butter with the remaining olive oil in a heavy-based non-stick pan over medium heat. Add the onion and cook for 5 minutes until soft, stirring with a wooden spoon. Throw the asparagus into the pan, then sprinkle on the marjoram and a little salt and pepper and cook for 4 minutes, stirring with the wooden spoon. Take the pan off the heat.

Cook the tagliatelle in plenty of boiling salted water for 2 minutes (they should be al dente, not soft, because they are going to be baked in the oven as well). Put the sauce back on the heat, throw in the pasta and toss for a minute, sprinkling over half the parmesan. Pour the pasta mixture into a large bowl and add the ricotta and egg mixture. Mix delicately but thoroughly.

Transfer the pasta mixture to the baking dish and sprinkle with the rest of the parmesan. Bake for 10 minutes until a golden crust appears on the surface. Serve hot.

Ricotta and mozzarella cannelloni

CANNELLONI DI RICOTTA E MOZZARELLA

Cannelloni are as versatile as lasagne and ravioli in terms of their variety of fillings and sauces. And of course, the quality of the ingredients and the thinness of the pasta are equally important to their success.

400 g basic pasta dough (see page 11)
20 g butter
250 g ricotta
150 g mozzarella, diced
1 tablespoon chopped basil
120 g freshly grated parmesan
1 quantity tomato sauce II (see page 52)
sea salt and freshly ground black pepper
extra virgin olive oil
1 quantity bechamel sauce (see page 62)

SERVES 4

Roll out the pasta dough into thin sheets (see pages 17–18) and cut into 12 cm squares. Lay the pasta on lightly floured tea towels while you make the filling.

Preheat the oven to 180°C. Grease a baking dish with the butter.

Place the ricotta, mozzarella, basil, 2 tablespoons of the parmesan and 4–5 tablespoons of the tomato sauce in a bowl. Mix thoroughly to amalgamate, seasoning to taste with salt and pepper.

Have a large bowl of iced water next to the stove. Cook the pasta in batches for 2 minutes in plenty of boiling salted water with a dash of olive oil. Drain using tongs or a large slotted spoon, then immerse the pasta in the cold water for a minute and place on tea towels to dry.

To assemble the cannelloni, divide the ricotta mixture among the pasta squares, leaving a 5 mm gap from the edge of the pasta and shaping the filling into a sausage no more than 3 cm in diameter. Moisten the far edge of the pasta square and roll from the filling towards the moistened edge.

Spread the base of the baking dish with a little tomato sauce. Place the cannelloni in the baking dish in a single layer seam-side down, so that there is no space between them. Top with the rest of the tomato sauce, then the bechamel sauce. Sprinkle over the remaining parmesan and bake for 20 minutes or until light golden. Serve hot.

Three-weed lasagne with blood orange and marjoram

LASAGNE DI VERDURE E RICOTTA CON ARANCIA E MAGGIORANA

This is a creation of Logan Campbell, executive chef at Lucio's, who warns: 'Perhaps I will not be very popular for changing what many consider the ultimate comfort food, but there is method in my madness. I made this vegetarian dish to utilise some much under-appreciated leaves, such as stinging nettles and chicory. With the addition of ricotta and a citrus sauce I hope to lift and lighten what can sometimes be an "undo my belt and sleep it off" kind of meal.'

For the photo, we made the lasagne with rounds of pasta and baked it in individual dishes, but it can also be made in a large dish and served at the table in the usual way.

400 g basic pasta dough (see page 11)

1 kg chicory

1 kg stinging nettles

500 g warrigal greens (or spinach)

800 g ricotta

finely grated zest of 1 lemon

1 egg

1 egg yolk

300 g freshly grated parmesan

1 teaspoon freshly grated nutmeg

olive oil, for greasing

1 blood orange, peeled and segmented, to garnish

1 tablespoon marjoram leaves, to garnish

SAUCE

300 ml blood orange juice (from about 4 blood oranges)

1 teaspoon good-quality red wine vinegar

200 g butter, diced

sea salt and freshly ground black pepper

SERVES 4

First make the pasta dough and, while it is resting, prepare the greens.

Bring a large saucepan of water to the boil. Pick the leaves from all the greens, making sure to wear gloves when handling the nettles. Blanch the greens for 3–4 minutes, then refresh in iced water. Drain, squeeze dry and chop finely.

In a large bowl, combine the ricotta, lemon zest, egg and egg yolk, 200 g of the parmesan and the nutmeg. Add the greens and combine well.

Grease a 30 cm × 20 cm baking dish with a little olive oil and preheat the oven to 180°C.

Roll out the pasta dough into very thin sheets (see pages 17–18), then cut into five 30 cm × 20 cm rectangles.

To assemble the lasagne, place one pasta rectangle in the bottom of the baking dish and cover with a quarter of the greens and ricotta mixture, spreading it evenly over the pasta. Continue alternating layers of pasta and greens, finishing with a pasta layer on top. Sprinkle with the remaining parmesan and bake for 15 minutes.

Meanwhile, make the sauce. In a small saucepan reduce the blood orange juice and vinegar until only 2 tablespoons remain. Turn the heat to very low and add the diced butter a little at a time, stirring constantly until all the butter has melted and the sauce looks glossy. Do not allow the sauce to simmer or boil. Remove from the heat and season with salt and pepper to taste.

Serve the lasagne on individual plates, drizzled with the sauce and garnished with the blood orange segments and marjoram leaves.

Shell pasta stuffed with eggplant

CONCHIGLIONI ALLE MELANZANE

Eggplant is a product of the south of Italy, but in any country it is a reminder of summer and the warmth of the sun. This flavourful dish, made with large pasta shells, is a good substitute for the great comfort food classic of macaroni and cheese!

2 eggplants (aubergines)
sea salt
200 ml extra virgin olive oil
1 clove garlic, finely chopped
500 g ripe tomatoes, peeled and seeded
    (see page 51), then diced
freshly ground black pepper
handful of basil leaves, chopped
400 g conchiglioni
80 g freshly grated parmesan
butter, for greasing
150 g mozzarella, diced

SERVES 4

Cut the ends off the eggplants, leaving the skin on, and cut into thin slices. Place the slices in a colander over the sink, sprinkle with sea salt and leave for 40 minutes so they sweat out their bitter juices.

Meanwhile, prepare the sauce. Heat 80 ml of the olive oil in a heavy-based saucepan over low heat. Add the garlic and stir with a wooden spoon for a minute or so until it just starts to change colour. Add the tomato and season with salt and pepper. Increase the heat to medium and cook for 8 minutes. Stir in the basil and cook for a further 2 minutes to allow the basil to perfume the sauce. Set aside.

Preheat the oven to 200°C.

Cook the conchiglioni in plenty of boiling salted water until very al dente – this will be about 3 minutes short of the recommended cooking time. You don't want the pasta to be completely cooked through, as it will cook further in the oven. Remove with a slotted spoon and place on a foil-covered work surface.

While the pasta is cooling, rinse the eggplant slices and pat dry with paper towels. Heat the remaining olive oil in a non-stick frying pan over medium heat and fry the eggplant in batches for about 2 minutes each side until golden. Drain on paper towels.

Place the eggplant slices in a bowl and dress with half the parmesan, 3 tablespoons of the tomato sauce and a little salt.

Grease a large baking dish with the butter and spread a little tomato sauce in the base of the dish. Fill each shell with eggplant mixture and place in the baking dish. Pour the remaining tomato sauce all over the pasta, then sprinkle with the mozzarella and remaining parmesan. Bake for 15 minutes.

Before serving, decorate with a little more basil, if you wish.

Baked stuffed pasta shells

CONCHIGLIONI RIPIENI AL FORNO

The giant pasta shells called conchiglioni are made especially to be stuffed and then baked. This substantial dish is perfect for a cold day; if it's raining as well, even better. Because baked pasta shells are a bit quicker and much easier to make than lasagne or cannelloni, this is a great dish for getting kids into the kitchen – they certainly seem to love stuffing the pasta shells.

120 ml extra virgin olive oil

1 onion, finely chopped

300 g minced beef

sea salt and freshly ground black pepper

a few gratings of nutmeg

1 × 400 g tin peeled tomatoes,
    passed through a mouli or squished
    with your hands

2 teaspoons tomato paste

250 ml boiling water

small handful of basil leaves, chopped

150 g breadcrumbs

2 eggs

100 g freshly grated parmesan

500 g conchiglione

1 quantity bechamel sauce (see page 62)

SERVES 4

Heat 80 ml of the olive oil in a heavy-based frying pan over medium–high heat, add the onion and cook for 3–4 minutes until soft and translucent. Turn up the heat, then add the beef and cook until brown all over. Season to taste with salt, pepper and nutmeg, then add a quarter of the tomatoes and all the tomato paste. Pour in the boiling water, mix well and simmer for 40 minutes, stirring from time to time. In the last few minutes, stir in half of the basil, then remove from the heat and allow to cool.

While the filling is cooling, make a simple tomato sauce. Place the remaining olive oil, tomato and basil in a non-stick frying pan. Season with salt and pepper and cook for 20 minutes over medium heat, stirring from time to time, then remove from the heat and leave to cool. Transfer the cooled filling to a bowl, add the breadcrumbs and mix well. Add the eggs and half of the parmesan, mix thoroughly and set aside.

Preheat the oven to 180°C.

Cook the conchiglioni in plenty of boiling salted water for 2 minutes less than the suggested cooking time on the packet. Drain the pasta shells and place them on clean tea towels. Allow to cool for a couple of minutes, then stuff with the filling.

Take one large or two small ceramic baking dishes and spread some tomato sauce over the base, then arrange the stuffed pasta shells on top in a single layer, open side up. Pour a little tomato sauce over each shell, top with the bechamel and sprinkle with the rest of the parmesan. Bake for 20 minutes or until sizzling and golden.

Rabbit cannelloni with Jerusalem artichoke sauce

CANNELLONI DI CONIGLIO

Logan Campbell, executive chef at Lucio's, who created this recipe, offers some valuable advice: 'The problem with rabbit is that it can turn out dry, unless you're very alert with your cooking times. Don't overcook it, and leave the rabbit to cool in the stock so it doesn't lose moisture. Roll this tender rabbit meat in cannelloni and you'll have a real crowd-pleaser.'

400 g basic pasta dough (see page 11)
extra virgin olive oil, for drizzling
40 g freshly grated parmesan
1 tablespoon thyme leaves, to garnish

FILLING

100 ml extra virgin olive oil
plain flour, for dusting
1 large farmed rabbit (1.6–1.8 kg),
    legs jointed and saddle cut in half –
    ask your butcher to do this
2 white onions, roughly chopped
1 carrot, roughly chopped
3 large ripe tomatoes, roughly chopped
1 bunch thyme
250 ml white wine
2 litres chicken stock
sea salt and freshly ground black pepper
100 g ricotta
50 g freshly grated parmesan
2 egg yolks
large handful of flat-leaf parsley leaves,
    chopped

SAUCE

400 g Jerusalem artichokes
½ lemon
2 tablespoons extra virgin olive oil
1 white onion, chopped
2 cloves garlic, chopped
1 bay leaf
1 litre chicken stock
80 ml cream
sea salt and freshly ground black pepper

SERVES 4

First make the pasta dough and then, while it is resting, prepare the cannelloni filling and sauce.

For the filling, heat the olive oil in a heavy-based stockpot or large saucepan over medium heat. Lightly flour the rabbit, then fry on all sides until golden brown. Remove from the pan and set aside. Add the onion, carrot, tomato and thyme and cook for 3 minutes. Add the wine and cook for 3 more minutes, then return the rabbit to the pan and pour over the stock. Season to taste with salt and pepper, cover and simmer until the rabbit is tender, about 35 minutes. Remove the pan from the heat and leave the rabbit to cool in the liquid.

When the rabbit is cool enough to handle, take it out of the pan and strip the meat from the bones. Put the meat in a large bowl and discard the bones. Strain the stock into another saucepan and simmer until it is reduced to half its original volume and is very thick. Set aside.

Add the ricotta, parmesan, egg yolks and parsley to the rabbit meat and season to taste with salt and pepper. Mix well, adding enough of the reduced stock to make the filling moist, but not wet. Refrigerate.

For the sauce, peel and chop the artichokes, dropping them into a bowl of water acidulated with a squeeze of lemon juice. Heat the olive oil in a medium-sized saucepan and sweat the onion and garlic for 3 minutes – do not brown. Add the bay leaf, stock and the drained artichokes and simmer until the artichokes are soft, about 20 minutes. Remove the pan from the heat, remove and discard the bay leaf, and allow the sauce to cool. Blend until smooth, adding the cream and seasoning with salt and pepper to taste.

Preheat the oven to 170°C and grease a ceramic baking dish (or line it with baking paper).

Roll out the pasta dough into very thin sheets (see pages 17–18) then cut into rectangles about 10 cm × 7 cm. To assemble the cannelloni, take a pasta rectangle and place about 3–4 tablespoons of the rabbit mixture along one of the long sides, leaving a 5 mm gap from the edge of the pasta and shaping the filling into a sausage no more than 3 cm in diameter. Moisten the far edge of the pasta and roll from the filling towards the moistened edge. Repeat until all the pasta and filling is used up.

Nestle the cannelloni, seam-side down, in a single layer in the baking dish so that there is no space between them. Add enough of the reduced stock to come a third of the way up the sides of the cannelloni, top with a drizzle of olive oil and a little parmesan and bake for 20 minutes.

Meanwhile, gently reheat the Jerusalem artichoke sauce.

Arrange the cannelloni on a serving plate, pour over the sauce and garnish with thyme leaves.

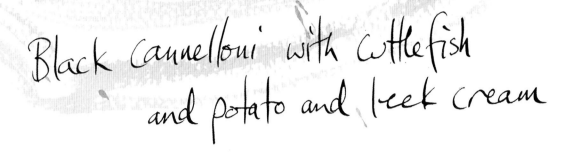

Black Cannelloni with cuttlefish and potato and leek cream

CANNELLONI AL NERO DI SEPPIA

Here is a fantastic 'new generation' plate of pasta from my family restaurant in Bocca di Magra. Although previous generations might have considered it vulgar to cook with black cuttlefish ink, its impact in this dish is superb: the subtlety of the black pasta and its cuttlefish filling is amazing, particularly with the contrasting colour and flavour of the cream of potatoes and leeks.

400 g black pasta dough (see page 14)
extra virgin olive oil, for drizzling

FILLING

200 g silverbeet
3 tablespoons extra virgin olive oil
½ white onion, finely chopped
1 clove garlic, peeled and bruised
1 red chilli, cut in half lengthways and
    seeds removed
300 g cuttlefish, cleaned and cut into strips
3 tablespoons dry white wine
sea salt and freshly ground black pepper

POTATO AND LEEK CREAM

300 g potatoes, peeled and cut into
    small cubes
15 g butter
100 g leeks, white parts only, thinly sliced
50 ml milk
sea salt and freshly ground black pepper

SERVES 4

First make the black pasta dough and then, while it is resting, prepare the filling.

Remove the white stalks from the silverbeet and wash the leaves, then chop finely. Heat the olive oil in a heavy-based frying pan over medium heat, then add the onion, garlic and chilli and sauté for 1 minute. Discard the garlic and chilli and continue to sauté the onion for another 4 minutes until it softens and becomes translucent, stirring often with a wooden spoon. Add the cuttlefish and sauté for 3–4 minutes until it turns opaque, stirring frequently. Add the white wine, stir once and then let it evaporate. Add the silverbeet and season with salt and pepper, mixing thoroughly. Cook over low–medium heat for 5 minutes, stirring from time to time. Transfer the mixture to a chopping board and chop finely using a mezzaluna or sharp knife. Set aside and allow to cool.

For the potato and leek cream, cook the potato in boiling salted water until tender (10–15 minutes), then drain. In a non-stick frying pan, melt the butter over medium heat. Add the leek and sauté for 3–4 minutes, then add the milk and the potato. Season with salt and pepper, mix thoroughly and cook for about 5 minutes. Transfer to a blender and blend to obtain a smooth cream.

Preheat the oven to 180°C and lightly oil a ceramic baking dish.

Roll out the pasta dough (see pages 17–18) and cut into sheets about 10 cm × 7 cm. Have a bowl of iced water ready. Bring a large saucepan of salted water to the boil, add a few drops of olive oil, then slip in the pasta sheets a few at a time and cook for 1–2 minutes. Lift the sheets out using a slotted spoon or tongs, refresh in the iced water, then drain and lay out on a clean tea towel.

To assemble the cannelloni, take a pasta sheet and place a generous tablespoon of the cuttlefish filling along one of the long sides, leaving a 5 mm gap from the edge of the pasta and shaping the filling into a sausage no more than 3 cm in diameter. Moisten the far edge of the pasta sheet and roll from the filling towards the moistened edge. Repeat until all the pasta and filling have been used up.

Nestle the cannelloni, seam-side down, in a single layer in the baking dish so that there is no space between them. Top with a drizzle of olive oil and bake for 20–25 minutes.

Meanwhile, gently reheat the potato and leek cream and divide among four plates. Place the cannelloni on top and serve.

LASAGNE SEMPLICI

On special occasions in the north of Italy, we make ravioli. But in the south they make *timballi* – pasta dressed with sauce, layered in a dish and baked in the oven. These range from very simple to very complex, such as *timpano*, where the pasta is enclosed in pastry. When I was working on this simple version of lasagne, I was reminded of the southern *timballi* because I decided not to use bechamel, instead building layers of mozzarella and egg, which is typical of *timballi*. And I am happy to tell you that the result is very tasty indeed.

60 ml extra virgin olive oil

½ white onion, thinly sliced

300 g minced lean beef

200 g minced pork

500 ml white wine

1 × 400 g tin peeled tomatoes, passed
   through a mouli or squished with
   your hands

sea salt and freshly ground black pepper

large handful of basil leaves, shredded

30 g butter, cut into small cubes

200 g mozzarella, thinly sliced

2 hard-boiled eggs, thickly sliced

100 g freshly grated parmesan

PASTA

400 g plain flour

4 eggs

SERVES 4

Make the pasta following the instructions on page 11, but using the quantities given here.

Roll out the rested pasta dough into very thin sheets (see pages 17–18), then cut into strips 25 cm × 12.5 cm or to suit the size of your baking dish.

Heat the olive oil in a heavy-based frying pan over medium heat, then add the onion and cook for about 5 minutes, stirring with a wooden spoon, until soft. Add the beef and pork and cook until browned (about 8 minutes), mixing and breaking down any lumps with the wooden spoon. Add the wine and let it evaporate (about 5 minutes). Add the tomato to the sauce. Mix thoroughly. Sprinkle with a little salt and pepper and add the basil. Let the sauce cook over low heat for 1 hour, stirring and checking it regularly. Add a little water if it seems to be drying out.

In the meantime, put a bowl of cold water near the stove. Cook the pasta strips 3–4 at a time in plenty of boiling salted water for only 10 seconds. Lift out with a large slotted spoon and place in the bowl of cold water to stop the cooking process. Carefully pick up the strips with your fingers, place on a tea towel and pat dry.

Preheat the oven to 200°C.

Grease the bottom and sides of a ceramic baking dish with a little of the butter. Spread a layer of meat sauce over the bottom of the dish and top with a layer of pasta. Over the pasta, spread another layer of meat sauce, some sliced mozzarella and some of the egg slices. Sprinkle with a couple of tablespoons of parmesan. Continue with another layer of pasta, meat sauce, mozzarella, sliced egg and parmesan, and so on, until you have used them all. Scatter the remaining butter over the top.

Bake for 30 minutes or until the top is crisp and golden. Take the lasagne out of the oven and leave to rest for 8–10 minutes, then serve straight from the dish.

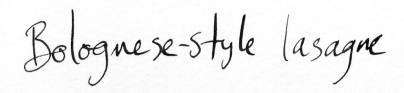

LASAGNE ALLA BOLOGNESE

Originating in Emilia-Romagna, this type of lasagne is referred to as _lasagne al forno_ ('baked lasagne'), and is not to be confused with other pappardelle-type pastas that in some regions are called _lasagne_ or _lasagnette_.

Lasagne is one of the most Italian of dishes, a great dish for a celebration. There are a few secrets to a good lasagne: the quality of the sauce, the preparation of the bechamel, the quality of the cheese and timing in the oven (you don't want it either undercooked or overcooked), but most of all the quality and thinness of the pasta. These are all things that you will master with time and practice!

20 g butter
400 g basic pasta dough (see page 11)
sea salt
olive oil
½ quantity classic Bolognese sauce
    (see page 56)
1 quantity bechamel sauce (see page 62)
120 g freshly grated parmesan

SERVES 4

Preheat the oven to 200°C and grease the base and sides of a baking dish with a little of the butter.

Roll out the pasta dough into thin sheets (see pages 17–18), then cut into rectangles to fit the size of your baking dish. Place a large bowl of iced water next to the stove. Bring a large saucepan of water to the boil, then add some salt and a few drops of olive oil (this will stop the pasta from sticking). Cook the pasta rectangles 2–3 at a time for 2 minutes. Lift them out using tongs or a large slotted spoon and immerse them in the cold water, then lay them on tea towels to dry.

If you have prepared the bolognese sauce in advance, gently reheat it. Spread some bolognese sauce on the base of the prepared baking dish. Cover with a layer of pasta, then another layer of bolognese, a layer of bechamel and a sprinkling of parmesan. Repeat until you have used all the ingredients, finishing with parmesan. Cut the remaining butter into small pieces and scatter on top.

Bake for 30 minutes or until the surface is golden and bubbling. Remove from the oven and leave to rest for about 10 minutes. Serve and enjoy.

Gnocchi

Gnocchi: are they pasta or are they dumplings?

I say they are both, which allows me to include my favourite gnocchi recipes in this book. These beautiful potato (or not) cushions are another masterpiece of *la cucina italiana*. They should be soft and light enough that you can squash them against your palate with your tongue to get instant flavour.

Gnocchi are so nourishing and comforting that in Italy, when you are sad or something has gone wrong, we say: '*Vai a casa che la mamma ha ta fa i gnocchi*' (Go home, so Mummy can make you some gnocchi).

There are many types of gnocchi, with different sizes, shapes and, of course, sauces, and we discuss many of them in this chapter – including some made without potatoes. These potato-less gnocchi have different names in different parts of Italy, but all are from poor and peasant origins. I have seen some being prepared by my mother or my Aunty Anna; others I have only been told about by members of the family. Some are the same size as regular gnocchi, while others are much bigger. Most of the time they are cooked in water and then tossed in the sauce, but occasionally they are cooked directly in the sauce. The one thing they all have in common is that they are *deliziosi*.

Potato gnocchi

To make potato gnocchi, it is important to use the right variety of potato. Floury potatoes work best, as they contain less water than new or waxy potatoes – this means that less flour is required and the gnocchi will be lighter. Desiree potatoes are the variety I suggest.

1 kg desiree potatoes, skin on
1 egg
200–250 g plain flour, plus extra for dusting
sea salt

SERVES 4

Place the potatoes in a saucepan of cold salted water. Bring to the boil, then turn the heat down a little and cook gently until the potatoes are soft when tested with a skewer – this should take 25–30 minutes depending on the size of the potatoes. Drain.

When they are just cool enough to handle (it is better to mash them while they are still hot), peel the potatoes and pass them through a mouli or potato ricer into a bowl. Cool completely and then add the egg. Mix it in lightly and quickly with a fork. Add 200 g of the flour, then add salt to taste and, using your hands, mix quickly to form a dough.

Flour your work surface well and place your dough on it. If it is too sticky add a little more flour, but be very careful not to make it too dry – too much flour will make the gnocchi hard and heavy. It should only take a few minutes to mix the dough into a homogenous soft ball.

Divide the dough into six. Working on a well-floured surface, use your hands to shape each piece of dough into a roll the thickness of a finger. Using a sharp knife, cut each roll into even pieces 2–4 cm long to make your gnocchi.

As you cut them, lay the gnocchi on a floured tea towel in a single layer – do not allow them to touch each other. When they are all done, roll each one over the tines of a fork (or use a special wooden gnocchi maker) to give them the classic grooves, which will hold the sauce. Or, if you prefer, press your finger into the middle of each gnoccho to give another classic shape.

The gnocchi are now ready to be cooked in plenty of boiling salted water. Place them on a plate, then tilt the plate over the boiling water and let the gnocchi slide into the water. (You may need to do this in small batches if your pan is not big enough.) As the gnocchi rise to the surface, lift them out using a slotted spoon, drain well then toss them with the sauce.

One of the best sauces to accompany gnocchi is fresh tomato sauce (see page 51), finished with plenty of fresh basil and parmesan, or the four cheeses sauce on page 98. Melted butter and parmesan is a lovely quick option.

If you don't want to eat them all at once, you can freeze the uncooked gnocchi – just sprinkle them with flour first to stop them sticking together.

Potato and spinach gnocchi with tomato and mascarpone

GNOCCHI VERDI AL POMODORO E MASCARPONE

Now we come to one of the many variations of gnocchi that dot the Italian landscape – this time mixing spinach with the potato to make the dumplings deep green in colour and lighter in texture. Spinach and potato gnocchi are tasty enough to be eaten with just a little olive oil or butter, but here I suggest a classic creamy tomato and basil accompaniment that will magnify the pleasure. I am sure that you'll feel the temptation, once you have eaten the gnocchi, to do the *scarpetta* (using bread to mop up the rest of the sauce on the plate).

250 g spinach, stems removed
600 g desiree potatoes, skin on
1 egg
250 g plain flour
sea salt
60 g freshly grated parmesan

SAUCE

80 ml extra virgin olive oil
1 golden shallot, finely chopped
300 g ripe tomatoes, peeled and seeded
   (see page 51), then diced
150 g mascarpone
sea salt and freshly ground black pepper
1 tablespoon chopped basil leaves

SERVES 4

Wash the spinach and wilt it in a saucepan over medium heat for a few minutes, using only the residual water on the leaves. Drain and squeeze dry, then chop finely.

Prepare the gnocchi following the instructions opposite, mixing the spinach in at the same time as the egg.

To make the sauce, heat the olive oil in a heavy-based frying pan over medium heat and sauté the shallot for a few minutes until transparent, stirring with a wooden spoon. Add the tomato and cook for about 10 minutes, stirring from time to time. Pass the sauce through a mouli or sieve and return to the pan over medium heat. Add the mascarpone and let it melt. Season with salt and pepper and sprinkle over the basil. Mix thoroughly until combined.

Cook the gnocchi in plenty of boiling salted water. Place them on a plate, then tilt the plate over the boiling water and let the gnocchi slide into the water. (You may need to do this in small batches if your pan is not big enough.) As the gnocchi rise to the surface, lift them out using a slotted spoon, then add to the frying pan with the sauce. Toss gently, sprinkling with half the parmesan. Serve hot, with the rest of the parmesan on the side.

Potato gnocchi with gorgonzola and pistachios

GNOCCHI AL GORGONZOLA E PISTACCHI

Gnocchi and gorgonzola is a marriage made in heaven: the creamy gorgonzola is a perfect match for the soft, pillowy gnocchi. When this dish was on our restaurant menu years ago, it proved a huge seller. I prefer to use the milder gorgonzola dolcelatte rather than the more robust piccante. The pistachios add a lovely texture and flavour to the dish, but you may substitute walnuts or pine nuts, if you like.

50 g butter

150 ml thickened cream

100 g gorgonzola dolcelatte at room
    temperature, cut into cubes

sea salt and freshly ground black pepper

1 quantity potato gnocchi (see page 256)

80 g raw pistachios, roughly chopped

100 g freshly grated parmesan

1 tablespoon chopped marjoram leaves

SERVES 4

Melt the butter in a large non-stick frying pan over medium heat. Add the cream and gorgonzola and season with a little salt and pepper to taste. Stir until the cheese has melted, then take the pan off the heat.

Cook the gnocchi in plenty of boiling salted water. Place them on a plate, then tilt the plate over the boiling water and let the gnocchi slide into the water. (You may need to do this in small batches if your pan is not big enough.) As the gnocchi rise to the surface, lift them out using a slotted spoon, then add to the frying pan with the sauce. Place the pan over low heat and mix quickly with a wooden spoon. Sprinkle with the pistachios, parmesan and marjoram and toss gently. Serve immediately, sprinkled with a little more pepper.

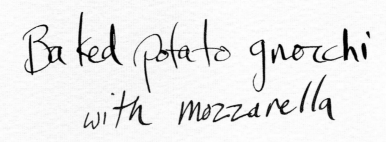

Baked potato gnocchi
with mozzarella

GNOCCHI GRATINATI CON MOZZARELLA

Here's a great Neapolitan approach to gnocchi, in which the gnocchi are both boiled and baked to give an interesting texture. In Naples these gnocchi are called *strozzapreti* or 'priest stranglers' (a term used for other pasta shapes elsewhere in Italy – see page 168), and are often served with the splendid Neapolitan ragù (see page 58).

1 quantity potato gnocchi (see page 256)
50 g butter
1 quantity tomato sauce II (see page 52)
10–15 basil leaves, finely chopped
200 g mozzarella, cut into 1 cm cubes
60 g freshly grated parmesan

SERVES 4

Make the gnocchi the day before you want to eat them. Place them on a tray, making sure they do not touch one another, and freeze them (this will make them easier to cook). When they have frozen, shake off any excess flour and place in freezer bags to store overnight.

Preheat the oven to 200°C and grease the bottom and sides of a ceramic baking dish with a little of the butter. Place 2 tablespoons of the tomato sauce in the dish and use the back of a spoon to spread it out evenly.

Melt the rest of the butter in a non-stick frying pan, add the remaining tomato sauce and simmer for about 5 minutes.

Meanwhile, cook the gnocchi straight from the freezer in plenty of boiling salted water. Place them on a plate, then tilt the plate over the boiling water and let the gnocchi slide into the water. (You may need to do this in small batches if your pan is not big enough.) As the gnocchi rise to the surface, lift them out using a slotted spoon.

Remove the sauce from the heat and add the gnocchi. Mix delicately with a wooden spoon and stir to combine well. Stir in the basil, mozzarella and 2 tablespoons of the parmesan. Pour everything into the baking dish, sprinkle with the remaining parmesan and bake for about 10 minutes until golden. Serve immediately.

Potato gnocchi with duck ragù

GNOCCHI DI PATATE AL RAGÙ D'ANATRA

In Italy this recipe is usually associated with Puglia, where this way of preparing gnocchi is a local speciality. The gnocchi are made with parmesan and nutmeg, which enables them to hold the sauce with a bit more strength. I lighten up the flavour and colour of the sauce by substituting white wine for red and omitting the tomato paste, and I shorten the cooking time by using only the duck breast, rather than the whole bird. This sauce can be used to dress other types of pasta, particularly tagliatelle.

60 g dried porcini mushrooms

2 duck breasts

100 ml extra virgin olive oil

1 small white onion, finely chopped

1 carrot, finely chopped

1 celery stalk, finely chopped

50 g prosciutto or bacon, chopped

1 herb bouquet (thyme, marjoram, sage)

100 ml dry white wine

1 × 400 g tin peeled tomatoes, passed
   through a mouli or squished with
   your hands

sea salt and freshly ground black pepper

60 g freshly grated parmesan

GNOCCHI

1 kg desiree potatoes, skin on

200–250 g plain flour

1 egg

sea salt

2 tablespoons freshly grated parmesan

a few gratings of nutmeg

SERVES 4

Prepare the gnocchi following the instructions on page 256, mixing the parmesan and nutmeg into the flour before adding it to the potato.

Soak the porcini in warm water for 15 minutes, then squeeze them with your hands, pat dry and chop. Set aside. Debone the duck breasts, discarding the skin but keeping the bones. Trim off and discard most of the fat, then cut the meat into small cubes.

Heat the olive oil in a heavy-based frying pan over medium heat. Add the onion, carrot, celery and prosciutto and sauté for about 8 minutes until the vegetables are soft and the onion is translucent.

Turn the heat up and add the herb bouquet and the duck meat and bones (for flavour). Brown the meat all over, then lower the heat to medium. Cook for about 6 minutes, stirring constantly with a wooden spoon, to allow all the flavours to meld. Add the porcini and wine and let the alcohol evaporate. Add the tomato, season with salt and pepper and cook, partially covered, over low heat for about 40 minutes. Keep an eye on the pan and stir from time to time so that it doesn't stick – add a little water if necessary. Remove the bouquet of herbs and the bones from the sauce and discard.

Cook the gnocchi in plenty of boiling salted water. Place them on a plate, then tilt the plate over the boiling water and let the gnocchi slide into the water. (You may need to do this in small batches if your pan is not big enough.) As the gnocchi rise to the surface, lift them out using a slotted spoon, then add to the frying pan with the sauce. Toss gently, adding the parmesan, and serve immediately.

Beetroot gnocchi with pancetta and goat's cheese

GNOCCHI DI BARBABIETOLA CON PANCETTA E CAPRINO

This is another creation of Logan Campbell, executive chef at Lucio's restaurant, so I'll hand you over to him to introduce it: 'Cooking and blending beetroot then incorporating it into potato gnocchi gives these guys an amazing colour and subtle sweet flavour. You do need to make adjustments to compensate for the addition to your gnocchi dough, but I've done all the trial and error for you. Some salty pancetta and tangy goat's cheese seemed like the natural accompaniments to the earthy potato and beetroot.'

60 ml extra virgin olive oil
200 g pancetta, cut into large dice
2 cloves garlic, finely chopped
200 ml chicken stock
sea salt and freshly ground black pepper
200 g firm goat's cheese
handful of wild rocket leaves

BEETROOT GNOCCHI

200 g beetroot
2 tablespoons red wine vinegar
1 kg desiree potatoes
250 g plain flour, plus extra for dusting
2 egg yolks
sea salt and freshly ground black pepper

SERVES 4

First make the gnocchi. Place the beetroot in a small saucepan and cover with water. Add the vinegar, then bring to the boil and cook until the beetroot is very tender. When the beetroot is cool enough to handle, peel off the skin. Roughly chop the flesh, then puree in a food processor.

Cook the potatoes in their skins until they offer no resistance to a skewer or the tip of a knife. Drain, then return to the pan and allow to steam-dry in the residual heat of the pan for 5 minutes. When the potatoes are cool enough to handle, peel and pass through a mouli or potato ricer, then add the flour, egg yolks and 1 tablespoon of the beetroot puree. Season with salt and pepper, then use your hands to lightly amalgamate the dough, but do not overwork it.

Dust a large plate or tray with flour and divide the dough into six. On a well-floured work surface, use your hands to roll out each piece of dough until it is long and snake-like and about as thick as your thumb. Cut into 1.5 cm pieces and roll each one across a gnocchi board or the back of a fork then place on the floured plate or tray, making sure the gnocchi do not touch each other. Cover and refrigerate while you make the sauce.

Heat the olive oil in a large heavy-based frying pan over medium–high heat, add the pancetta and fry until brown. Turn the heat down to low, add the garlic and stock, season with a little salt and pepper and leave to simmer gently while you cook the gnocchi.

Cook the gnocchi in plenty of boiling salted water. Place them on a plate, then tilt the plate over the boiling water and let the gnocchi slide into the water. (You may need to do this in small batches if your pan is not big enough.) As the gnocchi rise to the surface, lift them out using a slotted spoon, then add to the frying pan and toss gently until the gnocchi are coated and the sauce is glossy.

Transfer to a large serving dish, tear the goat's cheese using your hands and scatter it over the gnocchi, along with the rocket. Serve immediately.

Sardinian gnocchi with sausage

MALLOREDDUS ALLA SALSICCIA

Malloreddus is a typical Sardinian pasta that is also known as *gnocchetti sardi*. Traditionally, little lumps of the dough are rolled and pressed over a basket to get the classic grooved boat shape; the special screen-like utensil that is traditionally used is called a *ciurili*. The word malloreddus means 'young veal', which is probably an attempt to describe the shape, but they look more like worms than veal to me.

Made from semolina flour and water, malloreddus has become very popular outside Sardinia as well, and nowadays you can find factory-made versions of excellent quality in specialised shops. Like gnocchi, it is cooked when it rises to the surface. You can eat malloreddus with many different sauces, of course, but when I asked a Sardinian friend how he ate it, he replied, 'With sausage,' without even thinking about it!

60 ml extra virgin olive oil

3 cloves garlic, peeled and lightly squashed

300 g pork and fennel sausages,
   skin removed

3 sprigs basil

3 tablespoons dry white wine

1 × 400 g tin tomatoes, passed through
   a mouli or squished with your hands

sea salt and freshly ground black pepper

handful of basil leaves, finely chopped

80 g freshly grated pecorino

MALLOREDDUS

400 g semolina flour, plus extra for dusting

sea salt

pinch of saffron threads

SERVES 4

To make the malloreddus, place the flour in a mound on a wooden board or work surface. Make a well and sprinkle in some salt. Dissolve the saffron threads in 250 ml warm water, then pour the water into the well. Mix with your hands until into a dough, then knead for about 15 minutes, following the instructions on page 11.

Divide the dough into six. Working on a well-floured surface, use your hands to shape each piece of dough into a roll the thickness of your little finger. Using a sharp knife, cut each roll into pieces the size of chickpeas, then roll each malloreddus across the tines of a fork. Let them rest for at least 1 hour – or, better yet, make them the day before you plan to eat them.

Heat the olive oil in a large heavy-based frying pan over medium heat. Add the garlic and stir with a wooden spoon for about 4 minutes, just until it starts to change colour, then discard the garlic cloves. Add the sausages, breaking down the meat as much as possible with the wooden spoon, followed by the basil sprigs. Cook until the meat is browned all over, then sprinkle in the white wine and allow the alcohol to evaporate. Add the tomatoes and season to taste with salt and pepper. Reduce the heat and simmer for about 10 minutes, stirring from time to time. Remove and discard the basil sprigs.

Meanwhile, cook the malloreddus in plenty of boiling salted water until they rise to the surface. Drain, reserving a little of the cooking water, and add the malloreddus to the sauce. Toss gently for about a minute over low heat, adding the chopped basil and half the pecorino; if the sauce seems too dry, add a little of the reserved cooking water. Serve immediately, with the rest of the pecorino on the side.

Gnocchi with anchovies and marjoram pesto

GNOCCHI CON LE ACCIUGHE E PESTO ALLA MAGGIORANA

I was born in Liguria, on the north-west coast of Italy, where – particularly in my area of the Riviera di Levante – there is a strong culture of anchovies. In the past, Ligurians were not fishermen but sailors, having realised that it was more profitable to use big boats for the transport of goods. So the fishing was left to poor people with little boats that could not go far out to sea; hugging the coastline, what they caught was a lot of anchovies. This dish pays homage to these beloved little fish of the Riviera di Levante, and to the many beautiful herbs that grow wild in that part of the world. I hope you will try it.

400 g plain flour
200 g fine breadcrumbs
100 g freshly grated pecorino
freshly grated nutmeg
sea salt
20 anchovy fillets in oil, drained and
    finely chopped
1 tablespoon oregano leaves, finely chopped
2 eggs
1 egg yolk
120 ml dry white wine
freshly grated parmesan, to serve (optional)

MARJORAM PESTO

large handful of marjoram leaves
100 g freshly grated parmesan
1 clove garlic, peeled
50 g walnut kernels
50 g pine nuts
120 ml extra virgin olive oil
pinch of sea salt

SERVES 4

Place the flour on a wooden board or work surface with the breadcrumbs, the pecorino, a few gratings of nutmeg and a pinch of salt. Mix together very well and form into a mound. Make a well in the centre and add the anchovies, oregano, eggs, egg yolk and wine. Work for a few minutes until you obtain a rather firm dough. Form into a ball and leave to rest for 30 minutes.

In the meantime, make the marjoram pesto. Place all the ingredients in a blender and pulse until you have a creamy sauce that is not too smooth. Place the sauce in a ceramic bowl large enough to hold the gnocchi.

Divide the gnocchi dough into six. Working on a well-floured surface, use your hands to shape each piece of dough into a roll the thickness of a finger. Using a sharp knife, cut each roll into even pieces 2–4 cm long, then roll each piece over the tines of a fork.

Cook the gnocchi in plenty of boiling salted water. Place them on a plate, then tilt the plate over the boiling water and let the gnocchi slide into the water. (You may need to do this in small batches if your pan is not big enough.) As the gnocchi rise to the surface, lift them out using a slotted spoon and add to the bowl with the pesto. Mix thoroughly but delicately, adding a little of the gnocchi cooking water to loosen the pesto. Serve immediately – with a little parmesan, if you like.

Saffron gnocchi with mussels and asparagus tips

GNOCCHI ALLE COZZE E PUNTE DI ASPARAGI

Saffron was brought to the south of Italy some 3000 years ago by the Greeks, who got it from the Arabs. The Greeks regarded it as a medicine and an aphrodisiac: Alexander the Great, for example, used Persian saffron to treat his battle wounds; and Cleopatra used saffron in her bathwater to make her skin more sensitive during lovemaking. But, as far as I'm concerned, all that is just a waste of a good flavouring! Saffron gnocchi, mingled with my favourite seafood and tender asparagus tips, has become one of the signature dishes in Lucio's restaurant.

1 tablespoon extra virgin olive oil

6 cloves garlic, peeled

1 kg black mussels, scrubbed
    and debearded

12 asparagus tips

50 g unsalted butter, chopped

SAFFRON GNOCCHI

½ teaspoon saffron threads

1 egg

1 kg desiree potatoes, skin on

200–250 g plain flour

pinch of sea salt

SERVES 4

For the gnocchi, place the saffron in a small bowl, add a teaspoon of warm water and stir well. Mix the saffron water with the egg, then prepare the gnocchi following the instructions on page 256.

Heat the olive oil and garlic in a large saucepan over medium heat. Turn up the heat to high and add the mussels. Use tongs to remove the mussels from the pan as soon as they open, so they do not overcook (discard any mussels that won't open). Pass the mussel juices left in the pan through a fine sieve to remove any sand and grit, then set aside. When the mussels are cool enough to handle, remove the mussel meat from the shells.

Bring a large saucepan of salted water to the boil, then turn down to a simmer. Cut the asparagus tips so that they are a similar size to the gnocchi. Slip small batches of the gnocchi and asparagus into the simmering water, taking care not to overcrowd the pan. As soon as the gnocchi rise to the surface, use a slotted spoon to remove them and the asparagus tips.

Place the reserved mussel juices and the butter in a frying pan and bring to the boil. Add the gnocchi, asparagus and mussel meat. Stir gently to coat the gnocchi and serve immediately.

GNOCCHI NERI ALLE SEPPIE

This is a beautiful study in black and white. The potato gnocchi absorbs the black cuttlefish ink and dramatically contrasts with the white strips of cuttlefish. The onion needs to be diced so finely that it disappears in the cooking – at least visually, even though its flavour enriches the briny taste of the sea. I'd go so far as to suggest a little fish stock, to take that even further.

Squid ink is available in small sachets from selected fishmongers and specialist food shops. I recommend that you wear rubber gloves when making this gnocchi, so the squid ink does not stain your hands.

Prepare the gnocchi following the instructions on page 256, but replace the egg with the squid ink.

In a large frying pan, heat the olive oil and cook the onion over medium heat for 10 minutes until soft and translucent, taking care not to let it colour. Add the cuttlefish and sauté for 3 minutes. Add the fish stock as well if you want to intensify the flavour.

Cook the gnocchi in plenty of boiling salted water. Place them on a plate, then tilt the plate over the boiling water and let the gnocchi slide into the water. (You may need to do this in small batches if your pan is not big enough.) As the gnocchi rise to the surface, lift them out using a slotted spoon, then add to the frying pan. Stir well to coat with the sauce and serve immediately.

50 ml extra virgin olive oil
1 onion, finely diced
500 g cuttlefish, cleaned and
    cut into thin strips
100 ml fish stock (optional)

SQUID INK GNOCCHI

1 kg desiree potatoes, skin on
1 tablespoon squid ink
200–250 g plain flour
pinch of sea salt

SERVES 4

Flour-only gnocchi

GNOCCHI SOLO FARINA

These little gnocchi are made with only flour and water. They are light, delicate and delicious – and surprisingly quick and easy to make. You can dress them with rocket (see below) or try them with a lovely fresh tomato sauce (see page 51), basil and parmesan. Or you could bake them as for *gnocchi gratinati* (see page 260), or serve them with the broccoli sauce on page 130.

500 ml water
500 g plain flour

SERVES 4

Bring the water to the boil in a saucepan, then remove from the heat and throw in half the flour. Mix with a wooden spoon and, when the water has all been absorbed and nothing is sticking to the sides of the pan, transfer the dough to a floured work surface. Let it cool just enough so that you can work it with your hands, then incorporate the rest of the flour – this will take only a few minutes. If the dough is still too wet, add more flour while the dough is still warm.

Divide the dough into six. Working on a well-floured surface, use your hands to shape each piece of dough into a roll the thickness of a finger. Using a sharp knife, cut each roll into even pieces 2–4 cm long, then roll each piece over the back of a fork (or use a special wooden gnocchi maker). Lay the gnocchi on a lightly floured tea towel to dry for 2 hours.

Cook the gnocchi in plenty of boiling salted water. Place them on a plate, then tilt the plate over the boiling water and let the gnocchi slide into the water. (You may need to do this in small batches if your pan is not big enough.) As the gnocchi rise to the surface, lift them out using a slotted spoon, then gently toss with your chosen sauce.

If you don't want to eat them all at once, you can freeze the uncooked gnocchi – just sprinkle them with flour first to stop them sticking together.

Flour-only gnocchi with rocket

GNOCCHI SOLO FARINA CONDIMENTO ALLA RUCOLA

This sauce uses rocket as an alternative to spinach, and the result is a pleasantly peppery contrast to the soft comforts of the dumplings.

about 200 g rocket, stalks removed
3 tablespoons extra virgin olive oil
100 g prosciutto in one thick slice, cut into small dice
1 golden shallot, finely chopped
1 tablespoon thyme leaves
freshly ground black pepper
1 quantity flour-only gnocchi (see above)
60 g freshly grated parmesan

SERVES 4

Wash the rocket and spin dry, then slice very finely and set aside.

Heat the olive oil in a heavy-based frying pan over medium heat and sauté the prosciutto for about 4 minutes, stirring constantly with a wooden spoon. Remove the prosciutto from the pan with a slotted spoon and set aside. Add the shallot to the pan and sauté until translucent, then return the prosciutto to the pan. Add the thyme and rocket and allow the rocket to wilt for 2 minutes. Season with pepper (you don't need salt because the prosciutto is so salty).

Cook the gnocchi in plenty of boiling salted water. Place them on a plate, then tilt the plate over the boiling water and let the gnocchi slide into the water. (You may need to do this in small batches if your pan is not big enough.) As the gnocchi rise to the surface, lift them out using a slotted spoon, drain well then add to the rocket mixture. Toss gently and serve with the parmesan.

Semolina gnocchi with butter and sage

GNOCCHI ALLA ROMANA

Not all gnocchi are born of potato. This one is made with semolina flour, a coarsely ground flour made from durum wheat, which is the way they made their gnocchi in Rome long before the potato got off the boat from America. I think the presentation of these dumplings is different, inviting and elegant.

1.2 litres full-cream milk
pinch of sea salt
freshly grated nutmeg
300 g semolina flour
3 egg yolks
100 g unsalted butter at room temperature,
    plus extra for greasing
80 g freshly grated parmesan
leaves from 2 sprigs sage

SERVES 4

Preheat the oven to 180°C and lightly butter a ceramic baking dish.

Place the milk in a saucepan and bring it to the boil, then reduce the heat to medium. Add the salt and grate in some nutmeg to taste. Slowly add the flour in a fine stream, stirring constantly with a whisk or wooden spoon to avoid lumps. The milk and flour will soon start to form a sort of soft dough. Cook for 10 minutes, energetically working the mixture to make sure it doesn't stick to the bottom or sides of the pan.

Take the dough off the heat and let it cool a little. Add the egg yolks one at a time, mixing well each time, then add 30 g of the butter and 3 tablespoons of the parmesan. Mix thoroughly, then pour onto a cold, clean, slightly damp work surface. Wet the blade of a large knife and use it to spread and flatten the dough to a thickness of 2 cm. Leave to cool to room temperature. Using a biscuit cutter or a small glass, cut the dough into circles about 5 cm in diameter.

Melt the remaining butter in a non-stick frying pan over low heat, then sprinkle in the sage leaves. Heat for about 30 seconds, then take the pan off the heat.

Place the gnocchi in the baking dish, slightly overlapping each other. Pour the melted butter and sage on top, sprinkle with the rest of the parmesan and bake for about 20 minutes until the gnocchi have a golden crust. Serve immediately.

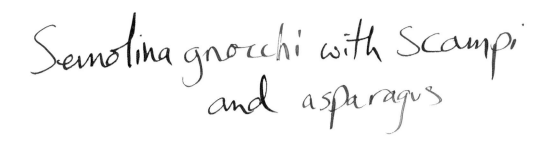

GNOCCHI DI SEMOLINA CON ASPARAGI E SCAMPI

Serving the gnocchi with scampi means that this is not a cheap dish – but it is ideal for a special occasion.

1.2 litres full-cream milk
sea salt
freshly grated nutmeg
300 g semolina flour
100 g freshly grated parmesan
3 egg yolks
20 g butter at room temperature,
    plus extra for greasing
1 egg, lightly beaten

SAUCE

800 g raw scampi
300 g asparagus
30 g butter
1 golden shallot, chopped
sea salt and freshly ground black pepper
30 ml white wine

SERVES 4

Preheat the oven to 180°C and lightly butter a ceramic baking dish.

Place the milk in a saucepan and bring it to the boil, then reduce the heat to medium. Add a pinch of salt and a few gratings of nutmeg. Slowly add the flour in a fine stream, stirring constantly with a whisk or wooden spoon to avoid lumps. The milk and flour will soon start to unify in a sort of soft dough. Cook for 10 minutes, energetically working the mixture and making sure it doesn't stick to the bottom or sides of the pan.

Take the dough off the heat. Incorporate half of the parmesan, then the egg yolks one at a time, and then the butter. Quickly mix everything to amalgamate. Pour onto a cold, clean, slightly damp work surface. Wet the blade of a large knife and use it to flatten the dough to a thickness of 2 cm. Leave to cool to room temperature.

Detach the heads from the scampi, discarding all but four of the heads (these will be used to add flavour to the sauce). Cut the scampi in half lengthwise and peel off the shells, being careful of the spikes. Slice the scampi in half lengthwise again and set aside.

Trim the asparagus, discarding the bottom third of each stalk. Blanch for 2 minutes in boiling water, refresh in iced water, then drain and set aside.

Using a biscuit cutter or a small glass about 5 cm in diameter, cut the gnocchi dough into discs. Place the gnocchi in the baking dish in four mounds of about five slightly overlapping gnocchi and brush with the beaten egg. Sprinkle the gnocchi with the rest of the parmesan and bake for 10 minutes until they have a golden crust.

Meanwhile, cook the scampi. Melt the butter in a large non-stick frying pan over medium heat. Add the shallot and sauté for 3 minutes, then add the reserved scampi heads, using a wooden spoon to squash them a little into the sizzling butter. When the scampi heads have changed colour and released all their wonderful flavour, discard them. Add the asparagus and scampi to the pan, and season with a little salt and pepper. Cook for 2–3 minutes, stirring gently, until the scampi becomes white. Add the wine and stir just until the alcohol evaporates.

Take the gnocchi out of the oven and, using a spatula, carefully pick up each mound of gnocchi and place it on a warmed serving plate. Pour a quarter of the scampi sauce over each mound. Serve immediately.

Silverbeet and ricotta gnocchi

MALFATTI DI BIETTI E RICOTTA

In some parts of Italy these large gnocchi made without potatoes or flour are called *malfatti* ('badly made'); in others, they are known as *gnocchi verdi* ('green gnocchi'); and, in Florence, *ravioli nudi* ('naked ravioli'), because they look like ravioli filling without the pasta. For these light gnocchi to hold together, the ricotta needs to be very dry – if it seems too wet, leave it to drain in a colander over the sink for about 30 minutes. Malfatti are very tasty and delicate and don't need much sauce. Here I suggest just melted butter and sage and lots of parmesan, but you could also serve them with fresh tomato sauce (see page 51).

1 kg silverbeet (Swiss chard)
350 g ricotta
2 eggs
120 g freshly grated parmesan
a few gratings of nutmeg
sea salt
plain flour, for dusting
80 g butter
1 tablespoon sage leaves, roughly chopped
freshly ground black pepper

SERVES 4

Remove and discard the white stalks from the silverbeet and wash the leaves well. Blanch the silverbeet leaves in boiling salted water for a minute or so, just until they have wilted. Drain, refresh in ice-cold water and squeeze dry, then chop very finely. Combine the silverbeet and ricotta in a bowl, then add the eggs, half the parmesan, the nutmeg and salt to taste. Mix thoroughly.

Have a bowl of flour ready. Flour your hands and, using a teaspoon and the palms of your hands, roll the silverbeet mixture into walnut-sized balls. When they are all done, roll the gnocchi in flour and leave to rest for 30–40 minutes.

Cook the gnocchi in plenty of boiling salted water. Place them on a plate, then tilt the plate over the boiling water and let the gnocchi slide into the water. (You may need to do this in small batches if your pan is not big enough.) As the gnocchi rise to the surface, lift them out using a slotted spoon, drain well and place on individual serving plates.

In the meantime, melt the butter in a frying pan over low–medium heat. Add the sage, let it sizzle for moment then pour the butter and sage over the gnocchi. Serve very hot, with a sprinkling of pepper and the remaining parmesan.

Pea gnocchi

GNOCCHI DI PISELLI

It may seem like a slightly perverse activity to cook peas, mash them and then turn them into spheres only slightly bigger than they were in the first place. Pea connoisseurs might suggest leaving well alone, adhering to the principle 'If it ain't broke, don't fix it'. But to my mind, these light-green dumplings have such a satisfying flavour and texture that they need only a little prosciutto, sage and butter to make of them something far better than the darker-green spheres they started out as.

400 g fresh or frozen shelled peas

100 g ricotta

1 egg yolk

1 tablespoon plain flour, plus extra to work the dough

80 g freshly grated parmesan

sea salt and freshly ground black pepper

80 ml extra virgin olive oil

80 g butter

80 g prosciutto, finely chopped

1 golden shallot, finely chopped

2 tablespoons sage leaves, roughly chopped

SERVES 4

Cook the peas in a small amount of boiling water until tender – about 6–8 minutes if fresh, 3–4 minutes if frozen. Drain and puree or mash very finely using a blender or potato masher, then place in a bowl and allow to cool a little. Add the ricotta, egg yolk, 1 tablespoon of the flour, 20 g of the parmesan and salt and pepper to taste. Mix thoroughly.

Flour your work surface and tip the pea mixture onto it. Using your hands, quickly work to a dough, adding more flour as necessary – it is ready as soon as it is no longer sticky. Divide the dough into six.

Working on a well-floured surface, use your hands to shape each piece of dough into a roll about 2 cm thick. Lightly flour a sharp knife and use it to cut the rolls into 2 cm pieces. Lay the gnocchi on a lightly floured tea towel to dry for 30 minutes.

Preheat the oven to 180°C and grease a ceramic baking dish.

Place the olive oil and the butter in a large non-stick frying pan over medium heat. When the butter has melted, add the prosciutto and shallot and cook for 4–6 minutes, stirring constantly with a wooden spoon. Add half of the sage and cook for 2 minutes, then remove from the heat.

Cook the gnocchi in plenty of boiling salted water. Place them on a plate, then tilt the plate over the boiling water and let the gnocchi slide into the water. (You may need to do this in small batches if your pan is not big enough.)

As the gnocchi rise to the surface, lift them out using a slotted spoon, drain well then add to the frying pan with the prosciutto and shallot. Place the pan over low heat and stir gently for a minute or so to combine all the flavours, then transfer to the baking dish. Sprinkle with the rest of the parmesan and sage and bake for 15 minutes. Serve immediately.

Ricotta gnocchi with green butter

GNOCCHI DI RICOTTA AL BURRO VERDE

The ancient Romans loved asparagus, and it's easy to imagine Pliny, the author of the world's first encyclopedia, tucking into this very dish as he wrote about the medical benefits of the long streak of green. This is a rich dish made with ricotta, covered with asparagus butter and boosted with parmesan.

300 g ricotta
100 g plain flour
80 g freshly grated parmesan
sea salt
2 eggs
2 egg yolks

GREEN BUTTER

150 g asparagus tips
150 g butter at room temperature

SERVES 4

First make the green butter. Rinse the asparagus tips under cold running water, then boil them for about 4 minutes. Drain and puree in a blender until you have a fine green cream. Using a wooden spoon, stir the asparagus cream into the soft butter until it forms a smooth paste. Set aside in a cool place.

Place the ricotta in a mound on a clean work surface and incorporate the flour, 3 tablespoons of the parmesan and a pinch of salt. Work it a little with your hands, then add the eggs and egg yolks. Knead until smooth, adding a little more flour if it seems too sticky.

Working on a well-floured surface and taking a handful at a time, use the palms of your hands to shape the mixture into rolls about 2 cm in diameter. Using a lightly floured knife, cut each roll into 2 cm pieces.

Cook the gnocchi in plenty of boiling salted water. Place them on a plate, then tilt the plate over the boiling water and let the gnocchi slide into the water. (You may need to do this in small batches if your pan is not big enough.)

Meanwhile, melt the green butter in a large non-stick frying pan over low heat.

Once the gnocchi have floated to the surface, wait another 30 seconds, then scoop them out using a slotted spoon. Add the gnocchi to the frying pan and toss gently, stirring through the rest of the parmesan. Serve immediately.

ACKNOWLEDGEMENTS

Four people were instrumental in making this a book I am proud of: Logan Campbell, Luke Sciberras, Julie Gibbs, and my wife, Sally.

Logan Campbell is the executive chef at my restaurant, Lucio's. He is a man of energy and imagination. He contributed numerous recipes, and he constructed the splendid dishes that we photographed.

Luke Sciberras is an artist whose work I am delighted to hang in my restaurant. He read the recipes, found inspiration in them, sat with us during the photographic sessions and, right there, on the spot, painted the wonderful images that surround and enhance the food.

Julie Gibbs is the publisher who commissioned this work and assembled the team that have made it both beautiful and useful. The team included Alison Cowan, endlessly efficient and patient editor; Anson Smart, thoughtful and meticulous photographer; Daniel New, talented designer; stylist Rachel Brown; photoshoot coordinator Megan Pigott; and senior production controller Elena Cementon.

Sally is the person who brings order and efficiency to my life and my work. She pulled this collection together from the chaos of my ideas.

AN APOLOGY TO BIGOLI

May all the people from Venice forgive me for leaving this classic Venetian pasta out of this book.

Bigoli are like thick spaghetti, and are made by pressing the pasta dough through a special machine, which is impossible to find! As for the sauce, bigoli are usually served in one of two ways: with a simple *salsa* of salted anchovies, olive oil, butter and herbs; or *all'anatra* (with duck). For the latter, traditionally the duck is boiled for main course, then the bigoli are cooked in the duck broth, drained and dressed with the offal of the duck. And there is the source of my dilemma. There aren't any recipes in this book that I wouldn't cook for myself, my family and my friends – and I didn't think anybody would want to eat pasta with duck offal followed by boiled duck. That's why bigoli are not represented in the book.

But now here I am, thinking about all the *gondolieri* going home for lunch and eating bigoli, the pride of Venice, and starting to feel a bit guilty.

So let me take you quickly through how to make my version of bigoli *all'anatra* for four. First, make 400 g of pasta dough and use the palm of your hand to roll small pieces of it into thick spaghetti about 20 cm long – or buy yourself a packet of bucatini. Cook two duck marylands (leg and thigh portions) in plenty of boiling salted water with an onion and two stalks of celery for about an hour or until tender. Remove the duck and vegetables with a slotted spoon; keep the duck broth and discard the vegetables. When the duck is cool enough to handle, remove the meat from the bones and cut into small pieces. Pan-fry 200–300 g of chopped duck livers with olive oil, butter and diced onion. Add some sage and the duck meat and mix thoroughly. Bring the duck broth back to the boil and cook the pasta in it, then drain, reserving some of the duck broth. Add the pasta to the pan with the sauce, tossing gently and adding some of the broth if needed. Sprinkle with parmesan, serve immediately . . . and feel Venetian.

INDEX

VEGETARIAN DISHES

This edition published in 2012 by
Grub Street
4 Rainham Close
London
SW11 6SS

Email: food@grubstreet.co.uk
Web: www.grubstreet.co.uk
Twitter: @grub_street

First Published by Penguin Group (Australia) in 2011

Reprinted 2015

Illustrations by Luke Sciberras
Photography by Anson Smart
Styling by Rachel Brown
Typeset in Univers and Cochin by Post Pre-press Group, Australia
Colour reproduction by Splitting Image, Clayton, Victoria, Australia

A CIP record for this title is available from the British Library

ISBN 978-1-908117-42-7

Printed and bound in India

This book is printed on paper from sustainable sources